To Carol, a true friend,
Blessings,
Jean E. Van Lente
7-11-13
9-22-19

*9.8 Meters
Per Second
Per Second*

1. Mark Richard Grimmette, 1997. A biography of the most decorated slider in the history of the United States Luge Association.

9.8 Meters Per Second Per Second

Jean E. Van Lente

Bormann Publishing
Kalamazoo, Michigan

9.8 Meters Per Second Per Second
Copyright ©2013 by Jean E. Van Lente

Bormann Publishing
P.O. Box 3173
Kalamazoo, MI 49003

All rights reserved. Except as permitted under the U.S. Copyright Act of 1976, no part of this publication may be reproduced, distributed, or transmitted in any form or by any means, or stored in a database or retrieval system, without the prior written permission from the copyright owner.

First Edition 2013

Scripture taken from the *Holy Bible, New International Version*. Copyright © 1973, 1978, 1984 International Bible Society. Used by permission of Zondervan Bible Publishers.

LCCN 2012913270
ISBN 978-0-9860255-1-8 (pbk)

Book design by Patricia Rasch. Front cover photograph © 2002 Nancie Battaglia. Inside front cover photograph courtesy of Edward Halcomb. Sketch of luger by Mark R. Grimmette.

Printed in the United States of America

Dedicated to:

Mark, Fawn, and Karrie

Contents

Foreword xi
Preface xv
Acknowledgments xvii

Part One: More Sparks

1. Why Not? 5
2. Where There Is a Mountain 8

Part Two: Ecstasies and Agonies of Childhood

3. Whee! 14
4. Uphill 20
5. Mercy 25
6. Christmas 29
7. Loss 37
8. Gone Fishin' 42
9. Halloween 46
10. "Everybody Abandon the Farted Ship!" 50
11. Liberation 54
12. "Baucis and Philemon" 58
13. Nice to Talk to 64
14. Two Flat Tires 68
15. Just Say "No" 73
16. A Boy's Room 76
17. "Undertoads" 80
18. Losses Skirt Christmas 84
19. Grandmothers Hurt Too 90
20. All Nature Sings 96
21. Hugs and Kisses 104
22. What Generations Pass Along 113

| 23 | Goings On Across the Street | 122 |
| 24 | New Pursuits | 132 |

Part Three: On Wings

25	Upswept	161
26	Sought	177
27	Shoot the Chute	194
28	Bounding Boundaries	203
29	Poured On a Pod Down 30 Stories	218
30	Sore Soaring	231
31	Grab the Kufens	253

Appendices

Appendix A: Commemorative Plaque: June 2010 260
Appendix B: Luge Tracks Around the World 262
Appendix C: The Sport of Luge 278
Appendix D: Discussion Questions for
9.8 Meters Per Second Per Second 289
Notes 293
Select Bibliography 305
Photo Credits 307
About the Author 308

Foreword

I was sitting in the Olympic Training Center lobby in Lake Placid, NY – it must have been about 1986 – when a group of athletes arrived from the luge track in Muskegon, Michigan. As a kid from the New York area, they seemed quintessentially Midwestern: clean-cut, friendly and all-American. They were all about 15 years old, like me, but I'd never seen anything like this group!

At the time, I was aspiring to join the Junior National team, the top-level of the sport for youngsters in the U.S. There were about 20 kids in the same boat as me. We were a fun-loving, yet competitive bunch, all living away from home at an early age and enjoying life to the greatest extent possible. The new arrivals shared the same aspirations.

In time, the Muskegon group started to mesh with the group of athletes in residence in Lake Placid. Despite being slightly square (we Lake Placid kids thought we were SO cool...), I soon had a new group of friends to joke around with.

Mark Grimmette seemed like one of the square ones, with his Reeths Puffer high school jacket and neat haircut (we all thought his jacket said Reefer Puffer and got many cheap laughs out of the joke...). He was a high school football star and a hell of an all-around athlete, but lacked any of the typical jock pretensions. He was good-looking, but didn't seem to know it. He was so nice that you wondered what was wrong with him!

In high school and college, it seems like you meet someone and become best friends in a very short time. This was the case with Mark and just about everyone at the Olympic Training Center.

As it turns out, Mark was the real deal. A real, genuine nice person. I still feel this way after being friends for 30 years. In fact, I don't think I've met anyone nicer.

Mark and I moved up through the ranks of the Junior National, National and ultimately Olympic Teams. Luge is contested in the disciplines of men, women and doubles. Mark and I were both doubles racers, but with different teammates. Despite the fact that we were racing against each other, Mark and his teammates Jon Edwards, and eventually Brian Martin, always worked well with Chris Thorpe, my teammate, and I.

By working hard together in the summer months as a team, we pushed ourselves harder than we ever could have imagined. The same ethos continued once the track was iced and the team hit the road. We were dedicated and focused on winning.

Mark had a few years in the mid-90s when he decided to try his hand as a men's competitor. After some success, Mark returned to the world of doubles, spending a season racing with Larry Dolan before eventually teaming with Brian Martin. I knew Mark and Brian would be a good team, but little did anyone know just how great they would eventually become.

Part of what made Mark such a good teammate to Brian, and what makes him a great coach today, is his sense of fairness and his patience. He'll take blame when he deserves it, but will assign it when it deserves to be assigned. When Mark points out something you could improve upon or calls B.S. on something, you have that sick sense that he is 100% right, in a very fatherly kind of way. He never raises his voice and is almost always even-keeled.

Our team has certainly tested Mark's patience. As the nice guy on the team, he was subjected to an inordinate amount of good-natured practical jokes. From pennies under his bed sheets to oral anesthetic gel in his toothpaste, Mark's been the victim. During our fireworks phase in the early 90s, Mark had three jackets replaced in one season. He was never able to dodge a skyrocket or an explosive very well.

As a racer, I have a few big moments that I consider career highlights and Mark's presence is a huge part of why they are remembered so fondly.

The first was at the 1996 Lillehammer World Cup, which kicked off the 1996-97 season. Mark and Brian were making their race debut after paying their own way to Europe for fall training. The U.S. was an emerging power in the sport and our doubles program was particularly strong, thanks to our hard work and the support of team coach Wolfgang Schaedler.

When race day arrived, the U.S. doubles teams, led by 17-year-olds Christian Niccum and Matt McClain, took the top three spots, making history as the first-ever (and only to this day) U.S. luge medal sweep. Chris and I were second, with Mark and Brian taking bronze. Mark made a comment that he didn't care who finished where, as long as all three of us were on the podium. That's a team player.

The season turned out to be a very good one for Chris and I, as we took the overall World Cup title.

The next season, it was Mark and Brian's turn to take the overall World Cup title, as Chris and I went into a slump. Mark played a significant role in getting us out of that slump, taking rides with me to see if I was doing anything wrong and evaluating my riding style. Keep in mind that we are weeks away from the 1998 Olympic Games at this point. While Mark and Brian were clear contenders to win the gold, they took the time to help Chris and I.

Finally Chris and I emerged from our slump and barely took one of the two Olympic team spots, with much help and consultation from Mark and Brian. During the seven training runs given to doubles teams, Chris and I were ranked first, second or third every run… except for the last one before the race. That was the run where we decided to really go for it. The run felt perfect, but to our surprise, we were ranked tenth.

The next morning, we were driving to the track to compete at the Olympics. I started to wind myself up about why we were so slow. Mark turned to me and said, "Just do what you did for the first six runs. You guys will be fine." It was the best advice coming from a trusted friend. He said the exact right thing at the exact right time, when he had every right to focus on his own performance.

The icing on the cake was standing on the Olympic podium with Chris, Mark and Brian. Just like in Lillehammer, none of us cared where we finished, as long as we were on the podium together.

Today, the next generation of luge athletes are fortunate enough to learn from half of the best doubles team in USA Luge history, as Mark is now the team's Director of Sport Programming.

Looking back, Mark has remained the same honest and true friend for all these years. I feel very fortunate to have Mark as one of my best and most trusted friends. I know the upcoming pages will show Mark for the great person he is.

Lake Placid, N.Y. Gordy Sheer
January 9, 2013 Marketing Director,
United States Luge Association

U.S. silver medal winner in doubles luge
XVIII Winter Olympics at Nagano, Japan
1998

Preface

Luge is the "fastest sport on ice." Presented here is the biography of Mark Grimmette, the most decorated slider in the history of the United States Luge Association. The story is as much a first as he is a first. One day, Mark dared the author to write a book about his luge career. There is no other.

Mark, at 13, grabbed the opportunity to luge when it presented itself right under his nose across the street. His ascendance to total number of titles in the sport, to the extent no other American has ever achieved, is a journey of talent, character, determination, faith, and exhaustive effort.

Mark preferred doubles. Doubles requires two experienced lugers to communicate and work together on one sled. In a sense, partners must learn to harmonize as closely as Kitty and Peter Carruthers, Misti May-Treanor and Kerri Walsh, Fred and Ginger, Crick and Watson, and Hillary and Tenzing. Mark and the partner he doubled with the longest, Brian Martin, worked not only hand-in-glove, but calf-and-shoulder together to succeed. Essentially, two young American men trained from nothing until they dominated the luge tracks worldwide.

The author's story is a biography of Mark to the age of his retirement from luging at 39 in 2010. From journals the author kept beginning with Mark's birth to 1994 are mined, in good times and trying ones, the development of a world class champion in United States luge. Mark dedicated himself and, in time, he excelled in doubles luge against the powerhouse teams of Germany, Italy and Austria.

Mark's story shares how he consistently exemplified the virtues intrinsic in luge to make him recognizable as a champion in the sport.

My hope is that you will take away a treasure-trove of inspiration and learning from his story.

West Michigan   JVL
January 1, 2013

Acknowledgments

Much credit goes to Mark Grimmette for infusing the words herein with his reality. To completely thank everyone who zealously helped me with the production of this book, I must begin with Karrie Childs. To her I owe a huge debt because she gave valuable technical skill, as well as the thoughts of her heart. I extend heartfelt gratitude to Fawn Volkert for her graciousness in blessing this book in the early stages with her encouraging spirit.

In addition, I thank Shane Childs and Keela Grimmette for sharing precious time and knowledge with me to help assemble the book. I am grateful to Debra Halcomb, Ed Halcomb, and Kathleen Montgomery for their generous input, resources and support. The writing itself put me in mind of my endearment toward my parents, Henry and Leona Bormann, and their encouragement, even from the grave.

I have thanked many people in the pages of the book for supplying me with continuous pages from the press in its diligent covering of Mark's career in doubles luge. Here, I thank them all again.

To the sources who have kindly given me permission to reprint excerpts from their original material to help build the text, I am deeply indebted and grateful. A big shout out goes to the *Muskegon Chronicle* and its sports editor, Tom Kendra, for their generosity to me in this effort.

I gratefully acknowledge Gordy Sheer, editor of the *U.S. Luge Team: The Official Media and Information Guide of the United States Luge Association*, 1999-2000, for his support, encouragement and permissions.

A few sources requested they be listed in a particular way in a conspicuous part of the book, apart from "notes" and "bibliography."

Here they are noted in the order they appear in the book:

By Dylan Thomas, "Fern Hill," from *The Poems of Dylan Thomas*, copyright © 1945 by The Trustees for the Copyrights of Dylan Thomas. Reprinted by permission of New Directions Publishing Corp.

From *The Metamorphoses* by Publius Ovidius Naso, translated by Horace Gregory, translation copyright © 1958 by The Viking Press, Inc., renewed © 1986 by Patrick Bolton Gregory. Used by permission of Viking Penguin, a division of Penguin Group (USA) Inc.

By George Oppen, "Boy's Room" and "On the Water, Solid," from *Collected Poems*, copyright © 1965 by George Oppen. Reprinted by permission of New Directions Publishing Corp.

© 1998, *The Plain Dealer*. All rights reserved. Reprinted with permission.

By Tomas Tranströmer, "Homeward," translated by Robin Fulton, from *The Great Enigma*, copyright © 2006 by Tomas Tranströmer. Translation © 2006 by Robin Fulton. Reprinted by permission of New Directions Publishing Corp.

Part One

More Sparks

2. Mark and Mom on the pinnacle of Cobble Hill in Lake Placid, New York, September 17, 2011.

3. Mark and Brian Martin slide to bronze in doubles luge at the Winter Olympics in Nagano, Japan, February 14, 1998.

Why Not?

"Transformation"

To turn a thing around,
Use two hands and an eye.

To turn a heart around,
Wait,
That it may die.

Jean E. Van Lente
1999

If Muskegon, Michigan's own "Bird Lady," Margaret Drake Elliott, could "compile for more than fifty years the Muskegon Christmas Bird Count for the National Audubon Society,"[1] and in her more mature years assemble the book *A Number of Things* of nature writings, surely a book is possible for me to lately unravel. She was a writer, poet, herbalist, naturalist, "Friendly Teacher Lady."[2] If Margaret Drake Elliott was married in 1927 and her book first copyrighted in 1984, she must have been in the range of 77 when the book was finished. Maybe I have a little time left to write a story.

Studs Terkel, social worker, social organizer, interviewer, and oral historian succeeded in writing his memoir at the age of 94.[3] Conqueror of Mt. Everest, Sir Edmund Hillary produced *View From the Summit* at 79 in 1999. Even Albert Einstein, almost 70, prepared a paper on "unified field theory."[4] I'm just a pup at 64.

As apropos, a little spice in the genre of Erma Bombeck may be folded in the mix. Her humor many times reduced me to spasms of gasping laughter through the years on topics too mundane, yet universal to miss the mark. Humor was by his side as Mark Grimmette grew to manhood. And humor rallies us as we look back over a span of forty years. Nudging us is the awareness there is a lot to look back on.

How does a new calling find us? Or us, it? Mark is a 41-year-old man now. He is just retired from a first calling it could be argued in all its uniqueness and notoriety, found him.

Margaret Drake Elliott quips in her book, "The age of exploration and discovery is not gone as some would have us think. Young people, especially, sometimes think there is nothing left to be found, that all has been revealed. However, this past year through the efforts of the Michigan Natural Features Inventory, three new species – two plants and one animal have been discovered."[5]

Those are worthy words for Mark. He has experienced lower back pain and decreased quickness in recent years, changes that caused him to retire from doubles luge, the "fastest sport on ice." Indeed, he made the sport a career for twenty-six years. But Mark finds life is not yet over. He finds himself immersed in new hobbies and challenges and discoveries as Sports Director and Manager for the United States Luge Association. And, in fact, September 14, 2011, Mark revealed he prefers woodworking to luge. What a surprise! Avocations by their very nature can be so much more satisfying than vocations. Mark likes to cut boards from felled trees and follow his projects through, beginning from scratch.

Margaret Drake Elliott, too, had her finger in oodles of enterprises. Anne Verne Fuller tells us in the "Foreword" to Mrs. Elliott's book, *A Number of Things*, that Mrs. Elliott was a "member of the Board of Directors of the Muskegon County Museum from its inception in 1937."[6] And, as I was born and raised in Albion, Michigan, I was surprised to read Margaret Drake Elliott taught "Biology at Albion College from 1925 to 1939."[7]

Mark has actually served on the Board of Directors for the U.S. Luge Association as athlete representative at least fifteen years.

Mrs. Elliott aptly quotes Robert Louis Stevenson on the "Title page" of *A Number of Things*: "The world is so full of a number of things, I'm sure we should all be as happy as kings."[8]

Where There Is a Mountain...

"Check"

Check
Rear view mirror in passing;
There's not that much to see.
Round it small is all front view;
    A glance behind should do.
A bended curve, tree-lined,
    Perhaps a lake to middle we.
Sky above and earth below,
The ribbon winds away.

Charge
Eye on eyes while it is day
To places stretched before,
Fuel burning in the core,
    Used up where there is more.
Place handle, push up, pour,
    Derived unthinkingly.
Sky above and earth below
'Tween coasts' outshining ray.

Jean E. Van Lente
1997

9.8 Meters Per Second Per Second

September 17, 2011, on a sunny 60° pre-fall morning in the Adirondacks, Mark delivered me to the base of Cobble Hill along the paved road and sidewalk between Mirror Lake and Lake Placid in New York. Shedding jackets and sweatshirts, we proceeded up Cobble Hill. Did he say anything about exposed roots or 75 degree angled sheer rock faces? But his firm hand always grabbed mine to aid my stumbling progress.

At the top we discovered balsam firs, white pines, and quaking aspen. Mark crushed the balsam needles to treat my nostrils to that fresh aromatic balsam scent. We alighted on a huge sun-baked cliff, where we took in downtown Lake Placid in the valley below and the further spread of firs and maples on the mountains beyond. Mt. Colden and Whiteface Mountain loomed high on the left. Moving right, we beheld majestic Iroquois Peak, Algonquin Peak, and Wright Peak. Iroquois, Algonquin and Wright, the peaks Mark chose to etch in the headboard he carved, stood imposing on the horizon. The carved bed was always cozy and warm for me when I came to visit.

Mark declared, "Last year, when I took you up Henry's Woods peak, you said, 'I've never climbed a mountain before.' I decided each year I would introduce you to a new and more challenging mountain." The view was so beautiful it took my breath away. "Next year, we'll try Mt. Joe or Cascade Mountain. Then, maybe next we'll do Mt. Pokamoonshine or Pitchoff, that one more in the foreground."

I asked when we would do Mt. Marcy at 5,344 feet. It is the tallest of the Adirondack mountain peaks. Mark assured me Mt. Marcy is on his list. "That mountain is not so hard, but it is long." He was right; it's 14.8 miles round trip. I reminded Mark I am getting older, not younger, so his mountain peak list should be going from more difficult to easier and easier. But, he observed I wasn't even breathing hard at the top, so he thought I could handle what he was preparing for me. Maybe seventeen years of running helped?

As we headed down Cobble Hill, Mark, 40, began to skip rock-to-rock on a run. He explained as he leaped that one of his early trainers, Dmitri Feld, taught the routine to him and his doubles partner at the time, Jonathon Edwards, to help them prepare to luge.

For a moment, he was trying to be young and fast and balanced and coordinated again. I recalled from memory Dylan Thomas's plaintive "Fern Hill": "Time held me green and dying/Though I sang in my chains like the sea." [1] But, wait, that's not Erma Bombeck. She might have said, "Go ahead, you nimble neophyte and accentuate the twenty-three years I've got on you. I can visit the loo twenty times more at the end of a climb than you could ever try to imitate."

He confided, "The 'season' traveling all over the world is getting harder for me. Nobody knows." And I was reminded of "The Love Song of J. Alfred Prufrock": "I grow old ... I grow old ... /I shall wear the bottoms of my trousers rolled." [2]

Of course, Erma may have parried, "Whose life are we talking about anyway?" Whereas, Job agonized, "Will you torment a windblown leaf? Will you chase after dry chaff?" *Job 13: 25 New International Version.*

We listened to the quaking aspen leaves and saw them pirouetting in a rush in the breeze. And Job cried, "At least there is hope for a tree: It is cut down, it will sprout again, and its new shoots will not fail. Its roots may grow old in the ground and its stump die in the soil, yet at the scent of water it will bud and put forth shoots like a plant..." *Job 14:7-9 NIV.*

Why is the aspen known for its strength in adversity? Its roots send out underground tendrils that grow new aspen until there is a grove for a hundred years. We, by contrast, at length languish and fade away, unless God enlivens us to be tendrils shooting from His root.

At length, the bereaved Job proclaimed, "I know that my Redeemer lives, and that in the end he will stand upon the earth. And after my skin has been destroyed, yet in my flesh I will see God; I myself will see him with my own eyes – I, and not another. How my heart yearns within me!" *Job 19:25-27 NIV.*

Heading for home to West Michigan, September 20, 2011, I stopped at the cozy Adirondack Cafe near Keene, New York. Two entire walls are devoted to the peaks and their names: Mt. Tahawus,

9.8 Meters Per Second Per Second

Mt. Colden, Mt. Iroquois, Mt. Algonquin, Boundary Peak, Mt. Wright, Mt. Phelps, Mt. Skylight, Little Haystack, Great Haystack, Boreas Peaks, Great Slide Mountain, Mt. Marcy, Gray Peak, Mt. Clinton, Mt. Seymour, and Mt. Von Dorien. But, what about the ones Mark knows as Cascade, Whiteface, Pitchoff, Hurricane, Pokamoonshine, and Mt. Joe? Upon inquiring, the proprietor told me the names were from old, old maps and may not even be right.

One year later, Mark and I were parking my rented Suzuki in downtown Lake Placid. We maneuvered in behind a black BMW, which sported "46er" on the license plate. Mark explained to me what that term meant. The owner had climbed all forty-six mountain peaks over 4,000 feet in the Adirondacks. We watched as a short, wiry, white-haired gentleman of maybe eighty sauntered amiably over to the BMW with car keys in hand.

Two days later, Mark and I walked the two-and-a-half mile brick walk around nestled Mirror Lake, with heavy, pillowy gray clouds layered about and around the mountains, which surrounded Lake Placid. Mark alerted me to the names of Adirondack mountains engraved and equidistant from one another embedded in the walkway. Even with all the names I had already learned, I realized I had not yet been introduced to them all. The likes of Dix Mountain, Gothics, Giant Mountain, Nippletop, Santanoni Peak, Saddleback Mountain, Rocky Peak Ridge, Macomb Mountain, Seward Mountain, Upper and Lower Wolfjaw, Sawteeth, Couchsachraga Peak and still others stood out as individual personalities rimming tiny Lake Placid.

Mark loves Lake Placid for its mountains and its snow. The cold can be very sharp, but to Mark even cold Lake Placid is cozy. True to his bent toward always improving, he suggested in our conversation that he thought the mountain names should be placed in concrete below where each one rises above Lake Placid to give a sense of place to each one.

I happened to be in Lake Placid Friday, October 12, 2012, when it snowed the first time for another season. People downtown were excited and everyone hailed the white, fuzzy flakes. Suitably, it happened on Mark's first open day at the track for lugers.

In fantasy, each of us may have his own version of the Adirondack lore. "Tmolus was cheered by everyone who heard / And who would have his say against a mountain?"[3]

Part Two
Ecstasies and Agonies of Childhood

4. Mark, Fawn and Karrie, 1983.

Whee!
Journal I: 1977 and 1978

"Eyes Rested"

Eyes rested
    after pain,
Protracted,
    forget
Till reflected
    in poetry
Of open eyes.

Lullabyes
    to children sing,
Fleeting,
    remembered
As echoed
    their pain
From parent ties.

Bow not
    little ones,
Outside to play
    together.
Circle,
    join,
Clap hands and sing.

                    Jean E. Van Lente
                              1997

Muskegon, Michigan, in 1974, was so much more than I ever could have hoped for. Before 1975 was half over we were in a new house. Four-year-old Mark, captivated, observed the building of the house and his one-year-old sister burbled with innocence and an adventuring spirit.

We vacated the Beverly Hills apartment and moved in to the new house to the delight of the children. We were enveloped by comforting oak and sassafras and maple and white pine woods. Lady slippers could still be found underneath leaves. We popped wintergreen berries into our mouths for treats and the delicate lacy ferns raised the forest floor everywhere. Walking sticks climbed our screened patio door.

Friends and next door neighbors, Jim and Bette, right away, mowed a path from their back door to our front door. We had built 300 feet from Fenner Road. Ben and Amy, Mark and Karrie became fast friends.

Best of all, vast Lake Michigan, alive, was embodied a quarter of a mile away. The matchless treat-to-the-feet berm of alluvium, soft sands on the shore mollified all burdens of thought. Pushing into the twinkling waters on a hot summer's day or climbing the mountainous frozen ice floes on a sunny winter's day bade us never retreat. From the house we could hear the crashing waves tossing and speedboats churning. Even in dead silence, Lake Michigan, ever-present, beckoned to us in our unconscious minds.

5. Lake Michigan, April 21, 1996.

Lake Michigan, ahhhh! Mark, Karrie, and Fawn used to sit huddled together in the Radio Flyer red wagon when they were little and down to the lake we would go for a swim. One summer day, we were getting ready to go to the beach. Karrie asked, "Mom, are you going to wear your zucchini?" On the way back, Fawn found four packages of condoms. The children were delighted and overcome with curiosity: "What's it for?" "Is it for catching fishies?" and Mark, "Are ya supposed to put water in them?" They played with the little critters all evening until, filled with water, they finally burst.

Days held endless pastimes for a young boy open to discoveries. Mark soared on his bicycle and hit the nails square with a hammer building many a tree house around the acreage with Ben and Michael and Jimmy. May 6, 1979: Picture Mark cruising down Fenner Road on his yellow bike celebrating life, singing, bobbing his head to a beat. Interspersed were shouts; he periodically removed his grip on the handlebars, zig-zagged. He was carefree and happy.

In winter, I would take the children across the street to the big hill to slide in Muskegon State Park. That hill was unnerving enough in its steep descent. Mark absolutely loved it when I took them to the really big hill at Sherman Park with a toboggan and saucer. Sherman was a dreadful, harrowing hill. Over and over, they went screaming with sheer delight, up and down, flying in mid-air off the bumps on the snow-packed hill. Many times we were the only ones there. Mark would beseech, "Keep your legs in!"

On one occasion, when Mark, Karrie, and I slid at Bronson Park hill, afterwards we stopped at the High Wheeler restaurant. I asked them what they thought of the dancing High Wheelers there. Karrie, 3, shot back, "Yeah, you go boogie and fall on your whoopsie!"

Before long, John bought cross-country skis for Mark. He was on them across the street in Muskegon State Park every available minute. Sometimes, we skied to Lost Lake Bog. Once, a spirited friend, Heather, cross-country skied with Mark to the bog. On one rise, she tore off downhill, jumped over a ski hill, and beat Mark by getting down first. Alas, she broke her ankle in the landing. Mark helped her hobble to the house for aid. Years later, after he had won a luging race, Heather, trusty friend, told Mark he should have raced *her* and *she* would have beaten him!

Life wasn't just recreation; vocations also occupied the adults in all their fullness and demands. Employees of Community Mental Health in 1976, supervisor, Mike Canter and I organized a recreation program every month for people with developmental disabilities and mental illnesses in the community. The activities represented the only real support out there at the time, deinstitutionalization having just begun. We enjoyed the parks, played baseball, sledded, camped, swam in Lake Michigan, canoed, visited the Chicago Flower Show and attended a football game at Pontiac Stadium just for starters. These were first experiences for our participants, many of whom had spent their lives in institutions. June 15, 1978, we held a hygiene program with Jackie on the subject of bathing and laundry. Jackie demonstrated the rudiments of washing, all in a round, metal washtub. She was pretty cute, swaddled in bubbles in a green bathing suit. Mike took pictures. The audience sat riveted. Afterwards, Mark and Karrie helped me take the chairs back to the rack. The children helped me often in various program presentations.

After returning everyone home with the van, I stopped and bought a pop treat for the children and made them wait to open them until we got home. As soon as we arrived, we opened them up and dropped in ice cubes. Mark knocked his cup and spilled his root beer all over the floor. First, he said he didn't mean to do it, then he said he didn't like himself and began to cry. Karrie right away empathized with him and said, "I'll give you some of mine, Mark; I'll share with you!" Finally with some hugs, Mark calmed down enough to let Karrie share with him. I assured him it was okay, just a mishap.

Mark, 7, reported he told almost everyone at school that he was wearing his swim trunks under his pants. He also managed the usual mismatched socks. The young Mark was very particular about his dress. It was a tactile thing. If he felt the seams inside his shirts or slacks, he refused to wear them. Corduroys were in; jeans were out. Shirts had to be softly knit inside as well as outside. All of his clothes had to touch him just right or he wouldn't wear them.

As they often did, Mark and Karrie stayed with Grandma and Grandpa Bormann in Albion when John and I left for a Beaver Island vacation. Mark tried to help by taking down the clothes from the line behind the house, his apron growing heavy with clothespins; the apron was sinking further and further down his legs. Finally, he grabbed the clothes and wadded them under his arm, while he swatted mosquitoes. He proudly brought the whole mess in, where Karrie smugly told him he had left one towel out there in the bushes.

We were in Winter's Variety in North Muskegon February 9, 1980: Mark, Karrie, and I. I had an armful of yarn for Ada Fitzgerald, so she could make an afghan and we were proceeding to the checkout. Mark swung the bag containing four dollars' worth of Valentine cards I had spent thirty minutes selecting, three comic books, and one small bottle of creme de cocoa.

He must have inadvertently hit the shelf because creme de cocoa came oozing out, sticky. It spread over the floor of the aisle as it permeated the store with its pungent aroma. I was dumbstruck. Mark was bawling. Karrie was trying to pacify everybody.

I sent Mark to get the proprietor with a bucket. He came with mop and pail – sniffing. I lamely informed him it was creme de cocoa.

In a timid whisper, I said, "Do you have a wastebasket?" I stood with crumpled bag dripping. He said, "Well, no, just move on down here clear to the back around the corner and dump it." I flushed, "But it's going to drip all the way there." He glowered, "Yeah, I'll follow you with the mop." I whimpered, "Don't you have a wastebasket?" He: "But, then, I'll have to wash out the wastebasket."

So, cringing, I headed down the aisle dripping creme de cocoa. The mop was on my heels all the way as I tried to discern which direction to take and how far to go. Mark was inconsolably mumbling threats, first on himself, then on me and Karrie. He felt very bad. We salvaged the soaked valentines and ditched the comic books. We decided to square things up with Mark paying $3.50 to me for "damages."

Reminiscing, it was Mark whom we recall mowed down sassafras trees beside the driveway clear to the road while he tried to learn how to drive a car. June 5, 2010, we remember Jim Moyes "confiding" to a crowd of 300 at the Harbor Holiday Inn in Muskegon, that Mark never really could carry a football.

So much for coordination. In the course of growing up, Mark demonstrated his share of inagility. Mark has taken his ribbing over the years. But honestly, I don't know how anyone could lie on top of another body on top of a sled four inches off the ice going eighty miles per hour down a steep, curvy path and successfully make it to the finish without a modicum of coordinated skill.

Uphill
Journal I: 1977-1978

"America's War Zone"

In 1964
I saw the war
In Estorf,
In Belsen,
More in the occasional missing limb.
A story, a tear,
An insinuated envy of my virgin shores.
Then the war was twenty years past.

Paulette was five months
At an Anglican seminary
January to June 1997.
Now, fifty years past
She reports how much the war
Reminders
Are still
In England.

Yet I have only
To talk
With a handful of women
In my town
To re-experience over and over
Bits of bone,

Splintering, skin coloring:
America's war zone.

House
After home
Down
Any street,
Beaten, shattered,
Families
Spattered,
In ruin.

Jean E. Van Lente
1997

Beyond physical, we take a good look at mental, emotional, social, and spiritual growth. As through a rear view mirror, we look at past experiences. Newman and Newman teach:

> At the same time, children between 5 and 12 remain relatively dependent upon adults for material and emotional resources. Thus, the self-concept is likely to be most vulnerable during these years...
>
> The self-concept during these stages is based upon their own evaluation of their skills, their ability to behave in accord with cultural norms and moral teachings, and their continued sense of love and acceptance from significant others.[1]

Four years old represented for Mark a time which shattered his mental and emotional resources and rendered him deeply vulnerable in a way that made it difficult to bounce back. He fought through fears, confusion, loneliness, anger, and misunderstanding when his daddy left at the conclusion of our new house being built in 1975.

During this time we read many books before bed; his most cherished was *The Adventures of Huckleberry Finn* by Mark Twain. He often expressed his thoughts and emotions in the evenings when we read. At first, Mark seemed to feel he was cast in the role of "man" of the family. But he did not know how he was going to handle what he thought was expected of him because he was only a little boy. "Now, O Lord my God, you have made your servant king in place of my father David. But I am only a little child and do not know how to carry out my duties." *I Kings 3:7 NIV*.

He was hurt and became very insecure. Huckleberry Finn's adventures helped to assuage his feelings of vulnerability and to comfort him. He identified with the self-determination with which

Huckleberry courageously acted out his life on the Mississippi.

I was reading about primitive man, fossils, and buried bones to Mark and Karrie before bedtime, when Mark popped up with, "Will I be reborn in your heart when I die?" His train of thought seemed to be that if he dies will he come back to life and will I still be his mother. I promised him I would always be his mother. I assured, "When we die we know Jesus will take us to heaven to be with Him." He wondered if we'll recognize each other. Tears rolled down his face. Karrie comforted him, "Mark, you'll be with mama." Karrie squealed, "I don't want to be in that sand." I asked, "You mean like John's grandma?" She nodded, "Who put her in that box?" I told her morticians or people who work with dead bodies do that. I suggested to her that she listen in Sunday school. So I said to her, "Jesus died on the cross and came to life again and that means He will raise us up from the dead to be with Him."

In bed, Mark said he wished he wouldn't think about things like that. He knows *Battlestar Gallactica* is not real; he knows the TV story about the "killer" bear is not real, but he wishes he didn't ask that question Sunday: "Mom, will we be alive in 20,101?" Because he said he thinks about that.

We read the book about sea animals from Uncle Bob and Aunt Debby. Karrie got a charge out of the names: "butterflyfish, clownfish, lionfish, jellyfish, and starfish." So she made up her own: "TVfish, dishfish, floorfish, chairfish." Her favorite sea creature was the dolphin, which she renamed a "Karriedolphin."

Mark and Karrie were thinking things through. My difficulties coping were probably not helping them in their need for stability. I continued working in the recreation program at Community Mental Health. Alice Thompson, a park ranger, filled in often as babysitter during this period. She tumbled and rough-housed with the children and supplied gaiety to the home. The only thing about her was that she loved to fry foods in hot oil. I, chagrined, put up with strong cooking odors permeating my brand new house.

Mark and Karrie would often assist me with recreation outings for work. I'm sure today this practice would never be allowed. However, they loved helping me. Meeting new and challenged people expanded their world. They took pride in the assistance they were capable of giving to our clients.

I loved the children with all my heart and we enjoyed our many activities together. They had valuable friends in Heather, Ben, and Amy. Following rules was never a problem for them as youngsters because there weren't many. The rich environment close to lake and woods enlivened their spirits and their morale. It wasn't long before Mark attended Little Learner's Preschool, where he happily participated and made new friends.

Mercy
Journal I: 1977-1978

As a father has compassion on his
children,
so the Lord has compassion on those
who fear him;
for he knows how we are formed,
he remembers that we are dust.
As for man, his days are like grass,
he flourishes like a flower of the field;
the wind blows over it and it is gone,
 and its place remembers it no more.

Psalm 103: 13-16 NIV

A blessing came along late in 1976; he had a beard and wore green corduroys. His name was John. He, with his little daughter Fawn, who was Karrie's age, completed our family. John sutured what was torn; he glued what was broken. Mark, still emotionally fragile, sprang from his uncertainties and reticence and returned to being a secure, happy, curious little boy.

John helped babysit the children right away. Mark burst with joy to be around John. This new circumstance was nothing but great as far as he was concerned. John, though firm, loved Mark and Karrie as his own. Now, Mark felt free to play and compete in activities with his friends without worrying about Mom.

John played the guitar to sing the children to sleep. His deep, rich voice resounded through the house. "Yellow Submarine," "Yellow Bird," "Day Is Done," "Operator," "Leroy Brown," and "Put Your Hand in the Hand" were favorites and they called upon him to sing those songs again and again.

He and I established rules and enforced them. We took the three to First Evangelical Lutheran Church on Whitehall Road every Sunday. John and I prayed together to be loving, wise parents. My prayers cry throughout my journals, "Help me, Lord!"

We assisted the children in playing activities and sports. Newman and Newman advised on the subject of team play, competition, and the acquired importance of winning:

> Children are already sensitive to the pain of failure. The public embarrassment and private shame that accompanies failure are powerful emotions, even for the early school child...
>
> The more children identify with the team and value team membership, the more noxious losing becomes... Vince

> Lombardi has been known to say, "Show me a good loser and I'll show you a loser..."

Team sports teach children to want to beat their opponents.[1]

Early, Mark began to show respect for his friends; nevertheless, he was viewed by his opponents as a serious player. "Modest" often described his temperament, but Mark went about sports and games with a clear resolve to win. Whatever it took to best his adversaries, he was willing to pursue and attain. No compromises, no distractions, he carried within him an attitude to learn how to become better and better at everything he undertook.

As a very young child, he took advantage of Grandma Bormann's sidewalk in Albion. I found the schedule Grandma Bormann used when the children rode the coveted Big Wheel she had gotten them:

9-10 –	Mark
10-11-	Karrie
11-11:30 –	Mark
11:30-12 –	Karrie
1-2 –	Mark
2-3 –	Karrie
3-4 –	Mark
4-5 –	Karrie
6-6:30 –	Karrie
6:30-7 –	Mark

Grandma Bormann knew how to manage children and structure fair play. She had three daughters and she taught Sunday school for 20 years and she was a secretary at North Elementary School in Albion 18 years. She may not have been into sports, but she predictably trounced her opponents at bridge.

"... If anyone competes as an athlete, he does not receive the victor's crown unless he competes according to the rules." *2 Timothy 2:5 NIV*. One night, we were playing Chinese Checkers. I noticed Mark's slippery fingers move his marbles extra spaces. After the third time, I told him I wouldn't play anymore. Mark was enraged. He charged it was an accident and he accused me of being a quitter. I told him we would play again when he could play by the rules.

Later we were reading *Frog and Toad Were Friends*. We flipped a coin for reading "A Swim" or "The Letter." Karrie was eager until the point she realized it was "tails" and she had lost. Then she flipped the Chinese Checker board over and stormed to her bed howling. I brought her back and began to read when Mark turned the page back to "A Swim." He asked me to read that story because he didn't want Karrie to be sad. Karrie brightened and laughed at Toad in his swimsuit through the whole story.

Mark could not only learn to follow rules, but he could be merciful as well. Mark liked to win, but he learned very early that winning at the expense of "team" took away most of the elation of winning.

Mark was ready to pitch in gladly to any activity John introduced to him. Mark loved sports. Anything physical Mark enjoyed. He liked play and friends and competition. John and Mark dribbled the basketball on the cement slabs John had lain in the turnaround area of the driveway. They attempted to throw the basketball into the net. John had erected a pole which he had filled up solid with cement. Of course, over time, the iron pole warped, buckled, and split with this construction, but it certainly did not fall.

November 11, 2012, John shared with Karrie his memory of basketball with Mark. He let Mark know the rules: "I am bigger, I don't sweat, and I will always win." But, the day came that he wasn't quite prepared for, when Mark was sixteen. John jumped up to sink the basketball and Mark casually reached up, knocked the ball out of his hands, and with a twinkle in his eye put John on notice, "New rules!"

Christmas Journals I and II: 1977-1982

"Make Room"

As foretold and prescribed
To a faithless forefather,
God gave us Himself,
Then faithless forebrother.

What more could He give
Than Himself He has given?
What more can He bring
Than His name under heaven?

He dove to a haven,
Delivered bare,
Sweet baby Jesus,
Where no room was there.

Turn, trek, as you can
On bare desert sand,
On rough clods of clay,
Or stone pavement. Make way.

For, what more can I give
Than myself
In return?
A blue babe, extra room.

The ewe brought an eye,
Abiding shepherd his staff,
A wise man his presence,
A camel her hump.

The donkey a tail,
So
Rise now to meet Him
There, where you are.
Look, give ear,
Hear His voice; see the star.

He's coming again
-In splendor, victorious,
Christ Jesus, the Lamb.

Jean E. Van Lente
December 19, 1999

John chopped wood out back to make the house cozy from the crackling of the loaded "Better 'N Ben's" woodstove. Mark followed right behind him helping: splitting, chopping, stacking.

One day, Mark was angry because he couldn't ride with Karrie on the toboggan out to get wood. He stomped into the house. When we were ready to go in, we were greeted at the door with a sign: "Don't try to get in the house! It is locked!" Well, that came down real fast with a smile across his face when Marcia Van Lente came to visit.

Star Wars was popular. Mark was seven when he showed me his *Star Wars* cards. When I asked him where they came from, he said he let kids at school use his magic marker pen in exchange for a card. For Mark's eighth birthday, we went to see *Star Wars*.

·:·:·

By the second snow, December 16, 1979, erupted the rebirth of the drip in the bathroom. If we had to have a hole in the roof, what better place than over the toilet? No more long squatters! Karrie insisted on an umbrella to hold over her head. Mark, in amusement, spoke of the drip down his back as he sat. We each had the choice of sitting in agonizing suspense, wondering when we would get it, or looking up to be hit in the eye.

Aunt Debby accompanied Karrie, 3, to her preschool party. Later, Karrie pondered at supper, "I wonder if Mrs. Santa wears those things all day... I think maybe Mrs. Santa is one of my teachers - - she not real." I asked, "Karrie, did somebody tell you that or did you think about it?" Karrie demurred, "I thought about it myself." I asked her, "Were all your teachers there?" She nodded yes. I finally ventured, "Well, maybe it was a teacher's mother, Karrie." She grinned.

At 6, Mark told me he knew there were two Santas in the world. One was at JC Penney's and one was at the mall. As I stood on the sidelines at a distance, it looked as though he and Karrie were not speaking with Santa. But I was wrong. Afterwards, Mark told me Santa had a belly and he asked Mark not to sit on his knee. Karrie revealed he had make-up on; she pointed to the different parts of his face that were made-up. Karrie was obsessed with what she classified as "stuff" like powder, foundation, mascara, eye shadow, lotions, lip gloss, barrettes, and on and on...

By now, all the children were well committed to blocking off the hall to Mark's bedroom where they made surprise Christmas presents for the adults. They were holed up creating for days on end. Then, they needed wrapping. All the tags, ribbons, bows, and tape I so carefully bought as I estimated how much I would need – GONE! Bits and pieces flew here and there to wrap these priceless gifts of love.

January 1, the Van Lente Christmas party was held at First Evangelical Lutheran Church in Fellowship Hall. Gatherings with the multitudes of cousins were greatly anticipated. John had nine siblings. By contrast, Mark and Karrie had no cousins on my side. We visited Grandma and Grandpa Van Lente often at Silver Lake, Michigan. We had wonderful meals of roasted chicken and roasted, sweetened, halved potatoes or grand potlucks. The coffee pot was always on.

Gift buying became an exercise where I decided from the beginning to buy identical gifts for both Fawn and Karrie. I did not want either to wish she had gotten what the other one did. Colors may have varied, but they both opened gifts that were alike on holidays.

I began collecting Fontanini figures for a nativity way back in 1972. "Uncle" Jim and "Aunt" Theresa Zuidema were angels who cared for Karrie and Mark when we worked. They came over often to the house for dinner. One time, Jim, prolific woodworker, brought a handmade wooden creche for us. Mark was beside himself over the gift. "Boy, Uncle Jim and Aunt Theresa sure are Christians!" Every year, we took out the special nativity scene and the children loved it. When Mark was grown, he would buy me carved pieces for the Fontanini nativity from Germany and Italy.

Every weekday for years, Theresa and Jim were integral parts of the children's lives as caregivers. They received structure and affection from "Aunt" Theresa and "Uncle" Jim, who ran a tight ship. Mark saw Jim build with wood as he had seen his father build a desk when he was two years old.

6. Jim and Theresa Zuidema with us for dinner on Fenner Road, 1981.

When Dave Gonzales was building his house down the street, Mark could scarcely be found, he was so engrossed in "helping" him. I have often wondered at Dave's infinite patience in letting Mark hang around. Mark retained what he learned from Dave and Jim; his avid interest in woodworking and building grew from early experiences.

Mark loved wood pieces. He treasured nice samples and he later learned to construct wood articles. My family had a beautiful grandfather clock that stood six feet five inches in our house in the corner of the living room by the window at the bottom of the stairs. The clock was mahogany with a curved top decorated with lattice engraving all along the door. It had a small lock with a tiny key. It stood on round, pedestal feet. The face was of brass with black numbers and black hour and second hands. The heirloom had a brass and wood pendulum and three heavy brass weights, which gradually dropped and had to be manually lifted about every five days. The clock chimed on the quarter hour with the longest melody on the hour. The tone of the chimes changed with the weather. Humidity gave the chimes a flat, tinny sound with less body to the tune than when the humidity decreased. The inward parts were so delicate that when it stopped, only one man in Albion could fix it. His name was Scott Tuthill of Tuthill Jewelers.

My grandfather brought the clock back on a boat from the Black Forest in Germany when he visited relatives in 1914. My father inherited the clock. Truly, if you lived with that clock you never heard it chime. The ever-present predictability blocked out the sound from the conscious mind completely. Neither my friend Jane nor either of my two husbands slept well on the cot in the living room of my parents' home because of the relentless quarter chimes of the clock. Sometimes, my mother stopped it for them.

That old song was true with the lyrics:

> My grandfather's clock was too tall for the shelf,
> So it stood ninety years on the floor.
> It was taller by half than the old man himself,
> Yet it weighed not a penny weight more.
> It was bought on the morn of the day that he was born.
> It was always his treasure and his pride.
> But it stopped short never to go again when the old man died.

After Dad and Mother passed away, both Mark and Karrie wanted the clock. Mark crafted an intricate cardboard holder in which he set the fragile innards of the clock, so that they would be held still in his truck on the trip to Lake Placid.

In 2009, when I visited Mark in Lake Placid, he surprised me by saying he had decided to let Karrie have the clock. He had the inside workings still stable in his fashioned holder. He put it in my red Mercedes in the backseat to take home with me.

That turned out to be the trip of all trips. No sooner had I gotten onto route 401 in Ontario, Canada than something smacked me from behind. In my rearview mirror was the front of a huge Schneider semi truck. Once was not enough; he hit me again and again into the middle barrier while I fought desperately to keep the car upright. Finally, I came to a stop beside the road.

The driver from Nova Scotia told the policewoman he didn't see me. The Mercedes was totaled. It was a wreck. Only by God's grace did I emerge without a scratch. I could only guess what the impacts had on the clock. How could the heirloom possibly ever run again?

But Karrie was delighted to have the clock. She picked up the shell at Aunt Deb's house. That grandfather clock, almost one hundred years old, sits treasured in a corner of her dining room, silent. She's just happy to have it. If there's anyone out there who understands fragile clocks, some day we might need you.

December 15, 1977, Fawn and Karrie and Mark were playing in his bedroom. Suddenly, Mark cried, "Them girls are trying to get at my wiener...!"

I was cleaning off the top of the piano, when I happened onto a half-folded black and white newsprint photo of Marilyn Monroe in a bathing suit. She matched Mark's idea of a nice looking lady. He had asked me why I didn't wear make-up so I would look like her. In an effort to moralize on something like, "You can't tell a book by its cover," or "It's what's inside that counts," I told him she died young. He was all over himself with curiosity about how this poor creature came to such an untimely end.

Mark was dawdling while readying for school. John told him to stop working on his papers and eat his breakfast. Karrie stuck up for him in her usual vocal way, "John, you stop pickin' on Mark. Just leave him alone. I the boss of this house..." John swatted her butt and sent her to her room.

On the way to pick up Jeff for preschool, Karrie told me, "I hate John. I gonna throw him out in the snow and let the bunny rabbits eat him."

That afternoon John bet me half the grocery bill that when we got home, Karrie would be lovey-dovey. I bet him a quarter of the bill that she would still be prickly. He walked in and boomed, "Hi, Karrie!" She pulled her chin down to her chest with her tongue out and an impish grin came over her face; she put her hand up and waved with a "Hi!" John won.

April 4, 1978, John and the children planted cucumbers, tomatoes, cabbages, and corn. John worked diligently in the garden; he planted marigolds to discourage the deer. June 4, Mark chortled, "Mom, I'm so happy my bean plants have blossoms on them." What with deer, rabbits, oak worms, acid soil, and too little sun, John gave up gardening. Besides all the obstacles, Grandpa Bormann each month brought bunches and bunches of lush, beautiful produce from his huge fertile garden in Albion. Nevertheless, Mark, as an adult, takes great pride in his plantings in his yard and in his garden plot that he and Gordy Sheer have developed together.

John, Mark, and Karrie met me at my office. We hurried to the bank so that Mark could open a savings account. Mark seriously concentrated on all that was being said and written. I had just given my name and Mark started to sign his, when he said to the teller, "We're all in the same family though."

As he grew, Mark amazed us with his ability to gather resources and save money. Pennywise, in Lake Placid, he purchased a very nice house. Furthermore, it didn't take him long to start saving for retirement with some of his earnings.

Loss
Journals I and II: 1977 – 1982

"Life's Losses"

What should feel good,
But doesn't
All ways.

What ought to work,
But won't
Partly.

What turns out right,
But not
Sometimes.

What speaks a joy,
But can't
Fully.
    Then, oh, that dread
    Seems
    Halved at best.

When aches' beat
Strums, but
Not alone.

When rest comes
Too soon, but

Releases a while.

When the wrong turn
Delays, but
Gets us there.

When sorrow steals in on
Squeaky hinge, but
Stays by the door.
  Then dread is doubled.
  How could heaven be more?

Jean E. Van Lente
December 18, 1999

Mark obeyed John and never crossed him. And John included the children whenever, wherever he could. I noticed Mark's spirit return in double portion. Kay Briggs told Mark she saw John on TV and he was "just great." Karrie said she told the whole class. Mark told "Uncle" Jim Zuidema his dad was on TV and "he was just great!"

John ran for director of the West Michigan Environmental Protection Agency. He was active in CEASE, the movement he had begun to halt nuclear energy plants. December 9, 1977, we went to a CEASE party, where I won the door prize. This was just prior to the "Three Mile Island" incident that happened March 28, 29, and 30, 1978. After that coincident episode, there was no more need for CEASE.

June 5, John was preparing to speak for Community Action Against Poverty. He asked Mark what he thought a good parent is: Mark was distracted by a couple boys he knew going by, but he thought it was a good parent who tells you not to get on the table. John said he was going to focus on the value of finding ways to make a child feel economically important to the family.

Other Van Lentes involved themselves in politics. November 1979, Uncle Bob Van Lente won his city commission seat. He had been active in Save Our Shoreline. At that time, the movement drew a lot of opposition. On May 19, 1980, John, optimistically, threw his hat in the ring against veteran John Halmond for Muskegon County Commissioner. John lost. When I cleaned out the attic in 1999, there were all the sky blue poster signs on sticks left over from that campaign.

John gave blood – gallons of it – just as his father had before him. But, his father enjoyed fat, juicy hamburgers when he gave blood at, what is now, the refurbished Hackley House. In our day, we were never served anything but cookies and apple juice.

For exercise, John and I ran for years. He engaged himself in triathlons and a marathon. John would often bring home trophies and medals from his races. My routine included running about five miles around the block. I ran to Ruddiman, to the lake, and up over the Block House hill and down to the north campground at Muskegon State Park, and then home. I'll never forget the natural beauty of my running route. At one point, panting to reach the top of the final upgrade on Ruddiman, there always lay before me a peek at breathtaking Lake Michigan.

One visit to Albion, Grandpa Bormann took all Mark's blue ribbons from school and put them on top of the TV next to pictures of him and Fawn and Karrie. Grandma Bormann said Grandpa talked to their pictures every night before he went to bed. Grandma and Grandpa Bormann were part of everything. They drove to Muskegon every month. The children spent much playful time with them and the kids received all kinds of attention from them. Grandma always brought Mark's favorite strawberry freezer jam, which she canned in June when the strawberries were fresh from Grandpa's garden. Mark ate it inches thick on his toast or off a spoon.

All this involvement and concern served as model and encouragement to a growing boy. Mark even followed in the footsteps of his stepfather and Grandpa Bormann when he turned eighteen and he, like they, became a "conscientious objector."

⁂

"Losing one's friends and relatives means a loss of daily companionship, a shared world of memories and plans, and a source of support about values and social norms."[1]

August 6, 1979, Karrie, on a tangent of some kind, began asking many questions. At Grandma and Grandpa Bormann's, she wanted to know who the man was in the picture with Great Grandma Reichow. I explained it was Great Grandpa Reichow and that he had died. Later, I heard her ask John if his grandma was still "died." Then at the reunion, she kept asking if Great Grandpa Reichow was going to be there. My parents remarked on how pensive Karrie seemed. At the reunion, she kept wondering who everybody was and who they were married to. Karrie was so matter-of-fact with her insights and observations, it was not always easy to get at the depth of her feeling and sometimes raging emotion underneath.

Mark and Karrie had three grandmas they loved dearly: Grandma Grimmette, Grandma Van Lente and Grandma Bormann. It was a sad day as Mark was only ten and Karrie only seven when they attended Grandma Grimmette's funeral. She had died of ovarian cancer at the young age of fifty-seven. She and Grandpa Grimmette had taught them how to swim in their pool. For quite a while, Mark and Karrie shed tears in unobtrusive moments over the loss. Mark would tell me many years later, "I wish I could see Grandma Grimmette again."

April 10, 1978, I pondered how so many precious days with these children go by and I miss jotting their sayings and doings. I had not inherited my mother's keen memory; therefore, to make up for what I lacked, I felt highly motivated to record, record, record. Tangible and retrievable, history then was at my beck and call to remember and enjoy. Where my enthusiasm came from for recalling my past life I do not exactly know. In observing my children rapidly grow, however, I was palpably impacted by the realization my yesterdays slipped by forever – unless I wrote down their events.

Gone Fishin'
Journals I and II: 1977-1982

"A Hebrew Alephbet"

A smoking firepot; a blazing torch,
Ox, goat and camel under the porch.

A head, tooth and eye,
A hand, an ear.

A door, a window,
Cracks for lintel light.

A house, a club,
One fish, loaf of bread, le pain.
A nail in the wall,
A picture; a story to tell.

Seven starved rocks, each to feed
People sucking before eyes see light.

So spread out the table, clangor the bell,
Sadhe? – no que without you.

Till steps slow – Ithyein,
With the sign of the cross and taqa'.

Mem, as the waters roll on.

Jean E. Van Lente
December 20, 1999

9.8 Meters Per Second Per Second

One evening, Fawn, Karrie, and Mark danced for us to two full sides of the *Mickey Mouse Club*. Mark produced and choreographed. Karrie kept passing out leaflets and Fawn danced as the twirling dervish with a beat that wouldn't quit. Mark definitely showed the influence of the Russian dancers John took them to see. I marveled at these imaginative, dramatic productions and the children always basked in our full attention.

John made more whole wheat bread – the best yet! He bought 40 pound bags of whole wheat flour from the Unicopia Food Cooperative, where we did most of our volunteering and shopping. The children enjoyed helping with weighing, bagging, and labeling the bulk food at the Co-op. For a special treat, they enjoyed the ice cream sandwiches from the freezer. The scrumptious, natural cheeses from Unicopia added deliciously to the homemade bread and homemade pizzas. John and I thought the carob provided a great alternative to chocolate, but the children never seemed to appreciate it. Maybe we spent more money there than we would have at the grocery store, but to us, it was worth it because the food promised to be more tasty and wholesome.

June 7, 1978, we met with Pastor Gary Hansen to set a date to get married: July 20, 1978. We wanted to include the children in the ceremony. We found that they had mixed feelings about the occasion. Karrie, 4, gave us a hard time by refusing to wear a red sundress we wanted her to wear. They all had sneers in the photographs that were taken that day. Karrie sat with her legs open in one photograph such that everyone can view a spot of her white underpants. Yet, we knew that they were happy deep down to be a family.

Just about that time, I saw my first wrinkle. And what do you know, Erma Bombeck hit the nail on the head again:

... But, as I was telling my friend, Mayva, the other day,

"What's so bad about wrinkles? My goodness, they're beautiful! They give you character and depth."

"I couldn't agree more," said Mayva. "'Wrinkles are the jewels awarded survivors."

"That's beautiful, Mayva," I said, "but be fair! We're lucky. We haven't aged like our friends. I mean some of them look like an unpaved road."

"Don't I know it," said Mayva. "Florence uses that cream to erase bags under her eyes. The other day she erased her entire face."

"Oh Mayva,'" I laughed, wiping tears from my eyes, "I wouldn't believe we'd spent so many years together, you look so young. Sometimes I forget about your neck."[1]

·:·

April 17, 1979, Karrie was 5. We made a cat cake this year and her friends, Fawn, Amy, Ben, Michael, Vicki, and Kathy came over for a party. We always had parties, and often for Karrie's birthday, it was nice enough to be outside. The children were crazy for celebrations and traditions. If they involved guests coming over, that was even better. At one birthday, Karrie merrily sang her favorite song:

> If all the raindrops were lemon drops and gum drops,
> Oh, what a world this would be.
> I would stand outside with my mouth open wide;
> That's the weather for me.
> Oh, Baby!
> I don't care if the sun would never shine;
> I keep on wishin' for raindrops all the time.
> If all the raindrops were lemon drops and gum drops,
> Oh, what a rain it would be!

She had learned the song in kindergarten. She always sang it with enthusiasm and relish, regaling us with theatrics and a bouncy beat.

·:·

In October 1979, erudite Jim Kane, Jane's botanist professor husband, called to invite John to a Lions Luncheon. Jim, so fetching, and a good friend, said he gets a "kick" out of John. From that one invitation, John was active in Muskegon Lions until he left Muskegon in 2004, twenty-five years. It's how the Spirit moves; who knows what an invitation can mean where receptivity dwells?

It was Sunday, October 19, and it was the first time John wore a cream colored three piece suit. Well, all right! So, what was the sermon about but self-pride, conceit, and humility. Sometimes, you just can't win. Mark, one Sunday, decided to compliment Karrie on her shirt. "It's a nice flexible shirt, Karrie. I could see the sun reflect off it when I stood at the end of the pew."

Mark reached an A on spelling without even practicing. He bubbled over scholastic success of any kind. Karrie announced she and Michelle had won the "Poison Meatball" race at school! Karrie said, "All the boys and girls said, 'Karrie, you sure ran fast that time!' And they all clapped for me when we had to stand up."

⁘

When Mark was seven, Grandpa Bormann took the kids fishing off the dock at Duck Lake, near Albion. Mark screeched when he caught a fish. Karrie sang to the wind on the lake.

Grandpa Bormann took Mark fishing on Prairie Lake October 9, 1979. Mark, after waiting patiently a while, caught a ten and a half inch perch. The two of them then caught eight bluegill off the dock. They brought them home, cleaned and filleted them, and we ate them for supper. Mark proudly ate his perch.

Mark shared with Pete Sodini, the barber, how he found ten dollars on the ground outside the Shamrock tavern at Beaver Island and that the biggest fish he ever caught was at Silver Lake at Grandpa and Grandma Van Lente's. Thank goodness for our mild-mannered barber, Pete Sodini, who served as an institution all by himself in North Muskegon. He carried himself in his two-seater, one barber shop with a spirit of patience and serenity, always ready to hear a good joke.

Halloween Journal II: 1979–1982

What do ghosts like to eat?
How do witches keep their hair in place while flying?
What do ghosts add to their morning cereal?
Why do vampires need mouthwash?
What ride do spirits like best at the amusement park?
Why can't skeletons go out trick-or-treating?

(Spookghetti!), (With scare spray!), (Booberries), (Because they have bat breath!), (The roller-ghoster!), (Because they don't have any BODY to go with!)

One of the first memories the kids kept of Halloween was of the small, blue house near the corner of Fenner and Peterson Roads. They were very young and impressionable. The front door of the blue house creaked open by a witch, baring one large corner of a room, darkened and sputtering with blinking lights. Mark and Karrie, wide-eyed, watched a body slowly rise up from a coffin, stiff-jointed and laughing a deep grisly laugh. They still recall they did not reach for any candy at that house.

Halloween 1979, the spooky blue house wasn't spooky that year. A man asked, "What will you do with all that candy – get a bellyache?" Karrie bellowed, "I'm gonna get fat like a snowman!" To an older neighbor, Karrie said, "Thank you very much!" Mark was about to walk away, when he turned to the woman to ask, "Is my make-up smearing?"

One year we were driving down Highway 31 past Laketon on Halloween night, when I saw a man's body down the hill on the grass. He was barely visible. I stopped, went over and shook him and he groggily responded. I got him up and delivered him to a nearby house to get aid.

I still have John's "Halloween Candy Covenant" from October 31, 1980:

> Two consumptions of candy per day is the limit.
> School days: Once following breakfast.
> Once following supper.
> Weekends: Once following lunch.
> Once following supper.
> Dosage: 2 little or 1 big, b.i.d.
> Qualifications: Only following a decent meal.
> Consequences: Parents will decide.

John had the children sign the covenant. Sometimes maybe it worked and sometimes maybe it didn't. One school morning, Mark woke up first and began fixing his lunch. John awoke next and found him in the candy bag in the kitchen. John snuck up on him, startling him to death. He vociferously defended himself, "John, Mom said I could get candy for lunch last night when you were at your grandma's dying."

October 31, 1981, we had a perfectly beautiful Halloween. John had the first Friday and Saturday of his Stress Management course. I felt lonely when he was not around. But, Mark and Karrie and I picked up all the people with developmental disabilities for the special Halloween party at church. When we turned in the drive to Wes's house, I knew the day would pass quickly. Dressed as a girl, Wes, we discovered had gorgeous legs! Minus a shave, he had a made-up face and wig. His "get-up" complemented his personality. "Hi, kiddo!" He was a riot. He had to prance up to Mrs. McDermott at Pearl's house, so she could see him. Tommy was a ghost; Ron was a cowboy.

At the party, Wes gave a very touching testimonial that was quite a contrast to his garb. They called Janeen "Humpty Dumpty." Don won a game and a prize. Terry smiled the whole party. Alex needed no costume; himself was enough. Sherry refused to come in altogether. As cheerful assistant, Kathleen Cobler was heroic in the role of "leader of games" for the party.

Wes sang a song to Karrie. He told her he remembered when she was just tiny and she and Mark would come with me to do "pick-ups" for recreational activities. Mark used to "man" the van door and the stool used for climbing in and out of the van.

One year, John went trick-or-treating with us. We had a four-faced pumpkin. Parrishes on Scenic Road disturbed the mild fall evening with a very scary, cackly record going. And Polly, their parrot, squawked nonsense to make the spooky atmosphere more jarring and sinister. Halloween was particularly fun with marvelous weather.

A Halloween dance was held at church on a Saturday night. Mark confessed he liked it! Jane, my friend, confided the girls were waiting outside the boys' bathroom door for them to come out. Dennis was hiding in the bushes on the lookout for John, lest they get caught.

Halloween was on a Monday. The children joined by Carol, Vicki, Nathan, Dennis, and Michael, visited around the neighborhood. Mark, 12 years old, felt afterward that it was a little silly for him. It might be his last year trick-or-treating after all.

"Everybody Abandon the Farted Ship!"
Journal II: 1979-1982

"Fog"

The fog comes
on little cat feet.

It sits looking
over harbor and city
on silent haunches
and then moves on.

Carl Sandburg
The Complete Poems of Carl Sandburg
1970

The fog moved in from Lake Michigan, thick and soupy. Enchanting Lake Michigan will never let you see across her, but when a serious fog rolled in you couldn't even stand on the sugar sand and see the water's edge. The red lighthouse, invisible, throbbed its siren which permeated the gray blanket to warn watercraft. By noon, perhaps the shroud would lift and waft out of Muskegon. Muskegon's jewel would gradually return to dazzling blue on blue, its normal azure display.

Karrie and Fawn drew inside to play on a foggy weekend morning. They extended their rambling occupations all over the house. Then, they joined me in the kitchen and began extolling their grandpas, their cats, and all their favorite things. Karrie said she loved her three grandpas: Grandpa Grimmette had a swimming pool; Grandpa Bormann had "Dixie," the little black and white terrier; Grandpa Van Lente had a "Sara." And, oh, did Karrie adore her furry black and white cat, Freeway. We had Freeway eleven years and he only went to the veterinarian's once for a fight with what might possibly have been a raccoon. His little head was all bandaged up for two weeks with a neck collar to prevent him from rubbing his head. Bloody and stitched, Freeway lay around lethargically for days. He sported the collar around his tiny matted head and he looked just pitiful.

Grandpa Grimmette and Uncle Ron stopped by on their way home from hunting. Mark and Karrie came popping in with all their treasures to show them: baseball trophies, a hobby horse, masks made of egg cartons, which fit over their eyes and noses. Grandpa Grimmette in his down-homespun drawl let on he had had a slight heart attack, the scars of which showed up on the EKG. He said he had kept too many things inside. He urged John and I to come to Ypsilanti, Michigan to visit.

November 16, 1979, John went on a thirty-hour fast. He did that every once in awhile, especially after he saw *Ghandi*. Thanks to his running, John did not really have to worry about excess weight. And as far as food went, Mark never did a meal justice. A few quick bites and he had to be excused; he had better things to do. Keeping meat on him was a challenge. Even John's baked whole wheat bread, voluptuous pizzas, and his scintillating crepes Mark left half eaten. He liked lentil soup with hotdogs, which we often had. He also enjoyed one of John's frequent breakfast treats: "egg-in-a-hole." Out of hearty homemade bread, John cut a hole in the middle. He toasted the slice in butter in a fry pan and then cracked an egg into the center, turned it all over once and served the egg in the hole to his salivating brood. By contrast, when we had tofu, Mark went straight arrow to Dollene St. Martin's kitchen down the street to eat "something good."

One evening we went to see *And Justice For All* with Al Pacino and John Forsythe. Mark and Karrie were overjoyed to have Laurie Nelson come to babysit. The children seldom stayed with babysitters. But there were a few and, of course, they had their favorites. I think we paid babysitters fifty cents an hour.

I remember a time when I was returning a babysitter home around midnight. When I turned onto Peterson Road, I saw police and ambulance lights flashing and people congregating beside the road. I was allowed to go through. By the time I returned home, I was shaking, sharing with John I was certain the police would come to check me out. He doubted it. About three a.m., there was a hard knock at the door. A policeman said a pedestrian had been killed on Peterson and the driver had not stopped. They were looking for a car with a smashed front headlight. So they examined my Buick until they were satisfied I had nothing to do with the accident and they left.

Mark was once again pestering Karrie. He said he thought she was soft and cute and he liked her. She could render him helpless, however, by tickling him. That same day, the children were making a big deal out of everybody's farts. Mark's mantra inspired, "Everybody abandon the farted ship!" And away they would go.

⁘

The children were seldom sick. When they were sick, we had to juggle work with trips to the doctor and caring for them. In January, Mark had strep throat. We visited Dr. Harris for an injection. Then we played Edu-cards before bed to help improve sequential skills.

Unfortunately, John had a cold and an earache, so he dredged up his old Indian remedy. He heated up an onion and squeezed out the core; then, he placed the hot core in his ear and he said he felt better.

I noted I was struggling with whether I was perhaps overly protective and enmeshed or under conscientious. The children seemed to work out so many things on their own that I easily became immersed when it was not necessary. On the other hand, when the questions and emotionally heavy stuff cropped up, quite possibly I should have paid more attention. I was always praying for guidance.

Liberation
Journal II: 1979–1982

It must be considered that there is nothing more difficult to carry out, nor more doubtful of success, nor more dangerous to handle than to initiate a new order of things.

Machiavelli
The Prince

Deinstitutionalization was new. Years later, there was money to hire support staff, but not in the early years: 1976 through 1984. My caseload, composed of persons with developmental disabilities, was nearly one hundred individuals. The recreation program, 1976-1979, was the only community support before it, too, was dismantled. The developmental disabilities cadre had two case managers and one supervisor. I worked with the private big-hearted, sparsely paid adult foster caregivers such as Ruth Harvey, Tom Russo, Rosie Knight, Lillian Glass, Lloyd and June Gongalski, Mrs. Parker, and many others.

The case manager for the individuals with mental illnesses sat by the phone and manned the lobby because they were usually mobile. Whereas, careful plans involving many people were requisite in advance to care for a person with a developmental disability. The coordination always required much effort. And I was the only one on hand for years to handle the daily plethora of nonstop and often serious behavior problems in the adult foster care homes for persons on my caseload.

In total, numerous people were leaving institutions and as many returning to that setting. All transitions required reams of paperwork as well as planning. Caring, even-tempered Jim, at Muskegon Regional Center, functioned as liaison with the community. He surely remembers.

Wally, of the upper echelon, was fond of reiterating, "If you didn't write it down, you didn't do it." I am reminded of the animated bureaucrat in the movie, *Monsters Inc.*,: " ... always watching... " And when was the writing to happen? Night after night I wrote at home often seven in the evening until midnight to satisfy rules of documentation. We had no computers and no tape recorders then. Dynamite Priscilla, of Community Mental Health, surely remembers.

Priscilla had a wonderful staff, who, in the very beginning, had to file hand-written notes. Later they had to type tape recordings when we were able to dictate. The secretarial staff typed voices speaking into their ears all day long. That task must have been drudgery.

In addition, we visited Kalamazoo Mental Hospital weekly, which was two hours away from Muskegon. We saw the brick tower of the sanatorium in Kalamazoo rise alone against the sky as soon as we exited the highway. Bobbie and I traveled back and forth. Our job was to assess patients for possible discharge back to the community. We always ate at Big Boy, now Sophia's House of Pancakes, for lunch on the way out of town.

Piles of data were continually asked of us, which was extra work on top of the regular maelstrom. Otherwise, how could tax dollars be directed where they were needed? More time was usurped to attend in-services in order to learn about everything from social security to psychotropic drugs to behavior management. The reality resembled Sisyphus personified. I look back, however, and I am both humbled and proud to have been an integral part of the movement to deinstitutionalize in Muskegon County.

In all fairness, at one point, early on, Kathy offered me another position. I turned down the opportunity. Now I consider that decision a mistake. Promotions at mental health required certain advanced degrees. Clearly, I had little choice but to return to school. Finally, 1989 to 1991, Bernadette supported me to attend Western Michigan University to earn a Master of Social Work degree. For her kindness and indulgence, I will forever be grateful. But the work and classes took me away from my children in their teens.

The truth was I liked school. I liked doing the assigned work and receiving personal feedback from my instructors. I strived to do well. As I look back, some teachers and professors come easily to mind. Throughout Dalrymple Elementary and Washington Gardner High School, I remember Mrs. Graves, in kindergarten, whom I kissed every day before departing for home. Miss Felton taught sixth grade with a strength for writing. In high school, Mr. Steen, choir director, introduced us to staging musicals. With a name that fit, Mrs. Sharp taught English. Indomitable, Mrs. Fleenor taught debate. Her stature was such that if she were coming toward you, you might fear she would fall forward on top of you; yet, if you were behind her, you might be on your guard, lest she sit at any moment on top of you. Mrs.

Geyer introduced only the girls to home economics and cynical wit, Mr. Young taught math.

From my undergraduate years at Eastern Michigan University, I immediately flash back to Dr. Trowbridge for freshman English, Dr. Hefley, wizard of history, and Reverend Richard Kapfer, the Lutheran Church, Missouri Synod chaplain, whom I adored for his connect with students and his contagious faith and keen intellect.

A few professors stand out from graduate experience at Western Michigan University, such as Dr. Wertkin for research, Dr. Morris, Dr. Blakely, counselor, Dr. Flynn for administration, and Dr. Wijnberg for family practice. I remember these people more than fellow students, more than supervisors at work, more than my doctors. Indelible marks I carry with me in the form of recollections of teachers I loved and respected most highly. By the time I was forty-one years old, I had had a very good education with no debt.

In the meantime, Mark and Karrie and Fawn were observing what it is like to toil. They observed both John and I work very hard at our jobs. Consequently, they have all had good jobs and have worked very diligently at them.

"Baucis and Philemon"
Journal II: 1979–1982

"Book VIII: Baucis and Philemon"

The service for the soup poured at the hearth;
Then came the table wine and the next course.
Set to one side, nuts, figs, and dates, sweet-smelling
Apples in a flat basket, grapes just off the vine,
The centerpiece a white comb of clear honey.
But happier than the simple meal itself,
A halo of high spirits charmed the table.

Ovid
The Metamorphoses,
8 A.D., 1958, 1986

7. Grandpa Bormann's grape arbor, Albion, MI, September 1999.

Mark was eight when he watched *The Portrait of Dorian Gray*. He woke up at night with bad dreams from that movie. Mark was very sensitive to video of a virulent nature. When I was growing up, I was not unlike him. My heightened sensitivity was roused by lyrics of popular music. My moods changed just by hearing the words to ballads such as: "Breakin' Up Is Breakin' My Heart," "It Wasn't Very Long Ago," "The Loner," or "Why Hurt The One Who Loves You," all by Roy Orbison. As I look back, I see that phrases from love songs burrowed into my psyche until my view of reality skewed to match the meanings of the words to songs. Especially "lost love" lyrics persuaded me that they represented real life experience. This "cheatin' heart" internalization was not a good thing. The influence made me afraid to trust from the time I was a teenager and played Roy Orbison albums to send me off to sleep at night.

January 25, 1980, we were returning from "Aunt" Theresa's. Karrie, 5, asked about "down there" pointing down. She was talking about hell. She wanted to know if I would go to heaven, if she would, Mark, John, Fawn, Grandma and Grandpa, Dixie, the terrier.

The next day the three were watching Saturday morning cartoons as I was leaving for work. I overheard Karrie say to Fawn: "If you don't believe in Jesus, Fawn, you will go down there. You have to believe in Jesus or you will get sins and you won't go to heaven. Do you believe in Jesus, Fawn?" Fawn hastened with, "I do!" Karrie said, "Do you believe in Jesus, Mark?" Mark impatiently shot back, "Yes, Karrie, I do."

Interestingly, Mark said he thought God might be the sun. John pointed out there are many suns. The children seemed to be obsessed with questions about where God is and where the devil is. In the old Irish cemetery at Beaver Island, Karrie wondered if the caskets were down there with the devil.

Karrie asked, "What's God's dad's name?" I told her God doesn't have a dad; God was from the beginning. Karrie continued, "Is God a stepdad to Jesus?"

※

Cousins Alice and Jim Schneider, Laura and Ann came up from Ann Arbor, Michigan to visit. Jim brought little white bunny rabbits on Memorial Day. Fawn and Karrie sure loved those little rabbits. Mark helped Jim erect a hutch for them near the house.

Friends abounded. February 17, Jibri came with Eunice and Dave. They shared, played, entertained and had lots of fun together. Jibri was very responsive and really it was a nice thing to see them all get reacquainted so easily. Eunice also has a son, Chris. She, a Chicago-born friend and Western Michigan University graduate, sings with her powerful, beautiful, well-trained soprano voice throughout the community.

Birthdays always got a special homemade animal cake and a group of friends their ages to play games. I usually made up the games. Fawn, Ben, Amy, Michael, Heather, Kathy, Wendy, David, Vincent, and Orville were usually there.

Mark and Karrie can remember birthdays for Heather Kane at her house. I was even blessed by a number of birthday parties lavishly put on by my best friend, Jane Kane. She was, indeed, the consummate entertainer in those days. She was also the church organist at First Evangelical Lutheran Church for twenty years. Jane played the organ many years at Redeemer Lutheran Church and she still plays in a quaint old Episcopal church from 1792 in "Little" Washington, Virginia.

Besides her music, Jane taught ten years at Little Learner's Preschool. The preschool which was located in First Evangelical Lutheran Church, was supervised by Kay Briggs. At that time, her Heather and my Mark and Karrie were going through two years of preschool there. Inspired, Jane wrote a marvelous, practical book, which she published: *Art Through Nature*. 1985, Jane began as a chemist at Muskegon Community College. As safety officer, Jane worked at M.C.C. until she retired in 2004.

Our girlfriends: Jane, Darma, June, Henriet, Eunice, Berit and others joined each other whenever we could to gab and banter, have a sip of wine and generally restore each other. That wasn't luxury; that was necessity!

※

November 19, 1979, Mark was in tears before he went to bed. He had just had a squabble with Karrie. He was angry when we had that game at Karrie's birthday party and we had to look for a penny on the stump and the mitten in the tree.

The birthday he referred to was two years prior, when Karrie was three. The way he remembered it, Amy climbed the ladder to grab the mitten in the tree the *same* time he jumped up and grabbed it. I had said Amy won because she climbed the ladder. Mark, apparently, had been very angry with me about that decision ever since. He recalled I took him out of the game and made him sit on the porch. He was embarrassed and he thought it was unfair. I asked him why he didn't tell me he was angry then. He replied, "Because the other kids were there."

At nine, Mark was reprimanded by John for stepping on Karrie's cheek with his foot when she threw his book down the stairs. John chided him. Then John told me Mark began an odyssey of incidents of unfairness he could already recall in his young life. Some incidents were where he'd been unfair and some were where someone else had been unfair to him. John did not respond in any way; he just listened. Mark went on and on, accelerando. At last, he just couldn't think of any more and he quit.

At that time in the news Elvis Presley overdosed. The United States conducted a grain embargo on Russia for invading Afghanistan. January 23, 1980, Mark's birthday, President Carter sought release of hostages unharmed from Iran or a severe price would be paid. As it turned out, accidentally a U.S. helicopter on a rescue mission over Iran collided in mid-air with its fueling plane costing eight American lives. The Summer Olympics in Moscow were boycotted by the United States. Mark does not think the boycott was a good idea. After that precedent, in 1984, the Eastern bloc countries boycotted the Summer Olympics in Los Angeles. However, there China competed in its first Olympics in thirty years.

February 24, 1980, the United States ice hockey (Dream Team) won the gold medal at the Winter Olympics in Lake Placid, New York. Jim Craig was the goalie. They beat Russia 3 to 2 in the semifinal match, which was later called the "Miracle on Ice" and they beat Finland 4 to 2 in the finals. Judge James Rogers was Director of Protocol for those games. He remembers the mania and crazy hoopla that erupted after that event. Even though he was quite important in his role at the Olympics, Jim and his wife, Keela, were not allowed in the '80 Rink of the Olympic Center (now, the Herb Brooks Arena) for the final hockey game. A policeman told him the stadium was already filled over capacity. So, Jim and Keela went home and watched the smashing, historic victory on TV.

Securing the 1980 Winter Olympics for Lake Placid trekked arduously back to 1963, according to James Rogers, who knows what happened because he was there. Politics royally led the Olympics – pursuing train of Olympic seekers for quite a few years. The project was hard work and many times frustrating. At last, Lake Placid prevailed for 1980.

October 2012, I had the pleasure of seeing the two massive skating arenas and the fine Olympic museum in Lake Placid. Mark's grandfather-in-law, James Rogers narrated the entire tour and I was enthralled. The 1980 Herb Brooks Arena is alongside the 1932 Jack Shea Arena. Legends of the skating rinks: Sonja Henie, Jack Shea, Scott Hamilton, and Herb Brooks look out from high on the wall.

Keela Rogers serves actively on the board for the Lake Placid Olympic Museum; they meet every six weeks. Mark's outfit from carrying in the U.S. flag in Vancouver in 2010 is exhibited. Wonderful exhibits of medals, old ice skates and hundred-year-old bobsleds span many years, even before 1924 when the Winter Olympics began.

I have eaten sumptuous meals, too many to count with Mark at Keela's warm grandparents' in Lake Placid and they have regaled me with one cherished Olympic story after another. I have enjoyed their company immensely.

Nice to Talk to Journal II: 1979-1982

"So Precious Is Each Speck of Dust"

Wipe the top of the dresser
With your forefinger and
Call it dusted.

What do you do then?
Empty it in the refuse.
    BUT
God uses the refuse to
Glorify His Name.

So precious is each speck
Of dust that He lifts
Its seeming insignificance,
Shame and decomposition
To the empty seats.

At His banquet table -
There we will sit with
Christ in the unused seats –

The folded fingers of Christ
About us –
The kept of the refuse.

                Jean E. Van Lente, February 25, 2000

9.8 Meters Per Second Per Second

"In our society, it is extremely difficult for children to develop independent criteria by which they can judge the worth of their own work."[1]

I took Mark with me to the office. Tootie and Theresa asked Mark to help with brochures. After a while, they told him he could take a break if he was getting tired. Self assured, Mark replied, "I'm not tired. I've chopped through a whole tree without taking a break!"

Mark mended the holes in his own white socks. He had been wearing them for goodness only knows how many days. But he liked them, so he took the worn, gray-white, slightly odious socks off his feet and proudly darned them himself. Then, he put them back on his feet.

Mark practiced copying drawings free-hand. He was precise, meticulous. He had also made a wooden sawhorse he was proud of. We all were. He always had a project going. Noteworthy, was the consistency with which he worked to each project's successful completion.

Conditions were right, so we went ice-skating. Mark's ice skates no longer fit, but he handled the disappointment well. He took the sled and had fun anyway. One winter Sunday, we attended Father Dick's (John's brother) Catholic church on Fifth Street and his rectory for coffee. John had bought Mark new hockey skates, so that day after church, we all skated onto Muskegon Lake. We met Peggy, Mary Kay (John's sisters), Kait (John's niece), and Joe (John's twin brother) on the ice "ice-boating." Ice-boating consisted of a sled with a sail attached to catch the wind. That was fun.

While walking the half mile hike on the ice to the car on the south end of Muskegon Lake, Karrie was putting out her last-ditch effort from her weary little body. A little crying for someone to carry her wasn't successful. She began jabbering about legs and how many legs different animals have. She chattered about as many as she could think of to allay her fatigue until we finally reached the car.

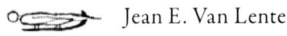

Fawn, 5, was going to have her tonsils removed. We had left Fawn off at her house after ice-skating and we were discussing this would be the Wednesday Fawn would have her tonsils out. Mark remarked he wondered how the doctor takes out tonsils. Karrie, 5, piped up, "With a chisel!" We asked her how she knew that to which she replied that Jesus had told her.

March 15, Mark broke his second window while he practiced baseball. But I could tell his eye-hand coordination was improving. He was growing up. "Mom, pitch to me. No, Mom, don't quit; pitch me some more!" John worked with Mark to help him perfect his overhand throw.

Mark was maturing and he was so nice to talk to with an easy way of engaging. He had an inviting, friendly, warm personality; he was instantly cordial to new people of any age. He reminded me of my grandpa Charley Reichow, my mother's father. Anyone who remembers Grandpa Reichow knows what I mean. I think large-as-a-bear, gentle Grandpa Grimmette made his mark on Mark as well.

It's hard to believe now that my granddaughters watch a TV screen almost as large as a sheet, but when our children were growing up, we only ever got channel 13 on the one 19" black and white television. Nobody complained. It was all there was. Atypically, all of us did watch *Escape From the Planet of the Apes*. Watching TV was just not a big activity in our house. The land and lake provided far more entertainment than the TV.

Later on, Mark took notice of the new electronic games. He explained to me in front of the woodstove about "D and D"; translated it meant "Dungeons and Dragons." He only played it once at a friend's house. He couldn't play it at home and he never went anywhere else on a regular basis where he could play it. He told me he liked "D and D," but added it was a small part of his life.

Mark preferred Intelevision to Atari. He remembers the thinking was the more popular kids liked Atari, while all the "geeky" kids preferred Intelevision. Reflecting in 2011, Mark said, "I really liked it." For the most part, Mark taught himself on the computer.

He took a couple computer courses, including a Fotran computer language course at the University of Denver in 1995.

⁂

I noted Mark was taking exception to his cute freckles. He decided to use Old Spice deodorant on them to make them go away. I suggested facetiously he would have more luck covering them up with toothpaste. The next thing I knew Mark was dabbing Crest toothpaste on each freckle. Once again, in self-examination, I wondered if I was guilty of being over-involved.

All of a sudden, Mark began having episodes of waking up about time we were going to bed and crying; he was scared enough that he wanted us to stay up until he was asleep. Mark had recently shown a special attachment to me. He wanted to kiss and hug me and jump in bed with me. This was uncharacteristic. John thought the clinginess coincided with Freud's "Oedipus complex," so John began calling Mark "Eddy-puss." These stages came and went. I decided not to react, except to measure up an extra bit of loving.

Karrie busily cut paper dolls with a vengeance. Then, she wrote a letter to Grandma and Grandpa Bormann about it. She and Fawn and Mark, for the most part, were self-directed in their activities. They pleased themselves by what they accomplished. Only in her early adolescence do I recall that we felt forced to urge Karrie to spend more time outdoors being active. She did not have friends nearby to play or hang out with. She became somewhat sedentary. We transported her to be together with her friends.

One day she scared us. After work, she was nowhere to be found. We checked with neighbors, with parents where she babysat, and throughout the park. No Karrie. We were just about to call the police when we heard her come up the drive on her bicycle. She said she had gone to visit Vicki on Scenic Drive. There is no way to describe the trembling fear and the quaking relief we felt through that experience. I thanked God.

Two Flat Tires
Journal II: 1979–1982

Then Ben-Hadad sent another message to Ahab: "May the gods deal with me, be it ever so severely, if enough dust remains in Samaria to give each of my men a handful."

The king of Israel answered, 'Tell him: 'One who puts on his armor should not boast like one who takes it off'.'"

I Kings 20:10-11 NIV

9.8 Meters Per Second Per Second

May, before the tourist season, we played "Capture the Flag" at the bathhouse with Swensons. Up and down the hills, all over the dunes we played, each team looking to find the flag first. I wonder if all these many years later, Dick Swenson remembers the fun we had playing that game in the dunes and forest next to Lake Michigan.

Bicycle riding, Mark joined John on his new Liberia 10-speed to ride from church home. Karrie, 6, had been promoted to the red bike. She was perfecting her bike-riding style for a week when she first learned. Namely, she earnestly practiced hopping on, getting started, falling, getting bruised, exclaiming loudly to the sky. One day, she came in proclaiming, "They don't make bikes like they used to!" Two days later, Karrie rode her bike alone! She was beaming, she was so proud. She hollered, "Strike up the band! Of course I can cause I'm six!"

Every weekend, John worked with Fawn until she mastered riding Mark's old bike. Fawn and Karrie rode their bikes May 23, 1980, when we all rode together through the park to Ruth Ann's Dairy Queen. On the trip through the park, John warned us to watch out for "Karrie, the kamikaze kid," that Mark modified to "comet kid" and John embellished to "comic cosmic kid."

Mark shouted, "I told ya, John. Karrie learned to ride a bike on a flat tire! She learned on the red jalopy Bill Webber sold us for $1.00." The day she finally kept her balance both tires were nearly flat.

But let's not forget Aunt Deb's Honda Civic. She bought it brand new in 1978. It was an ill-fated, silver jinxed bomb. First, it perpetually stalled. Soon, the key broke in the ignition. Next, the back light went out. On her way to visit a friend in Indiana in 1980, she smelled smoke from the rear. She brought the Civic over to the side of the road and stopped. Immediately, a male driver behind her stopped. Opening the trunk, she saw that her sack full of tampons were on fire.

Another man stopped, brought his fire extinguisher over and put out the fire. As Deb wondered what to do with her bag, one gentleman said, "Oh, just put it by the road. It will be picked up." Considering what was in it, Deb was a little embarrassed but she did as he said.

As soon as she returned to Kalamazoo, Michigan the end of April, she took her Civic to a mechanic to fix the light that had started the fire. Last, but not least, May 8, 1980, the fierce tornado that swept through Kalamazoo caused the collapse of the roof of Deb's Honda in the damaged garage. She lamented she would never forget her first car!

∴

Grandma and Grandpa Bormann visited. The junior choir sang. There they were all assembled. And there was Karrie in front singing her heart out, brown purse dangling in front of her robe and sunglasses on her head. February 25, 1980, on the way home from choir, Mark spoke of one of their best male singers who couldn't come because his voice dropped.

Our objective was to clean at church, but first we went to Pete Sodini's barber shop. Mark was vocally determined not to go in the first place. When his hair was cut, he was even more distraught because he thought Pete cut his hair too short. At church, who did we see but David Webber. David, with his experience with the "butch" haircut, could immediately empathize. He gave Mark a deep, knowing look and Mark was all right after that.

Amy and Ben got a dozen new little chickens. Amy, Ben, Karrie and Mark named them all. Karrie took a diaper over for the chickies when they wet. Animals held a big attraction. July 6, horse-loving Aunt Kathy said she bought a new buckskin gelding named "Shadow."

∴

Pam Torrey Poplawski told me about her beautiful twin boys, Adam and Stephen. It was so good to talk with her again. Pam and Ed waited a long time to have twins. My acquaintance with Pam went back to high school. Through college we lived and worked together. Pam and I waitressed at the Cracker Box restaurant in Glen Arbor, Michigan to pay for school. The owners were the boisterous, ever-contriving Jean and Dizz Dean. They battled years against the national park for naught. We lived the second year with lively, curious seventy-some-year-old Mrs. Rader in her house full of "working girls." We stayed in three bedrooms on Mrs. Rader's second floor of her old wood frame house in Glen Arbor. One day a squirrel wriggled his way into our bedroom. Pandemonium let loose until we scooted him out the window with a broom.

I fell in love with Lake Michigan there in Glen Haven. It was my joy to meet Bob Byerly, Dave Lieber, George Miller and Butch Burgeson. John Dean was always around for fun. He played in serial *Sergeant Pepper's Lonely Hearts Club Band*, over and over and over. Dottie Tobin and her daughter Donna worked industriously at the Cracker Box and afterwards, did we ever have fun. Young prepubescent Lance cleaned the toilets in the restaurant. He took an unmerited amount of teasing.

Speaking of college days, faces come clearly to mind: Cynthia, Diane, Nancy, Diane, Sue, Mary, and Pam. We had good times at King Hall and later at the Triangle Apartment in Ypsilanti. In 1968, I was honored to be chosen as a member of "Adahi" at Eastern Michigan University. Adahi was the honorary society for about twenty female students who were selected by the faculty for excelling in leadership, scholarship, and service. Of those of us honored, I was chosen president. Our faculty advisor was Merry Maude Wallace. There were about twenty thousand students at Eastern at that time.

In 1969, I was a graduate student taking "Wordsworth" and working at EMU as Assistant to the Director of Student Activities. It was my good fortune to work under Donald Kleinsmith, Student Activities Director. Nancy Zick Israel and I lived in an apartment together in Ypsilanti. It wasn't long before Nancy married and she eventually had three sweet daughters. As with Pam, the relationship between Nancy and I went back to junior high school. After Nancy married, I lived with Cynthia, a quiet one, who powdered the bottoms of her feet and tracked it all over the apartment. No matter, we enjoyed our time together.

At dance class I met Mark and Karrie's father. Rick became a biologist with a master's degree and we married. I remember March 22, 1970, he and I together were sampling water species. Rick found a dead sculpin. He told me, "I put him in a new preservative. He won't turn yellow that way. As a matter of fact, he looks a lot better already!" And I retorted, "Yeah. I'm sure he feels better, too."

We moved around frequently, first for ROTC and then for teaching jobs. We had two children, Mark and Karrie. Finally, Rick found a job as a biology instructor at Muskegon Community College, moving us from Aurora, Illinois to North Muskegon to the Beverly Hills apartments in July 1974. Mark was three and Karrie was three months old.

I found First Evangelical Lutheran Church around the corner without much trouble. And we undertook scouring the countryside for a place to build a house. Rick had a family well versed in construction. His brother Bob helped their father operate an electrician's business. Jim Westgate wanted to sell part of a section northwest of Muskegon on Fenner Road, a quarter mile from Lake Michigan. We had saved enough to purchase Jim's property.

Horace Gillette and Rick and I built a cedar house three hundred feet from the road in the spring of 1975. Horace Gillette proved to be an excellent independent builder. Our house was solid and tightly built. Mark remembered in 2012, the oak tree that curved over the Fenner house in the front yard. After a few years, it grew much larger and Mark was intimidated having it bend over his bedroom. John spoke of cutting it down. I beseeched him not to do it himself. We needed a professional.

One day, while I was away, John and Mark commenced cutting the oak down. They hurried to fell the tree and cut it up before I came home, because they knew I would be angry. I had told them not to do it. The tree fell, puncturing the roof. Mark recalled me coming up the driveway, getting out of the car, marching into the house and slamming the door shut without a word. They just went on cutting and stacking.

Mark labored to plug the hole in the roof. He plugged it so well that no leak ever developed from that incident. In 2012, Mark said, "I wanted to prove to myself I could fix the roof."

Just Say "No"
Journal II: 1979–1982

"Blueberries"

You ought to have seen what I saw on my way
To the village, through Patterson's pasture today:
Blueberries as big as the end of your thumb,
Real sky-blue, and heavy, and ready to drum
In the cavernous pail of the first one to come!
And all ripe together, not some of them green
And some of them ripe! You ought to have seen!

Robert Frost
Frost, Collected Poems
1970

July 10, 1980, John spent a rare sleepless night. The Fiat was kaput again added to many other stressors. That same day, Karrie had her hair cut at Peggy's and Mark and she were given fluoride treatments from Dr. Miller, D.D.S. Dr. Miller advertized their office was for "cowards" and they lived up to the promise as a comforting, cheerful, "jeepers-fighting" medical community in North Muskegon for years. One time, Dr. Miller even called me at home to see if I was okay after I had had some work done. The children inherited Grandpa Grimmette's teeth and, consequently never had a cavity. They had good teeth in spite of well water.

After seeing Dr. Miller, Karrie registered anger because her friend cut the curls off her "Darcy" doll. She would have to learn to say "no." Mark was upset because he chewed bubblegum a friend gave him, which he blew into a huge bubble. It burst and stuck to his face. Even rubbing didn't get it off. His face burned. He would have to learn to say "no," too.

John felt my family was deficient when it came to setting limits. He was probably right. It was my father who I could count on to say, "no" when I was young. But by the time I entered adolescence at 13, Dad was in no emotional position to be engaged, much less limit me. His major depression set in with a vengeance. He withdrew, embattled. He became so ill he was unable to make the smallest decision. All through my junior high, high school and college years and beyond, Dad's scourge was his depression. It is true when I should have been told "no," my father wasn't there. Neither did I hear the approval nor praise nor positive reinforcement I needed either. Yet, how he showered praise when I was young and he was well.

Still, Dad's intellect was keen, polished by his debating in school. I'm thankful for how he challenged me with the deep questions and perceptive comments directed at me and my life choices.

⁂

August 11, 1980, was the last day of my vacation. We had spent a thoroughly restful, relaxing week at Wojan's cabin on Beaver Island. Mark met ten and eleven-year-old girls at Wojan's cottage on Beaver Island. He asked John, "Am I old enough to have a girlfriend?"

Well, Mr. Beard came to clean our rugs after we got back. We headed out to go blueberry-picking as we often did. John made the decision to pick at Margie's even though nobody was home. There ensued a big discussion with Mark, who thought we should not pick there. John became rather short with him for not trusting parents. I rather supported Mark's thinking. There, in Daedalus' labyrinth of berries we picked seven pounds.

Then John found out Margie's family really didn't own the field and the owner didn't want pickers in there. I discussed it with Mark, who was upset. I took the opportunity to point out how John and he were different when it was an issue of caution versus taking risks. Mark was quiet all through the meal at Pirate's Cove. Karrie addressed John, "If you say you're sorry, Jesus will forgive you." It became clear Karrie was suggesting John ask for Mark's forgiveness and he would be forgiven. So, John told Mark that he had been right and John told Karrie she was *absolutely* right. Mark muttered to Karrie about why she had to bring the subject up and it was all too cute for words.

Out of the blue, Mark said to John, "John, you would've been thirty-one by now if you hadn't skipped first grade."

Mark's hero, Dave Gonzales, down the street, was still building his house and Mark was always around to help him. As Icarus was ever beside his father in learning how to fly, so Mark was ever beside Dave building that house.

Mark had been reminded to return from his friend Michael's in time for supper. Supper was ready, but no Mark. We headed for the beach and discovered Mark busily helping Dave put up rafters on the new house. Ironically, when I determined to put an ad in the paper for a retired carpenter to help teach Mark carpentry, he actually found his own way to learn woodworking. In later years, woodworking would become his true joy.

A Boy's Room
Journal II: 1979–1982

"Boy's Room"

A friend saw the rooms
of Keats and Shelley
At the lake, and saw 'they were just
Boys' rooms' and was moved

By that. And indeed a poet's room
Is a boy's room
And I suppose that women know it.

Perhaps the unbeautiful banker
Is exciting to a woman, a man
Not a boy gasping
For breath over a girl's body.

George Oppen
New Collected Poems
2008

I never had a brother, so I never ceased to be curious and amazed at what little boys do. August 30, 1980, I gleefully observed and recorded the contents of nine-year-old Mark's shelves in the walk-in closet of his bedroom:
    top to a snorkel
    Ban box full of puzzle pieces and checkers
    parts to *Star Wars* armored men
    card with Spanish words
    a black roll of electrician's tape
    a homemade receptacle for homemade Valentine's Day cards
    wadded up gold candy wrappers
    red crepe paper
    a stick
    another roll of electrician's tape
    rocks and pieces of coal
    a cover to a pill box
    2 toothbrushes
    2 hockey pucks
    a "Happy Birthday" pin and a "Happy Days are Here Again" pin
    homemade boxes from popsicle sticks and wood
    six Eveready flashlight batteries
    two Duracell nine volt transistor batteries
    one green bubble blowing bottle full of red corn kernels
    one miniature wooden stool
    assorted woven plastic bracelets
    another roll of electrician's tape
    one toy silver plastic "Private Police" badge
    two x-wing fighters from *Star Wars*
    one orange Ronald McDonald hamburger man
    orange cats, bats, witches, pumpkins on black for Halloween
    black electrician's tape wound around corks

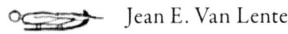

Scotch tape wrapped around wads of Kleenex
six bottle snaps linked together
a *Star Wars* torpedo
one slice of wood
a coin with *John 3:16* verse
five seashells
a box for a bomber fishing lure
six little wooden painted buildings
another roll of electrician's tape
a plaster of paris horse plaque
the putt end of a golf club
a sack of little colored stones for fish tanks
a plaster of paris "God Bless Our Home" plaque
two power mower spark plugs
two large double-end treaded screws
one paper snowflake
one Trojan-enz Youngs rubber (used as a water balloon when found coming back from the lake)
one bag of protractor pieces
staples
two smiling apple cider caps taped together with black electrician's tape
one huge box of empty toilet paper rolls
one huge box of multicolored egg cartons
The Adventures of Huckleberry Finn
a color book about fish.

The cataloging of these contents amused me to no end. Parents of sons may be able to identify the vintage of an assortment of the detritus listed as having been common at a certain age.

One common thread seemed to be the electrician's tape that he used to hold everything together. Grandpa Grimmette and Uncle Bob were the electricians who gave Mark his inexhaustible supply of tape. This stuff was as valuable to my son as my sterling flatware and porcelain collector plates were to me.

And what was Mark's reaction to my meddling and reproducing the list of his treasures? October 6, 2012, when queried, Mark, 41, brightened: "I remember those things on my shelves. I always had a plan." With the empty toilet paper rolls, he intended to make rockets. And he had planned to build "variations on spaceships" from the multicolored Styrofoam egg cartons.

Somewhat languished, Mark assured me I could not embarrass him any more than I already had.

"Undertoads"
Journal II: 1979–1982

"Active Years"

Sitting in a chair in my living room November 1, 1997.
    This was a new experience.
In twenty-two years I never sat in a chair
    In my living room,
Unless it was posing for a picture.
No Lazy Boy in my living room.
    Time just went like that.
I wasn't even still when Mark and Karrie were born.
    I remember bouncing up and down on the table.

Today is November 1, after a pleasant mild Halloween night.
    It is fifty degrees and raining,
A real soaker before everything sets in for hibernation.

Always something is going.
    A pan burns up on the stove.
The smoke detector goes off
    Because the cheese bun is smoking in the broiler.
The hose must be wound up before a freeze.
The floor must be cleared
    Before it can be washed,
    Before it can be waxed.
And then someone spills orange juice…
    The stillness this morning.

                      Jean E. Van Lente, November 1, 1997

Aunt Deb came for a visit. We had "beeeautiful" waves Monday, so we donned wetsuits to slosh in the waves. Mark and Fawn and Karrie lolled like ducks in the restless waters. They handled the fierce lake deftly. They bobbed wide-eyed, anticipating the next bombardment of waves coming at them. No one wanted to quit. But Fawn and Karrie wanted us nearby. Finally, Fawn went in, buried herself in John's jogging suit jacket and went to sleep.

Fawn and Karrie were growing. Karrie was going through an intense word assimilation stage. For example, "What is 'boob'?" With reference to the sermon: "What does 'narrow door' mean?"; "What do they mean by 'sheep'?" To Aunt Deb, as we walked from the lake and Karrie spotted "shit" on the road, "What does that spell?" "What does 'shit' mean?" Fenner Road was not always the positive influence we might have hoped it would be. I remember finding magazines which made me blush beside Fenner Road.

Karrie was heard intellectualizing about undertows. She had not been able to conceptualize "undertow," but she knew it meant danger. At Beaver Island, she screeched in fright at the seaweed in spots at the bottom of St. James Bay. She referred to that seaweed as "undertoads." "Be careful of the undertoads!" she warned Fawn and Mark.

I gave Karrie her Wonder Woman under-roos. Wonder Woman flashed garishly from the tee shirt and panties. For Karrie, Wonder Woman was a heroine and she was a girl besides. Sporting this heroine, Karrie emerged as a specious spectacle of a femme fatale.

Marking Mark's growth, he seemed suddenly to have arrived at pre-puberty. He described a dream on the way to church wherein he was walking between dates. He said all of the girls were attracted to him!

For his first assignment from the able, dedicated Mr. Suckow, Mark chose articles about electric cars. September 26, 1980, Mark reported elections were held and Eric Alderman did win. Karrie spoke of Andy Nofsinger winning "president-device." Mark chortled because he won the bottle of pop for being best football player in his class. He drolled, "Everyone knows I'm the best."

John pulled off getting all the children from what they were doing and took them to the Hackley Library on a Saturday morning. Mark loved to read and since he had a bit of a rough start, I always gave the credit to Mrs. Bagby, first grade teacher at Pennsylvania Elementary School. She deserves the credit for teaching Mark the joys of reading. An excellent teacher stands alone.

·:·

The sure sign it was fall out in the oak woods: we heard the acorns fall plunk, plunk, plunk on the roof. When the wind blew, it was an assault.

September 16, 1980, "How lovely the children are!" A news article in the paper talked about the dangers of Bendectin, the medication given for nausea during pregnancy. "Thank you, Lord, for three healthy children." The girls liked to cuddle, to please, to fuss, to mother, to squeeze, and be squeezed.

Aunt Deb noticed John had improved on the Gibson guitar my family gave him for Christmas. He played it every day so he was getting better and better. What would we have done without the nighttime lullabies?

Karrie and I baked sugar cookies. Actually, Karrie found the cookie cutters and she wanted to play baker. She wanted to do it *ALL*. It wasn't long before she had flour head to foot. She didn't like the shortening on her fingers. She did like the whiff of vanilla and said, "It tastes good!" She cracked the egg; it slithered onto the table. She was so mortified, she threw the shell into the batter. Then, she accidentally cut the chickens' legs off. First, she was dismayed but all of a sudden she smacked the remains onto the sheet muttering, "You'll have to do without it, chickie!" By then, flour was all over. To her credit, Karrie washed the dirty dishes.

·:·

Mark and I read a fascinating book, *The Quest for Michael Faraday* by Tad Harvey. Mark was introduced to the enraptured idea that "it is impossible to create or destroy energy. What disappears in one form must reappear in another form."[1] Mark was absorbed by electromagnetism, electrochemistry, and electrolysis. "... As the modern physicists probe deeper and deeper into the heart of the atom, the distinction between matter and energy all but vanishes. Dalton's atoms divide and redivide into smaller and smaller particles, 'What is matter if it is not also energy?' the physicist asks. And 'Where does energy dwell?'"[2]

Mark, also captivated by the night sky and the solar system, wanted to be an astronaut like the late Neil Armstrong, commander of Apollo XI, who was the first to set foot on the moon. This dream was not unusual I should think from other boys his age. What fodder for the imagination.

Through the twentieth century from Albert Einstein forward, the means were being put in place to learn what we are now learning about outer space and spacetime. Step by step the processes for making herculean discoveries were being established while our parents, we and our children were growing up. The Hubble telescope, operational since 1993, allowed us to view for the first time millions of galaxies.

Actually, Galileo Galilei first pointed his telescope toward the moon in 1609. His short book, *Siderius Nuncius* means *Starry Messenger*. But in a display in 2012 at the Kalamazoo Valley Museum, we learned that the first edition of Arnold Mason and Robert Hackman's four-sheet *Engineer Special Study of the Surface of the Moon* map set wasn't published until July 1960, not very long ago.

Losses Skirt Christmas Journal II: 1979–1982

"In Amazement"

Not that He came,
But to a stable bare.

Not that the table bore,
But beyond the cloth.

Not that hearts were full,
But that space was found.

Not that the veil was left,
But that it split at His birth and death.

Not to wonder how,
But as an infant small.

Jean E. Van Lente
1999

October 8, 1980: "How beautiful are the ever evolving abstract notions of children!" I cuddled Karrie in bed. I hugged her and told her, "I thank God for giving me two little girls." A few minutes later I heard sobs from her room. I switched on the light. There, between Barbie and Kelly dolls was Karrie crying. I said, "What's wrong?" as I cradled her in my arms. "I don't wanna die, Mommy."

"Don't be afraid, Karrie. Jesus holds each one of us in His hands; He cares for us and protects us. 'And even the very hairs of your head are all numbered. So don't be afraid; you are worth more than many sparrows.'" *Matt. 10:30-31 NIV.*

I remember how much Intern Miriam adored the children when she graced our church congregation with her gentle, tender, loving ways. She made a positive impact on the spiritual growth of our young children. Then, years later, she had a son of her own.

Mark and I were going at it. Mark was trying to place blame for his carelessness in losing track of important papers on everybody else. I was yelling at him. Karrie, over hot cereal, silently held her head in her hands. Then, she entreated, "You're makin' me go up the wall!"

·:·:·

John and I attended the NAACP dinner where the speaker's theme was: "Don't Park By Your Successes." I remember the flamboyance with which the plate was passed for the offering. It was most "unLutheran." Under no pretense, no reticence, with only jovial and spirited entreaties, we were encouraged to give to the cause while the plate went round and round again. "Let go of your money! Did you give in a bountiful way? Pass it again. Part with a little more!"

November 8, 1980, Ronald Reagan was elected president. John repeated his name a lot to help Karrie pronounce her Rs correctly. Relating to Mark's education, he came home from school flattered by being considered for a "creative problem solving" competition. He chirped, "Mom, Mr. Suckow says I got 'upper brain.'" He told John he had a "higher mind." John commented how funny it is to watch his self-image change from carpenter to baseball player to football player to "higher mind."

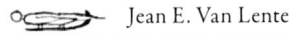

Inevitable growth stages went by. It looked like Karrie was going to lose her first tooth, a lower. She came in at 6:30 a.m. to say it was just about out and it was bleeding. At 11 a.m., Karrie's tooth was out with a little help. Karrie did not rejoice. She seemed to feel some sense of loss. Oh my, the new one may have a crooked start. Mark had had a brown front tooth since age 3, so he was glad to have that one out. He had jumped and hit his dresser by accident. For a long time, he didn't like to smile or show his dead tooth.

※

I called Bette, my neighbor, to see if it was really true they were moving the end of the month. On the last hymn at church and through the benediction, I was thinking again of sweet memories. I walked out wiping my tears. I felt very foolish. To see them go broke my heart. Mark said, "You mean Ben won't be here this winter to use our fort?"

November 11, in the early morning, I knew this was a day that was coming, but I never wanted to contemplate. The memories of our neighbors were all lovely. I took Mark and Karrie over and they lay down on the floor beside Amy and Ben.

Bette, warm and always creative, made me laugh whenever we were together. Jim was one who knew how and had all the tools. He had supplies for the cat when she broke her back leg. On the occasion John hit the pony in the head with the ladder, Jim knew what to do. Jim put the wormsoil on the garden. I don't know which one – Jim or John – cemented in the back patio and left the leveling board in the wet cement as it hardened, but I bet I can guess.

Jim made the best homemade plum cordial and cider. The lights on in their windows at night exuded a comforting glow. Bette would say, "Here , take a few eggs."

I'd sat in Bette's kitchen and laughed and cried my heart out. When Jim first mowed a path through the woods to our place, I wondered, "How do you make a path?" Every day you beat it with feet. The children erected forts in trees, brush, snow, huts, grass, tents, and blankets. The "ooogah" car horn blew very familiarly. The chickies, the piggies, the pony, the cats, and puppies we'll miss; we'll miss the sight of little Karrie toddling over to Bette's back door. We would miss them.

·:·

Karrie bellowed, "How come I'm the youngest one in our family?" The other day, she was experimenting with the word, "shape." At breakfast, she announced, "I'm in bad shape!" And to Mark at supper, "Shape up or ship out!"

November 27, 1980, was a washout for Thanksgiving, due to snow and slippery roads. We were heartened that Karen Kane could join us. She seemed happy to have a place to go while her family was traveling. Aunt Kathy reminded just how much snow had fallen that Thanksgiving. Grandma and Grandpa Bormann were stuck at home with the pies, Kathy and Dick resigned themselves to being shut-ins with the green bean casserole, and Aunt Deb ate her sweet potatoes and pickles by herself. Nobody dared drive the icy roads to Muskegon. As it was, we were left with a big turkey and lots of gravy and mashed potatoes.

With Christmas coming, Mark wove a web of string down his hall to keep everyone out of his room, because he was busy making Christmas presents. Except, one night, his covers became so hopelessly snarled that he flung a blanket over his creations and allowed me to crawl on all fours under the string to enter his clandestine bedroom. He let me straighten things out and cover him up. He barred me, however, from casting my eyes toward his closet.

We brought up the Christmas decorations from the basement to put it all out that afternoon. Mark dove excitedly into the box and pulled out the manger. We decorated the little tree we sat on the table by the humidifier. All the children helped. Mark seemed extra jumpy. Finally all was ready.

Mark, dressed like Santa, pulled a cardboard sleigh, driven by the plastic horse Aunt Toby had given Fawn. He projected a big round belly and wore a red plaid bathrobe, green knit cap, and a cotton beard. He was laden with presents all wrapped and ready to place under the fir. Eager to pose, he hastily gathered everything together he wanted me to be certain I got in the picture.

On Christmas Day, we were in Albion. I eagerly took an

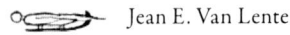

opportunity to see Pam Torrey Poplawski's twin boys, Adam and Stephen, and to meet her husband Ed. Karrie held Stephen. She thought those babies were so cute, and, indeed, they were. On the way home, Karrie mused, "When I was a baby, everybody thought I was real cute." I assured her, "Well, yes, but don't you think people say that about all babies?" Karrie thought, "Yeah, even Mark."

After Christmas, Mark could not get enough of cross-country skiing. We drove to Flaska's. Mark and John skied along the beach. At the first hill, Mark announced, "Here I go and if I don't come back, in my will I give all my money to the church!" January 10, we went skiing at Koster's, Mark fell end-over-end down one run. Karrie tried it and she actually did much better with John's "kicker."

That evening we served tofu and miso for dinner. It was one of those evenings Mark fled down Fenner Road to Dollene St. Martin's to eat. Later, after the hard work of gathering wood, John and Mark started work on the "Visible V-8" model Mark had received for his tenth birthday. He was fond of assembling models with John. Mark had shelves full of airplane, car and train models he had put together.

In eagerness I reached Fawn and Karrie's bedroom to show them the two new pairs of dress shoes I bought for myself. I opened the boxes just confident they would share my glee. Fawn gave a fleeting, approving glance and ventured, "When they get old, can me and Karrie wear them?"

·:·

In latter January, Mark brought his droid factory on our trip to Albion to go to Great Grandma Reichow's funeral. He said, "Is R2D2 a real droid?" Karrie chimed in, "I'd like a droid so it could do all my work for me."

January 31, 1981, on our way to the funeral, Karrie, 6, said, "Wouldn't it be funny if Great Grandma Reichow got up in the middle of the funeral?" Mark, in shock, responded, "It wouldn't be funny, Karrie." After a long pause, Karrie concluded, "We would've got out of school for nothin'."

Mother appeared weary and heavy-hearted. A massive heart attack apparently caused Great Grandma Reichow to fly out of bed onto the floor or perhaps she fell to the floor while she was making her bed. Mother always liked to have the details. In this case, she would never know.

I was bereaved at Grandma Reichow's passing. I wanted pieces that smelled of her. Of her furniture, I wanted Mark and Karrie to both have a piece. I felt compelled to wash her clothes. And I felt a certain contentment that she and I had just had a nice long chat two days earlier.

Grandmothers Hurt Too
Journal II: 1979–1982

"Pouring Flour for Prune Bread"

For Mother's Birthday

Thank you, Lord, of breath and dust,
Today I may
Give unhurried thought,
Unchallenged and unwrung,
To thought that brought
Me here with her there.
Invited, my gifts to bring,
Awe full wrappings time has scattered,
Tape and ribbon hold
Thru topsy turvy searing snarls,
Stained wars and want. She's told.
Tales and folks from memory divine,
Holy ribbon unwinds.
"To Mother."
What succulent tear could so express,
Yet keep
A bond so pure?

Jean E. Van Lente
September 15, 1997

We chased outside to cross country ski after the big snowstorm. Aunt Deb came with us. Karrie made the trip clear to Lost Lake Bog. Well, on the way back she was tuckered out. She bore no patience for Mark's barbs that he hurled when he had lost patience with her. Such troopers! Mark insisted on taking the *BIG* hill to show Aunt Deb and me.

8. Lost Lake Bog, North Muskegon, Michigan, October 2000.

Mark, shortly after, complained his legs hurt. John quieted him by telling him it was "growing pains." John asked Mark why he had not gotten twigs for the woodstove. Mark blathered, "Oh, John, my 'growing pains' hurted me...."

April 1981, we took a trip to Florida via motor coach driven by John and navigated by Grandma Bormann. It was a long way from

Michigan and poor John got tired driving. But, Fawn and Mark and Karrie greatly enjoyed Walt Disney World and Sea World. Grandpa Bormann, zesty and very much himself, and Aunt Deb played table games with the children on the way there and back. Mother, wound tight planning, thinking, worrying, said wistfully she almost couldn't bear to see the trip end.

I remember the parade of Disney characters on the isolated back path with all their attention on Fawn and Karrie. "Big Thunder Mountain" and "Space Mountain" became the favorite rides. We marveled at the detail, the lighted main street at night, John shaving by the pool. We enjoyed blueberry waffles, Monopoly, Dad playfully splashing Mother. Treated to pecans and pink azaleas, we basked in our time together. "Thank you, Lord, for all of it. Bless my husband, my three children, my parents, sisters and all my loved ones. Take my fears and scatter them far away. Perch on my shoulder. Be with all in need, suffering, in pain, sorrowing. Help me pursue loveliness."

After our return on a Sunday, we visited Kane's for a delightful day and came away with a lush red geranium from Jim's greenhouse.

·:·

May, after Mark's Zephyr Oiler Little League game, which was coached by John and Frank Spytma, we hot-footed to Keefe's Pharmacy to get Mother's Day cards for Grandmas. We selected nice ones and Karrie then hush-hushed Mark over to the other rack and instructed me not to look. I gave Mark $1.00 to spend before I went to the counter. As I was finishing, Mark and Karrie came bouncing up to the counter hiding something behind Karrie's back. As I was walking out, Mark came bounding back the length of the store to fetch an envelope. I was waiting in the car, when Mark tore up to me asking for thirty more cents. They were gone what seemed like a long time before they came out. They grinned from ear to ear as they tried to convince me we didn't have to wait until Sunday because that was too far away.

Mother's Day, we went to see new little Eleanor. Or and Vince cooed as they hovered over their new little sister. Mike showed me the note Vince wrote the tooth fairy and stuck under his pillow. He had lost his tooth playing soccer with Mark. Mike told me, "Mark knocked it out!"

Does anyone in Muskegon not remember, while salivating, the Mike's Bread bakery, which graced our town for nothing short of eleven years? "Delicious," "hearty" and "natural" come to mind. Mike Canter baked through the night; Darma and their sons Or and Vince accommodated customers during the day with maybe one or two assistants from Goodwill. Breads, rolls, dessert bars, and brownies beckoned from a myriad of tempting displays. Darma's mother, a no-nonsense baker in her own right, brought in pies, glacés, and triple decker cakes. The bakery, in both of its successive locations in downtown Muskegon, contributed a unique business, unsurpassed for quality in baked goods and catering.

Impulsively, we decided to see Dolly Parton in *9 to 5*. After twenty minutes, I departed with Karrie for McGraft Park until John and Mark came out of the Harbor Theatre. It wasn't a show for seven-year-old girls. The previous weekend we had gone to the Civic Opera to see *Camelot*. We were enjoying the fun of taking the children with us places. We took them to *Music Man* to see Uncle Bob perform. On an off-chance they would enjoy the music, we took them to hear the stupendous Westshore Symphony Orchestra at the most beautiful theater a small town could have. Muskegon was so fortunate to have volunteers in sufficient supply to tenderly restore every inch of the cozy shell-motifed Frauenthal Theater.

⁂

Together, John and I began cleaning up the copper boiler from Great Grandma Reichow's. We had stopped at the annual mall antique show to purchase polish. There, Mark bought three baseball cards, which he promptly lost before we left the mall. Almost to Meijer, I insisted we go back. There they were by the curb outside Sears getting drenched in the rain.

Mark soon discovered he had a chipped fracture on his right pinkie after we had been to Olaf's Crow. John saw it. The accident had happened the day before while he played soccer. Mark was upset to imagine what a cast might feel like, not to mention what problems life would present with a splint. He worried that he wouldn't be able to do his work in school. But by the time he got home, he was cheered figuring out how to do things with his casted pinkie, such as flipping switches. A couple days later he bellowed, "It's fun to see what I can do with my finger!"

John's parents and mine joined us on the weekend. John cooked barbecued chicken on the hibachi. Yum! John complimented my mother. He commented, "She always wants to hear what the other person has to say. She doesn't talk about herself and she makes no detracting comments." Rather, he thought she is very nurturing in her way of drawing the other person out. She actually favored her father who was also that way and she told me she wanted to be like him. Mark loved her dearly and always called her "special."

Despite her professional, objective demeanor at work, she still suffered harsh treatment by a brash, arrogant new young boss, after she had worked well with the old one for over twenty years. She had never before been treated as though she were incompetent or obsolete and I remember she was heartbroken. Finally, she transferred to another secretarial job in the schools for her last two years before retirement. The lingering memory of how she had been upbraided by a new principal always bruised her confidence and her sensitive spirit.

9.8 Meters Per Second Per Second

9. Above: Grandma and Grandpa Bormann, Albion, Michigan, 1986.
10. Right: Grandma and Grandpa Van Lente, Silver Lake, Michigan, 1982.
11. Below: Grandma and Grandpa Grimmette with Mark, Ypsilanti, Michigan, 1971.

All Nature Sings
Journal II: 1979–1982

Shout for joy to the Lord, all the earth,
 burst into jubilant song with music;
make music to the Lord with the harp,
 with the harp and the sound of singing,
with trumpets and the blast of the ram's horn –
 shout for joy before the Lord, the King.

Psalm 98:4-6, NIV

May 17, 1981, Grandma Bormann first saw the bluebird out the back slider door, while we were all eating breakfast. All agog, we observed that ephemeral blue, wafting creature. We hushed as we watched him there next to the red cardinal. That weekend, Grandpa Bormann, with luck, had his first chance to see the albino robin we told him about. Mark noticed the first orioles. They loved to pair up and chase each other around in the garage.

June 1, as we were coming in from work, Mark sorrowfully told us the scarlet tanager died. At bedtime, he mournfully told of throwing dirt at the bird in the tree. The bird came down. Karrie went out to see that it was dead. Mark felt very bad and he buried the bird. We talked a little about what happened. November 21, we put birdseed out for the birds. Mark knelt so still for so long behind the broken oak staring at the birds, that I wondered if he was in a trance. Then he made a snowball and threw it at a couple black-capped chickadees.

In spring, Mark bounded in with something down in his hands. He put it in my face to see. He was so close to me I couldn't tell what was there until he said, "It's a TOAD, Mom! A cute little toad ... I think the grass is good for the frogs and toads!" Whereupon, he leaped back outdoors with it. Of course, there was the hideous yellow spider captive in the jar in the front yard, too.

August 12, Karrie jumped into the Buick , which had not been driven for one and a half weeks. Karrie was sputtering about a spider web as she got in; she wanted to know if it was all over her face. Mark, after checking out his fort, came running and sandwiched in next to Karrie. The motor was purring when Karrie let out a scream. She had seen a brown spotted spider running up her jeans. She screamed again.

I gathered presence of mind enough to get out of the car and pull Karrie out after me. Mark chided us. He began sympathetically hunting for the spider because the spider's leg was injured. He had it running on his hand as he moved out of the car, but he lost it. Then, he retrieved it from the back seat floor. He carefully laid the injured spider on the grass. "Don't hurt the spiders! They eat bugs – that's what John said." Exasperated, Mark bellowed, "We could make a horror movie with our house." Karrie trembled, "Yeah, a scary house of spiders."

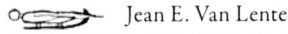

Mark screeched to have us see the huge, furry black spider in the backyard, toting an egg on her back. We were busy putting in a lawn, building flower boxes and painting window trim. John, in a frenzy, laid brick, seeded the backyard and fended off mosquitoes. We rejoiced in the beautiful weather! I loved the woods and the lake. The "lake effect" meant so much more than just snow; the lake's effect on me was tranquilizing and quickening all at once.

⋯⋰⋯

At the table, I told the children they could have one Double Stuff Oreo for dessert and, if they ate some asparagus, they could each have a second one. I put out three. Mark and Fawn snatched their cookies and I heard a shriek from Karrie because the one left had a chip in it. She cut loose while Mark chimed in unsympathetically, "Geez, Karrie, what do you think you are, the ruler of oreos?"

John brought Karrie to Peggy White's at 10 a.m. to get her hair trimmed. The front door to the house was wide open when he got back. We had front-door-shutting lessons all day. One of those hollow steel doors, it resisted fastening if the slightest breeze swept in from the west.

John unfortunately learned the one youth at Child and Family Services he was bragging about, suddenly "bombed." He ran away and stole three cars. Crazy business... John worked together with his dear-hearted superior, Richard Matt, and Betty, and the rest of the team for many years. I know they did their best to help many troubled and wayward youths. Child and Family Services' reputation possessed a long tradition in Muskegon.

One night after Mark's baseball game, I went overboard again jumping on his case. I lectured him about not playing his best. The next morning, Mark and I made a deal. He would pray for help to do the very best he could and I would shut up after games. Mark did swell in the very next game. He made a super catch, a throw to second just in time, and he began learning to tell the difference between a good pitch and a bad pitch. As a result, he "walked" every time.

On the way back from Mark's ballgame, Karrie instructed Mark, "You don't fall all by yourself; gravel helps ya." Mark clarified, "You mean gravity, Karrie. What is gravity, Karrie?" Karrie replied, "Little stones."

Kathleen Cobler told a funny story about a ballgame where Karrie was entertaining herself at the faucet until she was all wet. She sneaked to the car, undressed the "walking" doll she had brought with her and put on her doll's dry clothes.

Karrie hurried in, "Mom, Mark told me to get my tennis shoes on so I don't get 'striked' by poison ivy." She put on her tennis shoes in a flash in order to get back to Fawn and Mark and their building project. In a requited attempt, they began to build a second story to their tree fort. Mark was always trying to build things. He had previously shown me the picture of the picnic table he had copied from one of Karrie's play tables for her dolls. He was intent on constructing one.

In chorus, everyone wanted to go to the Seaway Festival parade. We made it downtown early to see all the pre-parade sights. The best was "Mr. Up-and-Down," the Dawn Donut clown. We met him and shook his hand, when Karrie saw that his right forefinger was off to the knuckle. She became obsessed by his disfigurement, wondering what might have happened to his finger. In concern and curiosity, she told John about it. John remarked on the need everyone has for closure.

·:꞊:·

July 11 the Van Lente picnic was held at the White Lake Golf Club with John's family and Nels and Mary Louise's family. These were two families related by both Alice and her sister and Ralph and his brother. They boasted ten and twelve children respectively. Picnics always held the sense of immense and the fun and variety a large gathering brings.

Whenever the Van Lentes got together, not only the local members came, but also those from far away. Sometimes, Gretchen, Jim and Bill were there with their families. Always, we looked forward to having Tom and Linda, Jennifer, Emily, and Joe join us from as far as Berwick, Pennsylvania, where they lived. Somehow, they never failed to pack up their family and migrate hundreds of miles west to Silver Lake where cousins enjoyed each other in their play and the adults bonded together once again for fun – sometimes mind to mind and other times for a little rowdy togetherness. Grandma and Grandpa Van Lente were the hub of the wheel.

It was a gorgeous light, airy Michigan summer day. We all left for Silver Lake. We climbed "razorback" dune and sailed on the day sailor. We swam.

···:···

For a food drive at church, I generously, I thought, donated a jar of peanut butter. When we reached home, John informed me, "We had used that, you know." So much for charitable overtures!

John helped his twin brother Joe paint his house, but his heart pounded for the waves of Lake Michigan. He scurried home to don his wetsuit to wade into the lake with his surfboard.

12. John Van Lente surfing in Lake Michigan, 1990.

That Sunday, we chose to eat at Mr. Steak's. I had told Karrie she may not have french fries and dessert. So, later, ordering, everyone at the table told Karrie to go ahead and order french fries. Karrie said, "No," and glanced sideways at me. The meal included french fries when it was delivered. We compromised such that Karrie ate a couple of french fries plus angel food cake with strawberries.

Dixie, the terrier, joined us too. Grandpa Bormann, knowing that his cigar was not very popular, walked around outside smoking and walking Dixie with Karrie at his heels.

⁂

John had suggested to Mark he ask Grandpa Bormann if he wanted to learn how to save money. Grandpa Bormann educated Mark about saving money. He advised Mark, "All you have to do to save money is don't spend it!" He told how he and another man were going to buy a store together before World War II. Each one was going to put in $200.00. Grandpa had saved; the other man had not. So, Grandpa paid $400.00 and bought the Pine Street Market store in Albion himself. Dad ran that store seven years before he served in North Africa during World War II. With boils all over his body while he was at war, he discovered he was allergic to chocolate. He believed he ate too much chocolate at his store and his allergy to chocolate lasted a lifetime.

We wondered how to control another ailment, Karrie's nail biting. Aunt Kathy promised Karrie that if she let her nails grow instead of chewing them, she would bring up nail polish. Karrie actually stopped biting her nails. Aunt Kathy remembered. The next visit, Aunt Kathy brought two dark, nauseating red colors, which she painted on Fawn and Karrie's fingers and toenails to their delight. Finally, with screeches from Karrie and Fawn, she painted Mark's two pointer fingers.

Mark continued working on the second story of the tree fort. He claimed he needed two-by-fours. Jeff and Nate were standing by. He was worried he said that, "the girls would come and 'terrilize' it." He was not about to let that happen. Finally, he joyously announced he had finished his tree fort.

The next Sunday, Mark wore the beautiful new-looking navy pants Grandma Grimmette had given him which had belonged to Uncle Scott. Mark wore them to church. After church, playing basketball, he tried to crawl under the garage door at Pastor Hanson's.

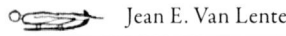

Alas, he rubbed through two nice round holes in the knees.

Karrie trounced in front of John and me when we were embracing. "When you kiss, be quiet! Gosh, you guys!" She had been just inside the door and, exasperated, she huffed out.

Mark complained his legs hurt again. Anyway, it was a good excuse for me to take a sick day. It was a beautiful day and a good time for me to spend some time with Mark. He commenced on the subject of: "If there's a war, do you have to go?" Also he asked me: "Do you get a shot to have a baby?" "No." "Well, how do you get one then?"

Fawn and Mark and Karrie are such marvelous creatures. Such a gift from God. "Lord, help me be the parent you want me to be. Forgive my weaknesses and make me strong. Thank you for your love. Teach them to love you. Amen."

⁂

September 12, John helped Lions with the crackerjack sale at the mall. He played his guitar for the first time in public. That event became a turning point for him. Gradually, he gained confidence to play his guitar and sing often on all kinds of occasions. He had a very nice, soothing deep voice.

The next day we met our favorite former next door neighbors at the Bear Lake Tavern for an overdue visit. The children were so excited to see Amy and Ben that they planned a dance in leotards and Mark dressed up as a Dolly Parton routine. They *had* to do it for *everybody*. Fawn said she didn't like it because we kept the show to just one song by Evie: "Step Into the Sunshine." They all wanted to do more.

Mark burst in from school and went right to work getting logs and stoking up the woodstove. He had wood-gathered all weekend. John and Mark also fashioned a windbreaker for the chimney. John rethreaded the well pipe, even though it was outside his comfort zone.

At supper, Karrie recalled how she had discovered the "callepitter" on the wall. Mark told how Mrs. Springstead dispelled the rumor she doesn't give homework. When she was forced to punish someone, her favorite method was to put her lipstick on real thick and give them a kiss.

Karrie and Fawn played and played inside as the weather turned cooler. They put on shows, played school, Barbie dolls, "Big house,"

"Little house." They blindfolded each other and led each other through the house and on and on. They sang and played the guitars. Is it possible they could be more darling now than ever? The children are so precious.

The girls finally drifted off to sleep. They fell asleep somehow to a record that purported the voice of a woman singing as her puppet in *Little Evie*. She was a ventriloquist and the noise from that scratchy record was never soothing. Mark and John were at the Catholic Central football game. With the rare uninterrupted time, I was able to do my Sunday school lesson and a few journal entries.

At Peggy White's salon, Janeen put Karrie's hair in braids. Karrie admired herself with braids as I was given a trim. She sidled up to Janeen, "My brother told me I look like Princess Leia." Janeen joined in, "You sure have a nice brother!"

Mark said nothing until we got in the car. "Karrie, I did not say you look like Princess Leia! You said, 'Don't you think I look like Princess Leia?' and I said, 'No, you don't look like her.'" Karrie just giggled and Mark shook his head.

This was Columbus Day, a holiday and a perfect fall day. Karrie took her braids out and squealed all over the house at the bushy kinks in her hair.

Evenings, we relaxed listening to John strum the guitar. Normally, still in school, he studied and wrote papers which was such a drag to see. He humored me by telling me he picked up a hitchhiker who turned out, coincidentally, to be the man in the boat last summer who had picked him up swimming far out in the lake.

Hugs and Kisses
Journal II: 1979–1982

"Make Room II"

Who, but a virgin
Loved, but not touched
For a home for the Spirit
To swell.

What, after all
Is rarer by far
Than suffering unknown
Outcast.

He came veiled
To a place
Unknown and unguessed,
To grow anywhere
Space is left.

We chased Him to Egypt,
Nailed Him to a tree.
Stripped, split all His clothing
Outworn, seamless piece
For the lot.

Gabriel announced the time had arrived,
Kingly shape for a landscape:

Mary's entry mild
To go out in amazement.

His backdrop: Love
Conceived for each child.

Jean E. Van Lente
December 20, 1999

John didn't let Mark get away with much. Mark didn't yet know how blessed he was to have what he had in John, but eventually he would. John was keen on Mark and the girls studying, playing to create skills, and learning obedience. My excitement stirred to see the children learn. Fawn and Karrie seemed to be having intellectual spurts. October 1981, they read everything. Driven, they wrote all the time: notes, pictures, signs, stories. In their Sunday school class, the girls learned to write "The Lord's Prayer."

John remarked to me as we ate Sunday brunch at Circles how the girls seem to take turns being confident. "One time, Karrie is the assertive one, while at other times, Fawn is." At Circles, the children brought up memories of Walt Disney World as they often had since April. Fawn always gleefully recalled the "Thunder Mountain Railroad" ride.

Karrie was doing her usual "fighting off of John's affection" routine. I gave Karrie the permission she was looking for, "You can give John a big hug, Karrie." She wrapped her arms around him in a big bear hug.

The season waxed fall. John was ecstatic over the beautiful leaves even in the gloomy, drizzly cold rain. Karrie spotted "Blackey" squirrel scampering out back in the trees and leaves. They wondered where "Greyie," "Superman," "Popeye," "George," and the others were.

John divulged, watching the Dallas Cowboys and Tommy Dorsett, that he doesn't fantasize anymore about being a big football hero... And I began to see signs of getting older. It was little ways gravity was winning out. I had shadows that didn't disappear with a good night's sleep, coarse hair on my chin and a gray hair! Mark reassured, "Don't worry, you'll always be my mom!"

I was taking a shower when Karrie came in talking a mile-a-minute as she sat on the toilet. I peeked from behind the curtain to see her sitting with the toilet cover down whizzing away as it dripped down the sides of the toilet. She moaned and rushed to get a pail with Mr. Clean to clean it up.

How thrilling to have Karrie teach Mark and me with untempered enthusiasm what she had just learned in her music lesson. She must have mimicked word-for-word what Mrs. Winter taught them. Of course, Mark, not to be outdone, had to learn and elaborate upon what Karrie taught him. Hands down at his side like a snail, arms out to reach the ocean, up to reach the sky, down to reach the ground, and he repeated those gestures again and again.

The sun was sparkling into our bedroom window piercing the frost designs. I knew that in Karrie and Fawn's room, the brightness would be shining through the eyelet valance ruffle to make an exquisite design on the wall. The girls loved their cozy little bedroom. And Karrie loved Fawn. She often tried to kiss her and hug her as we read stories. Fawn was, and is, Karrie's best friend.

13. Frost on a window on Fenner Road, 1999.

As Mark, Fawn and Karrie processed through the living room and kitchen to the *Music Man's* "Seventy-six Trombones," I tried to retrieve the things floating in my brain the previous few minutes. John and Mark began to play chess. Karrie proceeded to tell John about mental health client, Muriel's behavior at night class. "She said a bad word, John!" As John was praising Karrie, "I'm glad you don't feel compelled to repeat it," Karrie blurted out, "Damn!" Both Mark and Karrie picked up Muriel's line, "You can talk to me, but don't make me mad!"

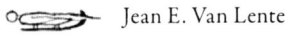

My friend, Henriet Vissia and I lunched at Peck Street BQ. Our chat was what I needed after a low morning with Mary; I had heard so many wounded accounts. On my mind was the barnyard - - stinky goats, barking dogs, and felled trees – going on next door inches from our serene property. I felt swallowed up with the fear of being swallowed up. Before many more days, I lunched with Jane, Heather, Darma, Eleanor, Mark, and Karrie at Aaron's. I had been with my family and friends. How could I feel sad?

Mark restocked the woodstove for me just before we went to bed and he instructed me on what to do after he fell asleep.

※

Tree-shaking Day! Ten inches of snow fell November 20, 1981 at 32°. Great glops of snow hung heavy on evergreen branches and oak branches where leaves had not yet dropped. All the snow weighed the trees down; the young ones were bowed to the ground. We rolled big snowballs to clear off the three hundred foot driveway. Mark and Karrie began creating their sliding slopes again.

We lost electricity by evening, so in response to generous invitation, we stayed with John's parents overnight. Alice and Ralph welcomed us and we had a lovely visit. Fawn and Karrie talked Grandma Van Lente into sewing clothes for "poor baby." Karrie scurried to bring her piano books out to play her tunes.

The next day, upon returning home, we slid down the hill behind the house. The tree smack in the middle of the track, of course, just made it more exciting. Finally Karrie and Fawn came in to practice their Christmas songs for the church program. Fawn had been chosen to be an angel.

On a special holiday trip, John took me to Ann Arbor to the Marriott. We went shopping to the Rider Shop, Cuisine LTD for tortes, and the Simulation Station. We bought three blue mittens with the middle one knitted for two hands in one. I have never seen another pair like them, where you could hold hands and keep warm at the same time. We enjoyed the whirlpool. We met a couple from

Canada a la prime rib and we visited Eastern Michigan University, my alma mater. The excursion made for a romantic, lovely adventure.

Meanwhile, Mark and Karrie stayed with Grandma and Grandpa Bormann. They played card games. Santa Claus visited. Grandpa gave them chewing gum. They were treated to the nativity scene on Duck Lake. Sunday, we saw Aunt Kathy and Uncle Dick in their new house. She now had a pen for her horses, "Red Hot Rose" and "Shadow." Grandpa walked in the back door and announced, "Everybody's drinking and here I am dry as a bone!"

December 14, 1981, from the North Pole in response to a school assignment, Mark received a letter:

Dear Mark,

And a cheery beery meery Christmas to you, too!

Thank you for asking about my family. Mrs. Claus was fine until she tried to wash my suit for the 19,892nd time and accidentally got sucked through one immense pantleg into the gyrating washing machine. I never heard or saw her again. Do you know where I could find a new one?

The elves are tearing their stringy, elfy hairs out trying to get all the toys ready. My best crew just about went blind trying to put together millions and millions of electronic games and mini-home computers.

Thank you for your fine letter. Old St. Nicholas will see what he can do.

Read what kind of a person old St. Nicholas really was on the sheet I have enclosed. Share it with your class.
      As ever,
      S.C.

Reluctantly, we wished goodbye to Christmas for 1981. We enjoyed good roads, good health. It worked out that Karrie and Mark saw Grimmettes. Mark tried his best to be Santa Claus in order to cheer up Grandma Grimmette, but she was so very ill at that time. It was the last time Mark and Karrie saw Grandma Grimmette alive.

We had a nice visit at Aunt Jean and Uncle Jim Reichow's on the centennial farm after the Candlelight Service Christmas Eve. A joyous Christmas Day passed at Aunt Deb's apartment. Mark, Fawn and Karrie so grown up, were spontaneous, yet appreciative. They behaved like three sweethearts. Of course, gift-giving at Christmas, overdone in my family, lavishly lasted an entire afternoon.

Van Lente's Christmas party was a great time! John's folks were tickled with the gift of a microwave. Eva, Anna, and Nicole played with the popular "Cabbage Patch" dolls Grandma Van Lente made for them.

·:·

After haircuts, Mark remarked, "I feel funny with this haircut ya know... like I got a load off my mind." Karrie was pouting over not getting the "high fashion boots" she wanted.

The grousing passed and Fawn and Karrie and Mark ate John's homemade stuffed-with-sauce delectable pizza. They bounded out back to bounce on the poor bent oak tree some more. Had it occurred to us, we might have given thanks in gratitude for all the money we didn't spend on toys and recreation for the children, given the free, limitless bounty nature herself provided for their utter enjoyment.

Mark came home from school and told me he played quarterback at recess. Postured as a champion, he said he threw a fifty-yard pass! I thought that was very good. But, when John came home and Mark told him his news, John had to be skeptical. Diplomatically, he tried to bring Mark back to reality. Mark got out the yardstick to begin measuring with the "Nerf" ball from the garage. He measured in the dark twenty-four yards. Maybe? Maybe we should have let him think fifty yards.

After roast beef, late, Mark set up a track with magazines and his good-sport-of-a-sister raced his little cars with him to see whose would leap farther.

At Lion's lunch, an amusing exchange between the "Tail Twister" and Mark took place as he quickly asserted that, indeed, he does not get an allowance Tuesday nights. The children posted their chore lists on the refrigerator and received stars for doing their chores.

·:·

We were heading for another sub-zero weekend with lots of snow. January 15, 1982, Grandpa Bormann went ice fishing twice at 0°; still he said he can't take the ice like he used to.

Mark told me he liked the white socks with the green band, but he added I should not give him the ones only so long and he showed me with his fingers, because they were Karrie's or Fawn's. He had tried those on before and they "didn't work." Fawn and Karrie side by side in their red and blue striped pajamas made one elfish sight.

As usual, the beautiful things slip by. Moments that are so full of meaning, of connecting, of love, bless us. Praise God. "I miss Grandma Reichow," Mark said. He added, "I wanted to ask her what it was like when Wilbur and Orville Wright flew the airplane at Kitty Hawk. There were so many things I wanted to ask her yet." I knew whereof Mark spoke; I felt the same way. At eighty-five, she died too soon.

Karrie kept trying to tell me what the next day at school was: "Patrotic" or "Parrotic" and so on. She wanted to wear red, white, and blue to school. She lay under her covers: "If you don't have blue, you can wear (pause) white and (pause) red; if you don't have red, you can wear (pause) white and (pause) blue; if you don't have (pause) white, you can wear (long pause)..." and by this time, she had gotten so thoroughly confused, she couldn't remember what colors she needed to finish. She was still trying, until I shook her and laughed.

Mark and Karrie and I took a brave impulsive sledding trip to killer Sherman Hill. Mark hollered, "Don't stick out your leg, Mom!" I stuck out my leg. Mark still remembers he was upset because we had to go home. I was relegated to crutches with a torn ligament.

Sunday, I was resting in bed when I heard Karrie coming in for one more thing and Mark called out, "Karrie, let Mom rest in peace!" At church, John was escorting me into the car with remarks like, "C'mon, cryp!" or "This is the first time I've felt like the boss." Mrs. DeVries suddenly passed by and called out, "You got a crutch; you ought to use it!"

On the way home from choir that week, Mark and Karrie were well-launched into their game of one-upmanship again. I cracked down and vowed if it went on, I would stop and dump them into the snow bank. Mortified, Karrie reacted, "Mom, you're either supposed to love your children or put them out in adoption!"

The next day, Mark and John got home from skiing at Grand Haven, Michigan. Mark, suddenly distraught, remembered, "Karrie, when you said, 'Mark doesn't wash his armpits,' that hurt my feelings. Besides, Karrie, I DO wash my armpits!"

What Generations Pass Along
Journal II: 1979–1982

"Later Adulthood"

In viewing their own children as mature adults, parents are able to determine whether they have helped their children to be able to meet the challenges of intimacy, work, and child-rearing with creativity and morality.

Barbara M. Newman and Philip R. Newman
Development Through Life: A Psychosocial Approach
1979, 2009

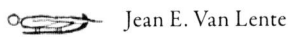

Mark and Karrie and I went to Albion to Grandma and Grandpa Bormann's while John attended Edo's class. We slid at Victory Park on Hannah Street, swam at the Albion College pool, and roller-skated at the new roller rink. Mark went ice fishing with Grandpa. They played "Old Maid" with Grandma. We ate delicious fresh fish, corned beef and cabbage, and Grandma's homemade beef noodle soup.

I tried, but I couldn't get Grandpa committed to taking Mark fishing. When he was getting ready at 7 a.m. Monday morning to go fishing with his good pal, Dick Schultz, Mark hopped out of bed and sat downstairs. He looked up at Grandpa who was trotting down the stairs and asked, "Are you goin' fishin', Grandpa?" Affirmative nod. "Can I go?" Long pause. "Well, are your boots warm? Do we have some plastic bags, Leona?" Grandpa thought Mark could go without breakfast to get going. Mark was thrilled that he caught three fish.

During one trip to Albion, Mark and Karrie went fishing at Prairie Lake with Grandpa Bormann. Grandpa shared he had said a little prayer before they left. It was 8:30 p.m., dark, and Grandma was getting worried. Just then, there came the old rusty blue truck down the hill, with parking lights on, from Prairie Lake. They produced a pail full of beautiful bluegill and sunfish.

For aficionados (no pun intended), like Jim Kane, I reveal my avid fisherman father's favorite fishing haunts. Summers he fished Duck Lake, Prairie Lake, Bolt Lake, Craig Lake, and Shedd Lake. Ice fishing with his buddies, they sought out Prairie Lake and the Gang Lakes near Coldwater, toting their ginger brandy. The ice melts around the edges of the lake first. Dad always kept right on ice fishing into spring by rowing his aluminum boat from shore out to the ice on Prairie Lake where he fished. When he was finished, he rowed his boat back to shore, hopefully with a mess of fish in his bucket. Nottawa Lake provided many filets of perch and bluegill for supper also. They knew the best spots to "get 'em."

Rollerskating, Grandma was angelically calm as she watched Grandpa teeter a bit as he got back his skate feet. He was sixty-nine years old. Hugh Washington made an announcement and everyone applauded Grandpa Bormann. He slapped his hands to his head. Afterwards, he figured they did that to warn skaters not to run into him.

Mark proceeded headlong into making eggnog. The blender was three quarters full when he tried to lift the pitcher by unscrewing it. Everything came splashing out the bottom. He was crushed. Poor fellow, but now he'll know.

We sent the three into Eberhard's grocery by themselves with a list. Confident, they came out having found most of the items on the list. We praised them for their collaboration, efficiency, and accuracy.

When Fawn and Karrie took a streak to "dress up," they wore long skirts, shawls, wigs, heels, purses with pulchritude. Sometimes the costumes were meretriciously scanty, sometimes matronly. One time the girls dressed up and Karrie was outrageous with a baton: "I'm here to judge the living of the dead!" Then she let loose with her belly roll laugh.

·:·

I called Aunt Deb and Uncle Bob to discover that Grandma Grimmette was so bad she was expected to die any day. It had been the family's intention not to call until she had expired. I called Grandpa Grimmette.

April 1, 1982, Grandma Grimmette died. Grandma and Grandpa Bormann, Mark, Karrie, and I went to the funeral in Ypsilanti, Michigan.

All that week Karrie had talked as she thought and cried. Mark said little. He only cried in the car on the way to Albion as Karrie wondered aloud about who would feed Brandy, who would make pancakes, who would watch them swim. Mark's eyes brimming, he said, "I'll miss her."

Grandma Grimmette's funeral was a cold, snowy, icy, windy day. We went to Immanuel Baptist in Ypsilanti. Next, we went to Textile Road where they lived. Grandpa Grimmette told my parents, "Jean and I understand each other." He gave me a ceramic shepherd boy carrying a lantern and a lamb from Irene's things.

In the worst weather, we crawled our way home. Mother always drove. By the time we finally arrived home in Albion, we all were very tired and drained.

Grandma Bormann had recalled some unbelievable things from the past, but then, she had a memory that would stop a train. She remembered where Washington Street was from 1939. She spoke of the day of Mark's baptism, March 7, 1971, eleven years prior, in Ypsilanti when it was snowy coming home. She remembered the house where the chapel now stands at Eastern Michigan University. She remembered where Forest Street was. I never really knew anyone else with as keen a memory as Mother had. It was second nature for her to retrieve exact detail of any time in the past.

·:·

April 5, 1982, we had a foot of snow. It was cold and drifting. The little birds were digging for food. For the third weekend in a row, we were in Albion for an inspired Easter and seventieth birthday celebration for Grandpa Henry Bormann and his twin brother, Uncle Herbert.

Debra brought her fiancé, Ed; we were all in the living room before church, passing the time. The conversation turned to how Mark and Karrie had gotten along the week prior. Karrie edified us all by telling us how she beats Mark: "First, I kick him in the nuts... then, I sit on him... and then I fart on him." By this time, I had left the area; Mother was telling Karrie to stifle and Dad's bottom lip was on the floor. Ed tried to hide his amusement.

I asked Grandma Bormann how the children were when they took them to breakfast with their friends, the VanMeters. She reported they were very good. On the way home, she said Karrie told her she hoped she was good because, "I don't want to be a disgrace to you, Grandma."

One evening, Karrie somehow heard us talking about something and she suggested, "Let's ask "St. John Writes," as though that were a person. Soon after, when Freeway the cat was jumping around acting strange, Karrie's explanation for it was, "Maybe he's in conscious pilot."

The next day, we had another lovely day swimming. August 15, we swam at Duck Lake. How contagious John's enthusiasm is. He dove off the drop-off and swam underwater to see the fish below. Fawn, Karrie and Mark tried desperately to dive and see fish, too.

John swam incredible marathon distances. His mother had been a strong swimmer as well. Karrie and Fawn later occupied themselves collecting clams and snails and stones.

The next week, Mark was at day camp all week. We visited the night of the overnight because it was supposed to be parents' night. We found his group far down the beach. He was ignoring us. Karrie had brought him a present – a bar of Sweetheart soap. She ran up to him to give it to him, but he saw what she had and shrank back with a mockingly prissy gesture and a look of disdain.

Fawn and Karrie pranced around in their leotards all morning before they left for Creative Movement classes at Blue Lake Community School with instructor, Peggy Hunt. All afternoon, as usual, they played for hours in the basement or bedroom or living room with the clothes and the dolls and all the accompaniments. John made vegetable beef soup in the woodstove oven. I cooked swiss chard and made carrot cake and pea salad for supper.

Big plans were taking place for the thirty-third birthdays for John and his twin brother, Joe. The children loved it. We were blowing up balloons the night before. Mark blew one up over and over until it got too thin and burst. John kept blowing one up until it popped and scared him. Karrie laughed that gusty, rolling laugh because she loved the preparations. Fawn blew the biggest, the blue Smurf! We arranged surfboards on logs for tables for the "little ones."

Mark and I went to the Community Mental Health ballgame against Muskegon Regional Center. Later, when we stopped at Mrs. Bird's to pick up the cakes, she was just decorating them. There was a bald face for John and a dark, bushy-haired face for Joe.

After a congenial party, John settled the children down by serenading them to sleep with his melodies on the guitar. Fawn liked, "Yellow Submarine"; Karrie's request was usually for the new one, whatever that might be.

The girls are so dear. On a sunny afternoon, I was laying bricks and they came prancing around the corner of the house in sundresses as maidens of Odin. They were ready to gather flowers in buckets. They gave each other rides in the blue wheelbarrow. Karrie sneaked up behind Freeway, grabbed him and plunked him into the wheelbarrow. Then, she gave her unappreciative passenger a ride. The girls took turns keeping Freeway in the wheelbarrow. When they let go of him, out he bounded away into the ferns as fast as he could go. Karrie and Fawn giggled and giggled over it.

14. Fawn and Karrie and Freeway, 1982.

John spent four hours in the thrashing lake, September 5, 1982. He and I were in the day before without wetsuits. Afterwards, at the Bear Lake Tavern, he told me my lips were blue.

To end summer, Grandma Bormann put up eighteen quarts of pears, which son-in-law, Dick loved, and tomatoes. I never canned anything until Mark and I together canned sweet pickles from all their home-grown cucumbers in Lake Placid, September 19, 2011. I was visiting him and Keela Dates, his fiancée, at the time. Keela made it known she liked sweet pickles. They turned out very tasty.

Board games were always popular with the children. After a rousing game of Sorry, we tucked in after devotions and Karrie wanted to give Mark a kiss goodnight. She planted one on him and he groaned, "Torture!" Mark asked to sleep in Fawn's bed because he gets lonely at night. He felt anxious after seeing a couple scenes on TV of emaciated children starving in Africa with flies on their faces. He murmured he didn't want to sleep alone.

Pastor's "Children's Talk" evolved around nicknames. We talked about our sobriquets on the way home. Fawn sported "Skinny Minny"; Karrie answered to "Little Russian Shotputter," "Bigly-bigly Boo," or "Karrie-Banary." Mark was "Mark Bark," or "Punk."

September 27, 1982, Karrie thought about Grandma Grimmette and she became saddened. She missed her as she thought about the times during the summer that she spent at the house on Textile Road.

·:·:·

Mark displayed a voracious appetite for physics and space phenomena. Information from Berkeley must have caught his eye in 1982; it caused quite a stir in his young imagination. He read a couple scientists' hunches erupted around possible early reversals in the earth's "magnetic field." They believed thousands or millions of years ago, under duress, the earth's magnetic field had changed 180° multiple times. Guessing, it was suggested at one time compasses may have pointed south instead of north.

One large meteorite crater in West Germany was said to have happened by a smack into earth by a meteor about the same time that a "magnetic reversal" occurred. The crater is called Ries Crater; it measures fourteen miles wide and is said to be fifteen million years old.

Theories abound. Juxtaposed, the idea of a "magnetic field reversal" and the idea that a crater possibly formed at the same time served as evidence, rather defied explanation. How clearly and thoroughly does a parent or teacher transmit the importance of discernment to a child? What are facts and what are theories? At the time, thirty years ago, I don't recollect that I said anything about it.

·:·:·

> At last the tree gave way; a boy was born,
> And dryads washed him with his mother's tears.
> They wove a crib for him of leaves and grasses;
> Envy herself, caught at an honest moment,
> Would sigh, then call him pretty as a picture,
> Painted as one of Venus's boy babies,
> Perhaps a twin, naked, and sweet as Cupid,

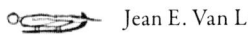

Nor could you tell which boy was which unless
One held an arrow and one stood empty-handed.[1]

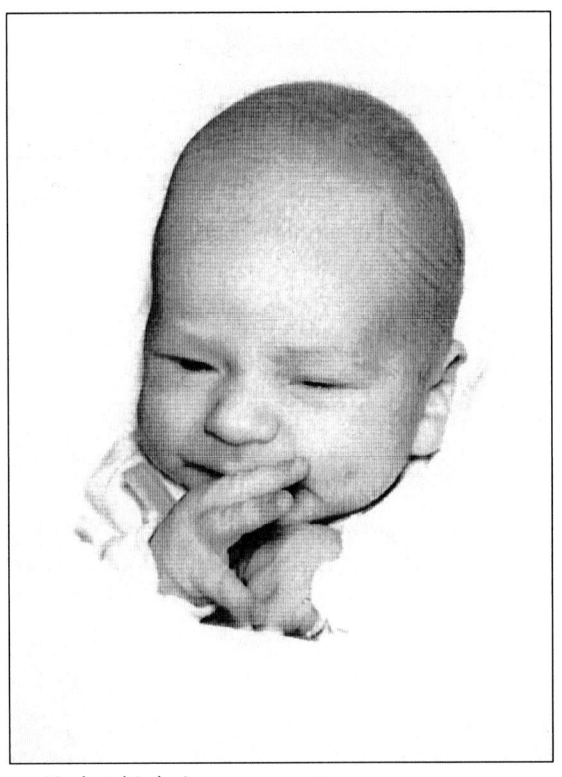

15. Mark at birth, January 23, 1971.

Mark's distinguishing characteristics as a baby grew with him. January 23, 1971, at 4:56 a.m. he was born eight pounds on a very cold day with one hand open and the other a fist. Many photographs would show that instinctive presentation of one hand open and one hand in a fist.

At birth, Mark held his head up. Within days he could lift his head and neck off the mattress. If he was held, he always wanted to sit, and not long at that before he had to be off and going. If he was in a good mood or planning mischief, he would rub his feet together. And when he was delighted, he made a long crescendo while breathing in. I remember him as a noisy child who resisted cuddling. He had expressive eyes, mouth and hands. From birth he displayed the dimple in his left cheek.

One of his first and frequent phrases was, "Here we go!" at about twenty-two months. Two other four-word phrases I often heard him say were, "I can't reach it," and "Let's read a book." One day he dove into the filled bathtub head first with all his clothes on. He showed an aptitude for jigsaw puzzles early on. At three, he told us, "I can't grow a beard; I don't have any of those toothpicks in my face."

Mark began referring to his new sister as "it." "It's crying," or "It's sleeping." In the first month, Mark picked Karrie up by the midsection and marched her across the landing to the next apartment to give her away to the neighbors. But soon, he decided she was more fun than not and he became very protective of "Curry." Later, at four, he could not have been more ecstatic to have another sister, Fawn added, only to increase his joy in life.

Mark continued to be shy and unconfident as he began preschool. During two years of Little Learner's Preschool, Heather, Boyd, and Lee were friends. He loved preschool and the camaraderie there. Heather has remained a good friend ever since. Mrs. Freeman, his kindergarten teacher, noted he liked to plan and dream. He liked to work and was known for his sense of humor.

Mark also loved wood building from the time he was two, when he watched his father build a trestle desk. Grandpa "Borney" Bormann's friend, Art Anderson, gave him wood scraps when he was four years old. From them, he made a toolbox, seed box, a coat hanger, a mailbox, and a clothes rack.

Mark delighted in gardening. One day, he proudly brought in a potato the size of a marble and carefully cut it in thirds for Karrie, me and himself. He rode a bike spring of 1977. The last day of first grade, he won two blue ribbons for the "50-Yard Dash" and the "Running Broad Jump." Mark's strengths only strengthened.

Goings On Across the Street
Journal III: 1982–1994

"The Home Visit"

COPD, diabetes, edema.
Test results not back – a tumor?
Five miles east and seventh house down,
'Round back in a 4-roomer.
Rap, rap.
Withered yews, parched grass;
Two-step an anthill; make it fast.
Tap, tap.
Plastic pieces, dry birdbath.
Knock, knock.
"Well come, but please excuse
My entry way lined with refuse."
HOH, six legs in sync;
Plant, lift. Plant, lift.
Pause, pause. Gibralter.

"Sit there – a table for your papers."
Two heads pictured close; drapes closured.
Curled schooled faces tucked in corners.
Bandaged foot inside a slipper.
"Foot rest?"
"That's done already."
Strips and lancets – insulin.
Jot, jot.

Dutifully answering questions.
Ring, ring.
"Under here – see over there."
Warm creases connect, tolerating
"Just about a year ago."
Plant, lift. Plant, lift.
Pause, pause. Gibralter.

"Just a year. How are you doing?"
Brush the pepper; shift the salter.
Nor hand to rest on several crumbs,
Etched, well-ingrained…
Caressing stubble on a sailor's prickly chin.

Jean E. Van Lente
September 30, 1997

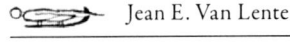

Oh boy... I scooted to the compost at 5:45 a.m. to toss out the shriveled pink and yellow mums Dad had brought. Just as I was about to heave them, something moved. A little skunk in the compost alerted himself. My heart stopped; I split for the house. We always had "little friends" in the woods. My early rise was intentionally to spruce up the house for a party.

Birthdays, as in the past, still promised special festivities. Guests, cake, games, and gifts, the children never tired of these capers. On Mark's twelfth birthday, Ben came over with his family for supper. It was always a glad reunion with them! April 17, 1983, Karrie finally had permission to open her gifts from Grandma and Grandpa Bormann, which she had brought back with her from having visited there spring vacation: a box of knitted Barbie doll clothes and a pure white furry Dakin Kitty on a blue pillow. John made pizza for Karrie, Fawn, Vicki, Kathy, Wendy, David, Anita, Michael, and Mark (the pest). Mark couldn't stay away from the fun of the treasure hunt. He relished the pin-the-balloon on the donkey's tail. He hooted when Kathy gaily announced, "I don't use shampoo; I use real poo!" Karrie opened cards from Aunt Kathy, Aunt Deb, Aunt Deb and Uncle Bob, and a call from her dad. They each had had enough celebration, I guess.

June 5, 1983, and why today? I don't know. It's been so long and so many things have happened. John took the children to see *Return of the Jedi*. I worked in the yard until they got back, all totaled seven hours. I was so sore in bed I thought I might never move again.

One typical evening family scene included John watching *T.J. Hooker* while his typewriter was in front of him. I sported upholstery samples, checkbooks, papers, a purse, folded clothes, "Wings" information, a church bulletin, and a book about trees all in my lap at once. I had just reprimanded Freeway the cat for curling up next to Karrie's face to sleep. He settled at the foot in that case. Mark finished the model, "The Christie."

The following afternoon, with uninhibited creativity, Mark, Karrie, and Fawn produced three skits: 1 "Spanish Restauranté," 2 "The Slum of New York," and 3 "Definitely Sick." For "Spanish Restauranté," Mark was Willy the waiter, Fawn was Belinda, Karrie was Zodina. For "The Slum of New York," Mark was Bum Bunker and Mac, Karrie was Jodini, and Fawn was Isabella. For "Definitely Sick," Mark was Mr. Clumsy the patient and Hank the janitor, Fawn was Deli Doctor, and Karrie was Nancy the nurse. They whooped it up and the off-the-cuff scenes were hysterical to watch. They loved engaging in theatrics together, once they were sure of a captive audience.

August 27, 1983, John participated in his first triathlon! By 1985, John was participating in his third triathlon, his second in Muskegon. His foot ached in the arch area. It threatened to be one of those spots that have to work out. Unfortunately, the injury occurred just before a triathlon; his running, biking, and swimming would be compromised in the race. Fawn and Karrie seemed ambivalent about watching the spectacle. Karrie spoke dryly, "I like to see everyone throw up." John came in 45th in that triathlon.

·:¦:·

"Given the degree of ambivalence in our culture toward sexuality, it would be difficult to imagine that an individual could experience puberty, pregnancy, or menopause without some emotional involvement."[1]

The children grew to increased sexual awareness. At the beach, Mark took a gob of green moss floating in the water and put it under his armpits to "gross" me out. Karrie took Fawn to the lingerie department at the new Hudson's store near Battle Creek, telling Fawn it was "sex education." Trying out new words, Mark came out with "hump" and a string of others, although some he wouldn't say....

I stayed home a day from work to help finish the move of Karrie and Fawn into our old bedroom, larger in area than their old room. We painted the spacious room pink. John and I moved to their old room. We were eating Red Baron pizza when Mark attempted to hog it all in mock ownership, calling provocatively, "But Karrie, I'm a growing boy!" Karrie retorted, "I'm a growing girl and besides, I'm blossoming!" Then, she went on to other questions of interest: "Mom, why do some people eat for two when they're pregnant?"

In a renovative plan, our placement unit at work: Marilyn, Mary Lou, Joe, Sue, Peter, Linda, and myself moved to the Department of Social Services. I loved the camaraderie. Bob, Karleen, Char, Barb, and Terry were always solution oriented, a lot of fun, and I admired them. We were able to work out many situations together for the benefit of community placement in Muskegon during that period. Ten years later, my career took on variety, when John and I moved to Cape Coral, Florida. I served as an in-home social worker for Able Care. But just as I was about to be promoted in 1996, I returned to Muskegon. The epigraph poem of this chapter calls up a poignant scene from that work. Fort Myers, Florida, encompassed a plethora of resources, given the large senior population there. My work proved satisfying. Cape Coral in 1994 still possessed large tracts of open undeveloped land. In 2004, when I returned, the landscape and prices had completely changed, the population having grown wildly.

·:·

Karrie decided it was time to measure herself again. She slapped herself flat to the wall as straight as a reed. Mark leaped to the scene to exclaim, "You're to the 'Not Yet' mark, Karrie!" Then, it was Mark's turn. He craned his neck to reach very tall. Mark had grown one inch, but Karrie had grown one and a half inches. Mark quipped, "Karrie, from now on take your height from the wideness."

Mark deigned to give Karrie a lecture, "Do you believe everything you hear, Karrie? You shouldn't believe everything, Karrie." Karrie reasoned, "Well, how do you know what to believe and what not to?" Mark proceeded to tell Karrie something that happened at school. Karrie returned, "I don't believe it." Mark imperialistically declared, "Oh, very good, Karrie, but this is true!"

Well, Karrie decided all on her own to have a doll sale. She debated whether to sell them dressed or naked. Finally, she dressed them and priced them and put a sign out by the road. When no one stopped, she pretended people were coming. It sounded so real I came from my dishes to see who was there. Karrie giggled. Soon, when Mark came home from Michael's, he felt Karrie's sign needed reinforcing; grabbing it, he took it to the basement to hammer on it awhile.

Still in school, John's professor held up his paper to the class as an example in "Ego Psychology." Soon, he would be finished with his master's degree. January 10, 1984, John attended the Alcohol conference in Kalamazoo. There, he developed a bad rash from soaking in the whirlpool too long. Why should he have to pay so dearly for a luxury?

Karrie did some thinking on babysitting. She wondered if she would make a good babysitter. At supper, Mark and Karrie demonstrated how the various babies, such as Kevin and Sandy, at Aunt Theresa's, fall asleep at the table. Timmy actually wet on Mark and he had to change into Karrie's shorts one day.

John arrived home from "Advanced Methods" in time for devotions. Mark ventured, "Goodnight, John… I love you." Well, John was visibly touched. He guessed that was a first.

·:·

By the time Mark was thirteen years old, he was joining John and Dave Gonzales and all the other volunteers to erect a wood-sided luge track across the street in Muskegon State Park. His initial distress because his favorite sliding hill was being overhauled and developed soon gave way to excitement and anticipation over the projected track to come.

Meanwhile, it became clear Mark was not the only one distressed. State Senator Phil Arthurhulz found himself fending off strong criticism toward his support for money for such a project. Mike Knight, Sports Council Director, threw in his influential weight to support the project.

·:·

We enjoyed having family over to visit. April 22, 1984, we celebrated Easter with my parents, John's parents and Aunt Toby. We tried to mimic the pork tenderloin with spinach we had enjoyed at Grootmüder's Töfel in Grand Rapids. It was delicious, but the weather was rotten. July 1, 1984, we hosted a Bormann reunion in Muskegon at our house in the woods. We had perfect weather and a good turn-out of Bormanns from as far away as Chicago. John grilled marinated chicken and turkey ribs to popular demand.

School was over for John and on August 17, 1984, he received his Master of Social Work degree. We celebrated with Grandma and Grandpa Bormann and Aunt Kathy with a dinner at Metropol.

September 3, John and I came to the end of a long and ambitious biking vacation. Meanwhile, Mark and Karrie visited their dad in

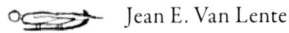

Colorado. That might have been the trip Rick took them to see the Olympic Training Center in Colorado Springs.

While they were gone, John and I undertook our biking trip to Wisconsin. First, we rode our bikes to Silver Lake, beginning in the rain, facing headwinds. We stayed overnight with Mom and Dad Van Lente. We rode north to Ludington, Michigan on our bikes the next day and took the "Beaver Islander" ferry to Door County, Wisconsin. We rode bikes all over Door County, including Jane Kane's birthplace, Washington Island. In slicing rain, we took the Washington Island Ferry crossing Ports des Morts there. By a week ending Sunday, we were surviving on only five hours sleep on the ferry. We trekked to Pentwater, Michigan and found the juiciest, most scrumptious peach on the ground in an orchard along the way. John shaved at the dock. We attended mass with Mom and Dad Van Lente. Later, Mom Van Lente made us a wonderful meal of turkey and poached egg on a muffin. On a rainy Monday morning, Mom and Dad brought us home by car after approximately three hundred miles of biking.

John was around now; he was happy he could attend to all his "starved birdies" without feeling torn by demands of school. Fawn, drawn to his lap with a cold, missed her mom. Karrie begged John to play the guitar and sing her to sleep. Mark started another plane model John brought him from Ann Arbor. Mark also helped John put washers on the bunk bed John had made for the girls; the washers were intended to stabilize the bunk bed.

It was too cold to swim this weekend. When that happened we missed the swimming.

Inexorably, winter came again. January 27, 1985, Mark had just turned fourteen and Karrie was old enough to go to camp overnight with her class. We were having fun teasing Mark about his friend, Heather, assigning him the tasks of birthday monies and the closing prayer for Sunday school. She called multiple times over the week to remind him. 8:40 a.m., Sunday morning, he was writing his prayer. I made a couple suggestions like praying the Word would take root and be like seeds to grow... Mark looked at me incredulously, "Mom, they'll all say, 'Nice prayer, Mark. Did your mother write it?'" The very last minutes, he came up with a prayer.

By 1985, Mike Knight was leading the new young lugers to pick up snow in local parking lots to pack on the track to form ice. For three winters actually, the weather in Muskegon did not cooperate for the luge. Mark would come in at 2 a.m. on weekends, take off his boots and the plastic bags that served as insulation under his boots and dump himself into bed. Mark took advantage when no one else was using the track to go down twenty-five or thirty times every day on the track sleds. His routine provided a hefty amount of valuable practice for him.

Muskegon's 600 meter track drew county residents as well as people from as far as Chicago. Something novel, winter lovers came to try it. I made mention of Mark's newly found interest in less than two lines in my third journal. Apparently, it did not dawn on me what might lay ahead from these humble beginnings in the woods.

16. Muskegon's first luge club, 1985.

February 1985, we took the family to Laramie, Wyoming to ski. John squashed all our things into a big cardboard box and tied it to the top of our Mercury fake-wood station wagon with his solution to all problems: rope. It was dry driving out, but on the return, we had rain around Chicago. Oh, boy!

On this trip, we visited Bill and Kathy, Nicole and Alison Van Lente. We slept on the floor at their house one night before we took up residence in our rented cabin at the V-Bar Ranch in Cheyenne. At that time, Karrie was fighting with a fear of being kidnapped probably stemming from the pictures of missing children on the backs of the milk cartons. So when she noticed a door in their bedroom in the cabin, she and Fawn were frightened that someone would come in during the night. Karrie and Fawn persuaded big brother Mark to sleep closest to the door before they could settle down for the night. Skiing was a lot of fun. The beautiful snow-covered slopes went on forever.

November 11, 2012, John reminisced with Karrie. He remembered a ski trip to Crystal Mountain with all of the children. Glancing down the hill, he saw Mark with beginners Fawn and Karrie in tow, teaching them to snow-plow. He told Karrie, "That is one of my favorite memories."

※

August 29, 1985, John's birthday, we were still in Albion after having gone to Stratford, Ontario, Canada to see *King Lear*. We canned pears from the huge pear tree behind the house next to the old crumbling outhouse. Grandma made John a carrot and pineapple birthday cake. We enjoyed fresh fish Dad caught. We ate sweet corn, swiss chard, cucumbers, tomatoes, and lettuce – all from Grandpa's garden.

When we returned from Albion, John reserved a spot at Pioneer Park and put up Nancy Zick Israel's tent for her and her three adventure-seeking little girls. He fixed the light fixture in the basement, talked business with Gregg Zulauf, and camped overnight at Pioneer Park with Mark and Dennis. What a honey!

Jane sent a card of joggers and a photo of herself and Jim side by side in waders with fly-fishing gear from their vacation spot. They were holding their poles straight up. They looked serious and I, amused, thought the photo resembled a daguerreotype of the puritan pair with the pitch fork. Everyone remembers the painting *American Gothic*.

Jane told me a funny story told to her about Karrie on the church bus to Colorado. Mark and Karrie were hitching a ride with the church youth group to Colorado to see their dad. Everyone stopped at a rest stop and were told to prepare for sleep on the bus. Karrie found the restroom and changed into her nightgown. In the morning, when it was time for the breakfast stop, Karrie unabashedly went into the restaurant to eat breakfast in her nightgown.

October 14, 1985, John, always available, was called in to the children's home where he worked as a social worker. He was back at 5:30 p.m. He found two girls on "Prep" had disassembled their bed. It was in six pieces. The agitated unit gradually calmed down as John methodically put that bed back together and nailed it solidly to the wall.

New Pursuits
Journal III: 1982–1994

"As a Comet"

As a comet streaks through the sky,
So the Bible trails through history.
A charged ionized tail
In a four dimensional plane, or ten?
With width, length, depth and time.

Every point of the comet's head
Enlightens in its place
As nobly as that head once lit
The tail it left behind.

Yet, being as it is but dust,
Ice, gas must finally be
The head in future trajectory.
Whereas,

The living Word knew no beginning
To His tale, neither size nor shape
As His trajectory
Is infinitely… He.

Vast, oh, so vast…
Beyond what eye can see
Is the Word on His page
Before me today
Whispering He loves even me.

Head, hands, fingers, toes,
Ax at the stump,

Veiled, troughed, wrapped in swaddling clothes.
We nailed Him to a cursed tree…
Ephrathah! He prevailed in victory
      To confound our reality
      For you and for me.
Papyrus or hide, numbered,
Leather bound,
Copied letters in columned array.
The treasures unfold.
One finger turns the page.

His head marks out
His infinite path
Beyond this space and time.
Must our voices call, "So long, farewell"?

Ah, rather, His tale, at every point,
Burns brightly as the head
For fueling our little lamps.
Reassured, watch now and wait.

Though on ahead He goes,
He's circling back around.
Hungry, He swallows death's tail to its nose,
Where safe in His presence I am…

To believe on the Name
Of that Word made flesh,
That He faced what we face – yet won.
He picks us up today,
God's glorious blessed Son.

Jean E. Van Lente
Based on *Romans 8:38-39 NIV*
August 10, 2001

Mark's voice was cracking; he had begun looking more manly in recent months. He had mentioned every once in awhile he could use some new underwear. He still hadn't gotten any when one morning Mark strode into the bathroom with a hanger, on which a pair of undershorts was stretched at the waist over both ends. Mark declared, "I'm stretching my underwear!" Guess what were in Easter baskets that year!

Mark had reached the age of concluding confirmation studies. November 3, 1985 was Confirmation Sunday. Like those few who remembered Mark's great great great grandmother, Wilhelmina Fredricka Louisa Nearnberg Scheunemann as being a very "serious" lady, her great great great grandson was a "serious" lad. And we asked God's blessings upon him. Friends Rob Eyestone, Heather Kane, and Eric Alderman joined him.

He diligently tried to learn and succeed, but he could also take some ribbing, too. Christmas 1985 was a boisterous day. Aunt Deb opened her diamond ring from Ed Halcomb. The next surprising gift was for Mark, who had attended a wedding earlier in the year. On that occasion, he told Grandpa he did not know how to dance. So Grandpa Bormann roared while Mark opened "Matilda," the life-size rag doll Grandpa gave him to be his dancing partner. Mark confessed later a little bit of embarrassment over the doll. Well, when we all chose stories to tell at Grandpa Bormann's eightieth birthday celebration in 1992, seven years later, Mark entertained the gathering with his story about "Matilda."

In his junior and senior years in high school, Mark was number "81" as "tight end" for the Reeths-Puffer High School football team along with his best bud, Rob. Mark rode his bike fifteen miles each way to practices. He basked in the camaraderie with his peers. Mark still names Reeths-Puffer coaches as first to teach him principles of training and conditioning skills. He became very fond of Coach Chiaverini for his ability to motivate his players and for his genuine caring. Mark's favorite quote was by Theodore Roosevelt and was given to him by Coach Chiavarini. (See Chapter 25.)

Karrie, also growing and entering young ladyhood, became fickle about clothing. Suddenly, she wouldn't touch those forty-five dollar navy blue shoes; instead, a blousy leg-of-mutton sleeved, oversized purple spring jacket suited her just fine. We suffered different tastes in clothes.

School brought good reports. Mark continued As and Bs in ninth grade. Karrie's sixth grade marks reflected her work the previous semester. She decided she was a "smart cookie," too, when all As crowded out one B in science. She was highest in her class in social studies and she involved herself in the school newspaper.

Fawn took flute lessons from the accomplished Mrs. Helen Dauser. She shone as a flautist. Her accomplishments even allowed her to play with her father on his guitar. When her flute broke, it was left to John to get the flute fixed. He also paid for new jeans. He was thinking, gee, why doesn't she just live here? We decided to get the special limited edition new flute Mrs. Dauser wanted Fawn to have. It was a nice one. Fawn earned ones at the Regional Orchestra Festival.

Fawn moved with her mother to Holland, Michigan. She was awarded the second chair in marching band and fourth chair in symphonic band at Holland High School. Fawn competed in Grand Rapids at Calvin College Solo Ensembles with a solo and a duet. All these children are so lovely.

I was yammering at Karrie to wear her hat to piano practice. It was cold. We stopped at Keefe's Pharmacy, where she dashed from car to store. And when we were ready to leave, I thought she was with me going out the door. When I went through the door, she wasn't there. But, she beat me to the car. When I asked her where she went, she informed me she had scooted out another door closer to the car so no one would see her with her hat on.

Fawn and Karrie acolyted together in November on Christ the King Sunday when Karrie couldn't get the Christ candle lit. Karrie scurried to retrieve a light off Fawn, but too late for Fawn had blown hers out. Mark nearly doubled over in the pew. And when they readied to leave after the service, Karrie just pretended to put her Christ candle out.

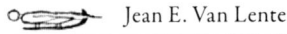

⁂

The time came when Dad could hardly breathe. In October, Aunt Kathy and I took him to Dr. Stinar's in Battle Creek while Mother had cataracts removed. Dr. Stinar arranged tests for Dad, but it wasn't angina and it didn't look like a tumor. His heart seemed to have an irregular heartbeat. Later, Mother took Dad back to Dr. Stinar's for a thoracentesis. He never had it because there was so little fluid left in his lung, it wasn't worth doing the procedure. I treated this as a miracle and an answer to many prayers. At this point, the thought of my parents passing continued to fill me with fear. Many times as I returned to my office I was afraid a sad message might await me there.

The children showed their concern and we checked in on Grandpa. He gradually improved, but he had to take his medicine. Dad always marveled God had given him twenty good years after his retirement. He knew he had been blessed and he was thankful.

⁂

John came home tired after the Unicopia Co-op meeting at the new store. It was never quite like the old store with the trolley car mural on the outside wall and the real wood floorboards and tall tin ceiling. Barb and Candy stayed on as managers. They had been the daily welcoming entourage for many years. What would Unicopia have done without them? Accounting savvy, Peter Sartorius carried the heavy load of board treasurer also for many years. He was probably the first to have to face the unfortunate reality that our beloved Co-op was going under.

Karrie told Grandpa Bormann she wished Mom would explain to her about "the birds and the bees." We needed to have a discussion.

Grandma Bormann dazzled us with stories about Karrie pasting on fake fingernails at their house and then trying to eat with them. Karrie told us she was changing her image. She had the permanent she wanted. She was eating more tomatoes and cucumbers. Grandma Bormann had taken her to get her ears pierced and Grandpa said to go ahead and get her braces. Both Fawn and Karrie wore braces.

We celebrated Grandma and Grandpa Bormann's fortieth wedding anniversary with an open house at St. Paul Lutheran Church in Albion where they attended and were active all their lives. A big crowd assembled to celebrate.

The night before, Grandma was wondering if Mark could still sleep in the same room as Fawn and Karrie. The girls were giggling. It seemed Fawn and Karrie sneaked a naked Barbie doll into the foot of his bed. As he climbed in, at first, he didn't feel anything; then the arms got tangled in his toes and he thought it was a spider and he let loose sufficiently to provide Karrie and Fawn with exactly what they were looking forward to!

Another popular event, Karrie and I helped Grandma and Grandpa Van Lente with their annual picnic for the employees at Goodwill. This activity endured as a long-looked-forward-to outing for the employees at Goodwill in Muskegon. On hand for the occasion always stood a couple of portable public toilets. Grandma Van Lente was a member of Muskegon Goodwill's board for many years.

1987, all the Van Lentes got together to celebrate Grandma and Grandpa Van Lente's fiftieth wedding anniversary at Hagar's Hideaway in Bluffton, Muskegon. Everyone was there. Ralph and Alice Van Lente modeled a giddy "new love" for each other for fifty years. And they reached beyond their sixtieth year anniversary before they passed away. Their joys were always the stuff of contagion.

·:⁂:·

Winter 1987, Mike and Peggy White Knight used a van to travel to Lake Placid, New York with a load of young teenage boys in tow. Mark, at 16, was among them. Lake Placid was the Olympic winter mecca for winter sports and, especially, luge. Lake Placid had held Winter Olympics in 1932 and 1980. The village boasted the only Olympic refrigerated track in the United States at that time.

Mark spent a week at the luge camp in Lake Placid, New York. He raced a set of three races called Junior Seed races, winning his division. Overall, he was third. As a result, Mark was invited to be on the Junior Candidate team of the United States Luge Association.

Grandma Bormann liked to tell she was staying with the children when Mark returned home. He was sick with such a bad cold she decided to keep him home from school one day to rest. Grandpa

Bormann wrote to Mark March 1987, "Mark, we are very happy about your getting that medal. I would like to have been there to watch you. Maybe next time there will be a longer season."

※

Mark trimmed Christmas trees in June and July at Barry's Greenhouse. He finished up his last day trimming the end of July 1987.

By August, Mark felt he couldn't do anything right. The first incident was that he lost his driver's permit. And he knew that he needed a bit more practice at driving. The first time Mark took his driver's test he failed because he made a left turn into a far lane instead of the nearest lane. The second attempt he failed because the headlights of our car were burned out. The third try, he turned left and banked the turn. He took the off-ramp and did a "4-wheel drift," that is, sideways with all four wheels. But he passed.

While Mark worked at procuring a driver's license, John and I were looking at a tubby ochre twenty-four foot sailboat called "Tigger." John's new hobby was sailing. He spent hours and hours studying everything he could find about the subject. We bought Tigger; then, we had to learn to sail her. Our first time out August 7, 1987, we had a rather slapstick sail, but the sails hoisted nicely. We were awed at the sheer grace of sailing. John found it almost too easy, too slow. "We need a dinghy," he announced. Grandpa Bormann provided his aluminum rowboat, since he felt his fishing days were over. It was promptly stolen.

We had a few choice first experiences like a rock in the water, running out of gas, John's multiple swims to and from the dock. John gave renditions of the "near misses" as he earlier in the day attempted to sail away from the dinghy solo. I purchased a brand new motor; that, too, was stolen. We were new at this.

Entertain a glimpse of a sailing trip in Muskegon Lake: John the captain, Jean, Fawn, Karrie. It was Labor Day. It was cold and looked threatening so we deliberated on the buoy. Finally, with dark clouds off to the north, we sailed anyway. We recall the storm, the rain. Down with the sails, on with the motor; the motor died. The look on John's face was priceless when the thought occurred to him that we might be out of gas. But no, he worked the choke, unpinched the gas line and the motor restarted. Alas, the motor died three times;

the second time we were dangerously close to the shore. John ran back and forth. I accidentally dropped the buoy line and pole. John motored in the worst wind to pick it up and, amazingly, he was able to get right next to the pole hook sticking out of the water. He forced the boat to turn the way it didn't want to, in order to attach it to the buoy. Not to mention how arduous the rowing was to and from Tigger in the chop. We were new at this. And the kids never really did grab onto sailing.

Orange "Punkin," our second sailboat, measured longer and sleeker than Tigger. John would eventually become an adroit sailor and we acquired a third sailboat, a 37 footer he salvaged from having been sunk in Florida in Hurricane Andrew: "Begin."

The poet, George Oppen put the immensity of the water compared with the vulnerability of a boat creatively into verse:

> On the water, solid –
> The singleness of a toy –
>
> A tug with two barges.
>
> O what O what will
> Bring us back to
> Shore,
> the shore
>
> Coiling a rope on the steel deck.[1]

·:·:·

We thought Mark, 17, was going to Lake Placid for four weeks in February 1988. He had been invited. Mark actually remained in Lake Placid months longer. He didn't come home until August 1, 1988. I missed him.

The United States Luge Association invited him to go to Austria to compete in upcoming November 1988, on the Junior Candidate team. He was going to go with the blessing of his favorite counselor, Bruce Galland and his teachers at Reeths-Puffer, including Linda Galland his English teacher. He always completed the work he missed while he was in New York. John monitored Mark's school assignments while he was in Lake Placid. I don't think I had either a grasp or realized the significance of what this all meant. I'd lost my little boy.

When Mark came home, he announced they were making a luge sled for him. He was very pleased. He tried on his rubberized blue luge suit. He actually wore the suit in the photo I gave to Reeths-Puffer, so he would at least be in the yearbook with his classmates. He is definitely singled out in the annual. The Reeths-Puffer Rocket Annual of 1989 devoted an entire page to luge in the sports section. What annual anywhere else in the United States would have created a whole page to esoteric luge?

Mark was reading deeply into body, mind, emotional and spiritual training in preparation for luge. He was into body-building and nutrition: "Karrie, I'm gonna put you on a different diet 'cuz I know a lot about diet now. Your diet is screwed."

In August, Mark built a luge-type platform behind the house; then he built the ramp. Mark could be observed at any moment with his eyes closed, bobbing and swaying his head about in an unconscious trance. He had to memorize the routes of the different tracks so that he would not have to look when he luged. He needed to hold his head back for good aerodynamics. Mark developed such strong neck muscles he never wore a neck strap; he was able to hold his head through five "Gs" at times. Five "Gs" meant he would be weighing the weight of a man 600-750 pounds. He also never wore a mouth guard. He was of the "old school."

Barbara J. Aardema was first in our area to write about luge. She came to the house, interviewed Mark and Joe Hagen and wrote a very informative piece. The article appeared in the December 1987 to January 1988 issue of the *Muskegon Magazine* published by Scott Publications entitled, "Luging – A Dream Becomes A Reality" :

> When Mark Grimmette was 13 years old, he heard the sounds of a bulldozer across the street and about 300 feet through the woods from where he lives on Fenner Road. He went over to investigate, and wound up helping construct a luge run at Muskegon State Park.
>
> …Members of the United States Luge Association [in Muskegon] whiz down the sloped, 600 meter curving

track at speeds up to 35 miles per hour, lying prone, unable to see where they're headed, just 6 inches above the cold hard ice.[2]

By 2010, in Vancouver, British Columbia, Canada, they were going down a track between 90 and 95 miles per hour. By then, Mark had been at the sport twenty-six years.

Mike Knight was quoted in *Muskegon Magazine* as saying, "Luging is a novelty; something to try, to say they did it." The article went on to say, "Mark and Joe competed with classmates from Reeths-Puffer High School on a luge team the past few years and are working with Knight to stir interest in the novel sport this winter."[3] Peggy White Knight always told many uproarious stories about the adventurous week long trip they took to Lake Placid in the camper with a load of teenage boys in 1987.

Barbara J. Aardema continued a little more technically in the same article:

> Luge is becoming more than a barely known exotic sport. Hagen and Grimmette are likely to be at the track daily... They will instruct novices on the basic techniques involving lying on the sled and steering with ankles against the "kufen" that curves upward from the runner [the bow].
>
> Now within one second of each other in a sport where thousandths of a second can determine a winner, Grimmette and Hagen are honing their skills in anticipation of the 1992 Olympics.
>
> Even after three years here, when the two went to Lake Placid last winter for additional training, they were considered novices.
>
> "There's no chance in '88; we're not eligible to try," says Grimmette. "To be eligible, a luger must finish in the top 15 in seeding races that occur between Olympic years."[4]

Hagen referred to luge as a very open sport in the U.S. There were only four luge runs in the country: Lake Placid, Anchorage, Alaska; Marquette, and Muskegon. Between twelve and fourteen is an advantagious age to begin training for luge. Because few athletes were giving it a try, a chance that someone from Muskegon might be named to the 1992 XVI Winter Olympic team in Albertville, France, tantalized the few young active sliders.

Originally, the curves of the Muskegon luge were: "Bumper," "Spike," "Thriller," "Cobra," and "Kiss and Tell." By 2010, the track had been redesigned and split up with the design of former Olympian, Frank Masley. The new names of the upper track are: "Grimmette's Peak," "O'Donna curve," "Bumper Curve," "Gooch Straightaway," "Frank's Bank," "Shady Curve," "Ping Curve," "Furnace Straightaway," and "Verizon Curve."

2010 was the first year of the all-year-round usable fiberglass track for sleds with wheels in Muskegon. Jim Rudicil, Director of the Muskegon Sports Complex, receives the kudos for that addition to the sports complex. Back in 1987, Lake Placid was the only world class luge track in the country, which was made of cement and refrigerated. The Muskegon track is neither cemented nor refrigerated. "Kunstbahn" is German for an artificially refrigerated luge track.

Barbara Aardema enlarged on the Lake Placid opportunity:

> Lake Placid's track is one thousand meters long. "Systematic training" refers to a slider starting first at the lower entry points and gradually moving up. Training camps are offered summer and winter. Serious contenders will [move from Junior Development team to Junior Candidate team to Junior National team and] travel to European tracks, competing on the United States' C and B teams, working toward a position on the [Senior National] A team ... [5]

A person must be a member of the USLA and must slide at Lake Placid ... Approximately, 50 people have qualified for the Olympic trials over the past 4 years. There is a "last chance" race set for January 4, to give 5 more top finishers a shot at the 1988 Olympic trials.

From the men's start at the top of Lake Placid's run, lugers may reach speeds of 70 to 80 miles per hour ... Lake Placid's track keeps its curves for the lower end. Years of international World Cup experience is required to make the Olympic team.

The *Muskegon Magazine* article extolled inside scoop about luge:

Now that the two are among the Muskegon area luge veterans, Grimmette and Hagen find themselves preparing for runs in a way they thought looked a little silly when they first observed it. As they mount their sleds, they close their eyes and run the course in their minds, turning their heads right and left, and dipping their shoulders according to the timing it will take to make the run before they shove off. Grimmette says they have also watched a sled careen down the course by itself. By observing the sled's path of least resistance, they figure how high or how low on each curve they should try to channel their ride.

"Every time you steer you slow down," says Hagen. "Yet if you don't steer enough, you ride too high on the wall," according to Grimmette. "It's better to scrape than to crash on the inside wall," adds Hagen, who knows from experience. [6]

Mark rode with Dave Gonzales out to Lake Placid October 29, 1988. He was headed to Calgary, Canada; Igls, Austria and Königssee, East Germany for one and a half months to compete on the Junior Candidate team. Mark and Jonathon Edwards of South Weymouth, Massachusetts began doubles team racing the fall of 1988. They were officially paired by the coaches. Mark was the top driver; Jonathon was the bottom driver.

John and I and the girls drove to Lake Placid to pick Mark up in December. We stayed at the St. Moritz Hotel, probably the cheapest, quaintest spot in Lake Placid. The woodstove was roaring full blast in the cavernous front living room. We heard the elevator squawking through the walls all night. And at -30° the next morning, our car didn't make a cough. That trip we brought Chris Thorpe, another luge teammate, back with us. He still had to figure out a way from Muskegon to Marquette, Michigan.

Mark marveled that what was a dream three years ago was turning into reality. He told us each time he went out to Lake Placid he found himself getting closer and closer to making the Junior National team. The *Muskegon Chronicle* quoted John:

"When Mark badgered us to go to Lake Placid, he was only 16 and I said let him go. He'll see how good everybody is and then he'll come back and concentrate on his studies."

Instead of coming home with a broken dream, Mark came home with a piece of paper. On one side of the paper were his times. On the other side were times from members of the United States Junior National team.

There wasn't much difference.

"Right then, I knew he was hooked on the sport," Van Lente said.[7]

In that same newspaper issue, Tom Kendra, Assistant Sports Editor par excellence, shared his first [and last, as it sounded] attempt at luging:

> After a few trips from the halfway point, I got to thinking: I'm still in one piece! I have survived! I'll just go one more time from halfway up and I'll be out of here.
>
> "Want to go from the top?" Jim asks as I get back...
>
> Sliding down from the top of the mountain, I was determined to go out with style. But unfortunately, I lost my perspective after the first turn. Once again, I became a pinball wizard. And I added a few more bruises. I had my eyes closed and wasn't thinking at all.[8]

17. Tom Kendra, Sports Editor, *Chronicle*, Muskegon, Michigan, June 5, 2010.

The week ending February 12, 1988, we received a note from Mark in Lake Placid:

> Dear Parents,
>
> I have completed three assignments in Algebra II and Trigonometry, 2 more chapters in Chemistry and did some work on my term paper.
>
> Love, Mark

John and I replied:

> February, 1988
> Dear Mark,
>
> How are you doing? It is cold and snowing here! Did you get a chance to luge? Is it wonderful?...
>
> Your driver's license came....
>
> Lots of love, Mom

> Dear Mark,
>
> I hope you're luging. I'd hate to think I was a liar when I told all my friends where you were and what you were doing.
>
> Some girl from Luther League called to see if you wanted a part in a play – 9th grader – Karrie knows her name....
>
> How's your book report coming? By my schedule, note-cards should be 75% done – outline done with first draft scheduled for middle of next week – final started by February 24th....
>
> Keep us posted.
Love, Dad John

Mark and Jonathon Edwards's first season together as doubles was 1988-1989. They were named March 18, 1989, to the United States Junior National Team. Mark was happy to make it for doubles. The United States Luge Association didn't have more than one good doubles team at that time. So, they were taken as doubles sliders. Mark told me, "Jon is light and quick, a good bottom driver."

On the Junior National team there were six men and four women. The coach was Lin Hancock and the manager and training conditioner was Dmitri Feld. Mark visited Colorado Springs, Colorado the end of May for some physical and psychological tests. He physically trained with the positive, ever hilarious Dmitri Feld in Lake Placid during 1988.

Mark, in earnest, told us he would be dedicating a lot more of his energy to luge. "I have to keep at top notch, so I have to train hard."

Mark called from Igls, Austria. In those days, it was often hard to hear each other by phone. Mark sounded very distant. I always got the names and numbers of the hotels where he stayed and the dates he would be there to call him.

·:⁙:·

October 6, 2012, Mark shared a high school story with me. His junior year in high school, Mark remembers he asked his secret heart throb to the prom. He recalls at first she said, "Yes," but when the guy she was apparently dating finally asked her to go, she told Mark "No." He was relieved she couldn't go with him, because he hadn't slept for a week after she said, "Yes." When she refused him, he said he slept much better. Sometimes, it takes twenty years to hear a good story.

Mark and Heather Kane, now seniors, together attended both the Christmas prom and the spring prom at Reeths-Puffer High School. They appeared young and stunning as I gazed after them, thrilled for them when they departed for the spring prom.

9.8 Meters Per Second Per Second

18. Mark and Heather Kane on spring prom night, May 1989.

June 6, 1989, Mark graduated with honors from Reeths-Puffer after making up all his work assignments. His counselor Bruce Galland, ever supportive, helped him and he and Mark became very close.

19. Mark and Rob Eyestone graduate from Reeths-Puffer High School, June 1989.

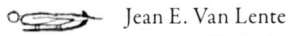

John taught classes in addition to leading social workers at Northwood Inpatient at Hackley Hospital and serving as social worker at Harbor House Treatment Center. He was promoted to director of Westwood Outpatient. He received notes back from Weidenhaver and the KLCO telling him what a super job he had done at his workshop in Lansing on the topic, "Dancing in the Dark" with reference to persons dually diagnosed with mental illness and substance abuse. John made apt professional use of his theoretical knowledge, extensive experience and people skills.

A couple years later, John presented workshops for "Dancing in the Dark" in Indiana, Minnesota, Ohio, and Illinois. He was chosen to be the keynote speaker for the Michigan National Association of Social Workers for May 1991.

I finished the first year of the MSW program after three weekends in July of Professor Tollectin and "Biofeedback." One year down and two more to go. The program through Western Michigan University proved strong in areas of clinical practice, program administration, and research.

One evening, Karrie floated into the car with Laura, her friend. It seemed Joe asked her to dance and, as Karrie put it, "No one told him to ask me either!" Meanwhile, fleet Fawn ran a 5:45 minute mile.

April 13, 1990, Dixie, the terrier just lay down and died on Grandpa and Grandma Bormann's linoleum bathroom floor. I can still see that little puppy chasing at Grandpa's heels or peeping out of his zipped jacket as Dad sneaked him into Meijer superstores with Grandma to shop.

That same day, John, after I asked him if I needed to buy deodorant, said, "I don't know if it's gone; I just keep rolling it under my arms."

Memorial Day, John and Mark worked together on our deep orange sailboat, "Punkin," in the morning. Later, Van Lentes got together at Silver Lake. Upon our return home, Mark in total glee and ecstasy heralded the discovery of another mouse with its throat slit in a trap. In mock funereal dirge, he ascended the stairs, glided out the back door and triumphantly catapulted the carcass into the woods. He sang the whole route with mixed cheers and shouts.

Grateful acknowledgement is given to the United States Luge Association editor Gordy Sheer, for permission to use information about the "History of Luge." This information is from the *Official Media and Information Guide of the United States Luge Association*, 1999-2000:

> Although the sport of luge is sometimes thought of as being relatively new, sled racing is actually one of the oldest of all winter sports. The word, "luge" comes from the French word for "sled." In Germany, it is known as "rodel"; the sport began in the Alpine countries of Europe.
>
> [Historical evidence goes back to the existence of sleds 800 AD with the Vikings.]... References to sled racing first appeared in chronicles from Norway in 1480 and the Erz Mountain area in 1552. The first international luge race took place in 1883 with 21 competitors representing 7 nations, including the United States. The race was organized by hotels in the Swiss resort of Davos and took place over the 4 – kilometer (2.5 miles) road from St. Wolfgang to Klosters.
>
> ...In 1953, the sport gained its own international governing body with the formation of the Federation Internationale de Luge de Course (FIL). [In 1955, the first World Championships were held on an artificial track in Oslo, Norway.]... and in 1964 luge was inaugurated as an Olympic sport at the IX Winter Olympic Games in Innsbruck, Austria.[9]

After 1964, without any formal United States luge organization, the United States Olympic luge teams were composed of American soldiers who were stationed in Europe at the time of the games.

Finally, luge attracted a few athletes who had nowhere to practice but on the 1932 Olympic bobsled run in Lake Placid... No formal national organization existed before 1979, so that American sliders remained in obscurity the two decades from the 1960s to 1980.

The United States Luge Association was chartered in 1979 as a direct result of the Congressional Amateur Sports Act of 1978. The XIII Olympic Winter Games in Lake Placid in 1980 brought the construction of the nation's first refrigerated luge run in 1979.

Part Three
On Wings

20. Mark and Brian Martin after they won bronze in doubles luge at the XVIII Winter Olympics in Nagano, Japan, February 14, 1998. Reprinted with permission.

21. Mark and Brian Martin smile to the cheering crowd after they won silver in doubles luge at the XIX Salt Lake City Winter Games in Utah, February 15, 2002.

22. Mark and Brian Martin with their sled, 2002.

23. Mark speaks with his two coaches: Wolfgang Schädler and Walter Plaikner, February 2001.'

24. Above: Mark and Mom at the Muskegon Sports Complex lodge standing next to the oil by local artist, Lee Ann Frame, March 1998,

25: Below: Jim Rudicil, Mark Grimmette, Lee Ann Frame, and Peggy White Knight at the celebration for Mark after he and Brian won the Olympic bronze medal, Muskegon Sports Complex, March 1998.

26. Above: Children came to see Mark's bronze medal, March 1998.
27. Below: Dignitaries came to see Mark's bronze medal, March 1998.

28. Above: Aunt Deb wearing Mark's bronze medal, Albion, Michigan, March 1998.
29. Below: Larry Page enjoys a moment with Mark, February 2001.

30. Above: Aunt Deb Halcomb, Merri Jo Charniga Grimmette, Rick Grimmette (Mark's father), and Ricky Grimmette (Mark's half-brother) in Park City, Utah, February 15, 2002.

31. Below: Cousin Alice Schneider with Mark in Park City, Utah, February 15, 2002. Gordy Sheer is behind Alice.

Upswept
Journal III: 1982–1994

Far better is it to dare mighty things,
To win glorious triumphs,
Even though checkered by failure,
Than to take rank with those poor spirits
Who neither enjoy much nor suffer much
Because they live in the gray twilight
That knows neither victory nor defeat.

Theodore Roosevelt
Given to Mark by Coach Ciaverini
Reeths-Puffer High School in
1988

In the early days, Mark was happy to be performing with the Junior National luge team. He had been frequenting Lake Placid since 1987. Now it was 1990. He continued advancing for four years. In 1989, he became a member of the United States Junior National luge team at eighteen years old.

January 26, 1990, Mike Mattson wrote:

Mark is still living on the fly in Lake Placid, New York.

Mark performed as a member of the United States Junior National Team. Mark received a medal for a 4th place finish in the Grosser Preis competition December 10, 1989, in Igls, Austria. The nineteen-year-old slid in junior men's singles against 36 competitors from 17 countries. That strong finish came during a six-week training session in Austria.

Mark said, "The United States as a team did real well in Grosser Preis. It was much better than I did last year and a big improvement for me this year."[1]

Mark earned a fifth place finish in the North American Luge Championships for U.S. and Canadian sliders January 6, 1990, at Lake Placid.... As soon as Mark was selected to the U.S. Junior National luge team March 1989, he performed in doubles competition with partner, Jonathon Edwards, of Massachusetts. They were not able to continue when John broke his foot training in Calgary, Alberta, Canada. Then Mark had to slide in singles competition. Mark confided to me, "I miss doing doubles." Although they trained in doubles, they hadn't been in any races because of Jon's foot surgery.

Mark's hope was to be promoted to a senior slider for competitors nineteen years old and above in the next season. His desire to be moved up motivated him to train hard in Lake Placid six hours per day.

During Christmas 1989, Mark was home. He saw the new luge track at Muskegon State Park. Ex-luger, Frank Masley had redesigned the track. Mark gave us his "take" on the new track: "I think it is a big improvement from the old track. Frank Masley did a wonderful job with it."

Mark was scheduled for training in Igls, Austria and Winterberg, Germany February 4-19, 1990. He also planned to compete in his biggest race of the year at an event called the Junior World Championship. Mark and Jonathon placed fourth. He and Jon were the top American team. Mark and Jonathon were selected as a doubles team to be members of the U.S. Senior National Select Team fall 1990. Further promoted, they became members of the U.S. Senior National A Team winter 1991, where they competed as long as they were a doubles team until 1995.

On our trip to Lake Placid March 2 and 3, 1991, we didn't see Mark luge because of the pouring rain. But we attended the first annual banquet with him. We enjoyed meeting Ron Rossi, Dmitri Feld, Wolfgang "Wolfi" Schädler, and Lin Hancock. Already, Mark and Jonathon were awarded second place in doubles.

Luge included a motley crew of senior sliders who traveled the "luge world" together. The third week of March 1991, as Mark later related the story, the lugers were on their way to Albertville, France for the first time. They had flown into Geneva, Switzerland and from there drove to Albertville. By mistake, they were taking the back roads. The traffic was a stalled snarl. Because of jet lag, they all fell asleep sitting in traffic.

They woke up and began to go. Gordy Sheer, Tim Wiley, Jonathon Edwards, Duncan Kennedy, Chris Thorpe, Robert Pipkins, and Mark started to joke with other vehicles, using the French phrase book. Out the windows, they yelled phrases like, "You bunch of camels!" Mark recalled a French driver was on their butt, when on a hill they were suddenly stopped in traffic again. Tim might have been driving and he got angry at the over-anxious driver behind. With the stick, he rolled back to touch the bumper of the car behind before he moved forward.

Mark described himself as the "fringe" guy. He didn't plan the capers, but maybe he went along with them. The group of lugers drove like crazy together all over Europe, year after year. I thanked God He protected and took care of them, even when they drove less than safely.

My journal of family stories continued. Fawn played her flute in two church services. We all met at Kalamazoo for her Solo Ensembles where she received 1s, which translated to "the best." John called Fawn at Socks Galore where she worked for her mother with more socks lines: a man walks around a mountain, so he needs one long sock and one short sock. He walks left to right, but he can't go right to left. Or, he told Fawn he needed five socks for a pet elephant.

Karrie was Student of the Month and we attended her induction into the National Honor Society. She moderated a program with John. They had been invited by Dr. Jimmy Jackson and Father Jake LaGoe to speak on the topic of "Adolescent Sexuality." It was an event given by teens; teens facilitated and moderated as part of the panel. Part of the talk included Aids and HIV because the goal was to control the spread of that virus among teenagers. She said later she felt honored to be a part of the program.

Mark, 20, disembarked the plane June 1991, in the Grand Rapids airport. He startled us, unrecognizable with long, curly, black hair and a thick black beard and mustache. He looked like the Gorgon triplets. I was so taken aback, I felt stupefied for a moment. Since Mark loved to surprise, it would never have occurred to him to warn us.

32. Mark, as he disembarked the plane in Grand Rapids, June 1991.

June 1991, was the month I graduated from Western Michigan University with a Master of Social Work degree. My trips back and forth to the Grand Rapids WMU Extension program had added up to at least three times a week for three years solid. The M.S.W. degree requires sixty credits as opposed to the usual thirty for any other graduate degree. The last week, I lost a complete ten-page paper I was readying to turn in. In a furious frenzy I had to start from scratch, with John helping me feverishly type the second paper in order to accommodate the deadline.

In one obsessive moment, I was snipping off dandelion seed heads in the backyard in an attempt to curb the spread. I put them in a bag. The next day I saw the bag had a hole in it. I walked in the back door muttering, "There's a hole in my bag of dandelion seeds." Mark turned to me incredulous, "You bought dandelion seeds, Mom?"

Christmas, we traveled to Grandma and Grandpa Bormann's and Mark said he was thinking of Grandma's cookies. She had been sneaking cookies to him all the while he was in Lake Placid. When he saw the round tin, he greedily thought, "Score!" He craved the pink and white braided candy cane cookies sprinkled with shaved peppermint. And they were in ample supply.

Mark, in great amusement, watched Grandpa take out rooster sheers to cut all his hair off. The tee shirt Santa brought sported, "Snowboarding is not about hairdos." Mark loved snowboarding. Nagano, Japan in 1998, was the first time snowboarding became a sport in the Winter Olympics. Where had this exotic sport begun, according to Mark, but on the winter dunes of Pere Marquette Park in none other than Muskegon. Sherm Poppen called the first snowboard, which he invented, a Snurfer in 1965.

Grandpa asked Mark for a demonstration of doubles luge. Mark used Karrie on the floor to show him how it's done. Actually, not until 1994 was it made legal to have female doubles teams or male and female doubles teams. But women haven't entered doubles yet; female doubles remains a virgin frontier.

Christmas Eve 1991, was sunny and warm; the snow was gone. The news announced Gorbachev's departure as the Russian leader. The Commonwealth plummeted out of the Soviet Union.

The 1992 Summer Games in Barcelona, Spain incorporated the news of the break up. Old Eastern bloc countries of Estonia, Latvia, and Lithuania now competed as separate nations. 1989, Germany's wall dividing East from West had toppled; in 1992, then, Germany entered a unified team. As Mark remembered, in 1992, South Africa rejoined the Olympics for the first time since 1960, having finally ended apartheid.

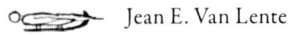

Mark pointed to the 1992 Summer Olympics also as first in making professional basketball players eligible for Olympic competition.

⁂

John made the cornbread he was famous for with the usual surprise on top for brunch, but we couldn't get to saying grace for all the calls from the media for the purpose of interviewing Mark. He managed to be totally gracious to each and every caller. Word was out that he and Jonathon would be contenders for the Albertville Olympics in 1992. We learned the media is not sparing when doing its job.

John crooned, "I just like our kids together... I like to see them interact together. Fawn and Karrie sing more confidently when they sing together."

Giving Barb Betts a storybook about "Woolly Mammoth" and one about mammals for her to read to her young sons, occasioned Mark to recall the books we read to him when he was young. His favorites were *Island of the Skog* and *The Adventures of Huckleberry Finn*. He remembered John reading the *Hardy Boys* sagas at night before he went to sleep.

On one trip to take Fawn back to her home in Holland, she wondered what story she would tell at Grandpa Bormann's eightieth birthday celebration. In a flash, she began to iterate the many mechanical problems we suffered with our old Mercury station wagon. All three children had experienced the same thing. There was a story!

Fawn and John played together their flute and guitar respectively, contributing special live music to Grandpa's birthday party. This, Grandpa really appreciated because he loved music and he sang with his beautiful, resonating, tenor voice all his life.

Grandma and Grandpa Van Lente stopped by on their return from six weeks in Florida to drop off oranges and grapefruits. Grandma sighed that by four weeks she was ready to come home.

Karrie turned eighteen. We gave her a "boom box." She made plans to attend Grand Valley State University in September. Fawn had turned eighteen a month before Karrie and she was planning to attend Davenport College in Holland. Karrie would live in a dorm and Fawn was moving into an old house in the center of Holland. "Empty nest" hit me hard. Yes, I prayed for their welfare, but, spiritually immature I still worried about them. At forty-five years old, I still hadn't learned to wait patiently on the Lord. What peace infused my being when finally a gradual fifteen years later, I could begin to turn everything over to Jesus with a more resilient life-restoring confidence. At a new place, I wondered what had taken me so long. Karrie earned a bachelor's degree, while Fawn finished a master's degree.

·:÷:·

We thanked those who had generously contributed to Mark's luge endeavor:

> Thank you for your support of Mark Grimmette's early luge training in Lake Placid. Mark especially thanks Muskegon and state officials for providing special opportunities for youth and adults through the Muskegon luge.
>
> We wish to bring you an update as we usher in 1992 with a Winter Olympics in Albertville, France in February. Mark and his doubles partner in Boston, Jonathon Edwards, consistently placed in the top three American doubles teams last year. As we write, they are competing in a World Cup in Sigulda, Latvia. Last Saturday, 11-23-91, in the Königssee, Germany World Cup, Mark and Jonathon came in the first American team and seventh overall.
>
> We wish them well at the Senior World Cups at Igls, Austria; Lake Placid, NY; and Calgary, Canada. The Olympic trials will be held 12-31-91 through 1-12-92, when the official Olympic teams will be selected.
>
> Glad tidings,
John and Jean Van Lente

December 1991, Ron Rop covered Mark and Jonathon Edwards's progress in trying to become eligible to compete in Albertville:

> Who could have envisioned how far the 20-year-old would take the high-speed sport that consists of lying on your back on what amounts to a double-runner sled?
>
> He's tested the icy curves on tracks in such places as Germany, France, and Austria at speeds exceeding 70 mph.
>
> But the biggest test of his luging career comes up this weekend when Grimmette and his partner... will be gliding down the track at Lake Placid, New York in hopes of earning a berth on the U.S. Olympic Team.[2]

Two doubles teams from the United States were going to compete. "The first team gets an automatic berth," said Mark, whose team was fourth after the first weekend of racing. Mark informed us: "The second team is discretionary. It's up to the coaches."

Mark practiced 2 to 3 runs each day in Lake Placid. He was concerned about the all-important start. He let on: "The weakest point in the track is our start. If you're $1/_{10}$ of a second behind at the top, you'll be $3/_{10}$ of a second behind at the bottom. We're really working on our start."

Per usual, before the 1992 Albertville Winter Games, the Olympic trial process took place in Lake Placid. They were not satisfied with their fourth place finish in the last race the first weekend of the United States Olympic team trials. Mark described, "Last week, the weather was nice for luge, but over the weekend it was rainy. Water dripped on the track and there was a surprise bump on curve five. Some teams handled the adjustment better than Jon and I did."

In contrast, on the Albertville track, Jon and he were the fastest American team. In that pre-Olympic training event, Mark and Jon finished sixth among the top teams in the world. So far, two Italian and two German teams had been the fastest in the world.

Mark told me over and over, "You can't imagine how hard it is to put two good runs together."

1991-1992, they set an American track record at the World Cup race in Königssee, Germany. They won the silver medal at the

NYNEX World Cup in Lake Placid and ranked sixth in the overall World Cup standings.

Mark and Jonathon were runners up to the XVI Albertville Winter Games. They finished just behind the qualifiers. We learned that we never know until the last minute, as in the end of December or early January, who the Olympic teams will be. My friend Jane and I had made extensive plans to go. After Mark and Jon did not qualify, Jane, though disappointed, generously gave her tickets to Mark. Mine went to Karrie. Jonathon, Mark and Karrie attended the Albertville Games. Mark was informed in dire words that he would be responsible for his sister.

As an alternate, Mark said he had a lump in his throat when he witnessed teammates filing in during the opening ceremonies. The record of zero medals for American lugers in the Olympics still stood by the end of that Olympics. Karrie told me later how Jonathon had mentioned that with their average times on that track, they might have been in fourth place had they competed.

September 27, 2012, toward the end of the start races in Lake Placid at the York International Start facility, I found myself being reintroduced to the chairman of the USLA board, dedicated John Fee. He launched immediately into telling me a story about Mark from 1992 at the Albertville Olympics. John was working for CBS and he wanted to do a segment of athletes demonstrating luge. He looked around, but no athletes. He saw in front of him, however, the unlikely, eager, untried young faces of Mark Grimmette and Jonathon Edwards. They were there as the alternate team. They were not required to be there, but they came for their sport. John Fee never forgot their drive and determination from that incident. He said, "Kids don't do that." John concluded with a sweep of his arm, "And what happened but the next two years and the next four years and the next four years!"

Mark and Jon's best year was 1992-1993 on the World Cup season with a second in Albertville, France, a third in Winterberg, Germany, and a fourth in Lillehammer, Norway. They were fourth overall in the 1992-1993 World Cup standings. Mark and Jon demonstrated very good results competing at the Senior National Doubles Championship and the Junior World Championship. They placed third and then fourth. They were the first American doubles team that year and the top American team.

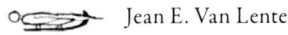

In the 1993-1994 season, they were the second American doubles team by the end of the first three World Cups. The first American doubles team at that time was Chris Thorpe from Marquette, Michigan and Gordy Sheer from Croton, New York.

Mark described to me the low point of his career was October 1993, on a blustery day on the track in Sigulda, Latvia, which Mark cites as one of the better tracks in the world. There, Mark has enjoyed some of his best races, but he has also had some of his worst races in Sigulda, too.

This particular race was a World Cup. He and Jonathon steered off the start handles and hit the right wall. Next, they hit the left wall so hard the front of the sled pointed up into the start curve and the back end whipped around. They were backward in the track. Mark, in that split second, wasn't sure just what to do. Jon pushed Mark so they intentionally crashed the sled. They finally stopped sliding at the end of curve 6. Together, they turned the sled around; they took some time to regain their composure and positioned themselves back on their sled.

Meanwhile, everyone who was gathered at the end of the track, began to wonder where they were. In front of all the coaches, watchers, and cameras, they slid to a finish of one minute twenty seconds on a track where the typical run is forty seconds. Mark uses the story to show that anything can happen, and does.

History would show this moment as a one and only unique time to be vying for the Winter Olympics. The decision was made at the level of the International Olympic Committee (IOC) to split up the Summer and Winter Olympics, so that there would be an Olympics every two years instead of both every four years. Lillehammer, Norway would be coming up in just two years in 1994 for the XVII Winter Olympics.

Mark and Jonathon worked hard to progress to a prime position to compete and win a U.S. berth on the 1994 XVII Lillehammer Winter Olympic team. Not until Igls, Austria did Mark begin to make slight changes in his positioning on the sled. Suddenly, the pair began to gain speed. By the time they arrived in Lillehammer to participate in the Olympics, they were sliding much faster than they had been earlier in the season.

"Grimmette thanked the people who made the track a reality [in

Muskegon] and helped him get involved in the sport, including the late Mike Knight and Dave Gonzales. 'I hope I can make the sport more popular,' said Grimmette, 22, who has been competing in luge for six years. 'It's much more popular than in 1992. It has been very good to me.'"[3]

Instead of the customary, last-minute Olympic trial race process to determine the Olympic luge team for 1994, the USLA began a new two-year Olympic trial process based on the results of two World Cup seasons and the World Championship competitions. Due to how well Mark and Jonathon finished in the World Championship of 1992-1993, they pre-qualifed for the 1994 Olympic team in Lillehammer, Norway.

To confirm their spot on the team, they were required to finish fifth place or better in any one of the fall World Cups on the 1993-1994 World Cup luge season. As it turned out, Mark and Jonathon slid poorly through the fall of 1993. But, they managed to win a berth on the Olympic team by finishing fifth in the final World Cup race in Winterberg in 1994. The result confirmed their spot for the 1994 Winter Olympics in Lillehammer.

February 1994, Mark and Jon were headed to Lillehammer to compete in the doubles competition at the XVII Winter Games. John and I went to see them compete. The snow-blanketed land held us mesmerized in its beauty. We felt enveloped by the warm welcome from the Norwegians and we saw first-hand how hearty they are in the winter snow and cold. Mark beamed, "It was incredibly exciting to march in the opening ceremonies... hearing the cheers."

Faye Redmond and Donna Little made a big banner, "Good Luck Mark Grimmette from Muskegon County." We spread it at the bottom of the track. The cameras panned on the banner and it was a wonderful moment.

The luge tracks are all shaped differently. One can never see the whole track at once. So we picked a spot where we would have a good view. The sliders came closer and closer rumbling like thunder. The closer they got, the louder it got. We had to look quickly as they flew by or miss them.

Mark and Jonathon twice hurtled down the track to place fourth after both runs. Fourth was the best finish ever for an American luge team in the Olympics. It was the highest U.S. achievement since

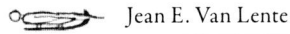

1964, the year luge was first made a sport in the Winter Olympics at the Innsbruck Games in Austria. Thirty years and not even a fourth place, until now.

Chris Thorpe and Gordy Sheer placed fifth right behind Mark and Jon. These two doubles teams had a long history of competing fearsomely against one another. They were always neck and neck. Mark and Jon finished $^4/_{10}$ of a second off the medal pace in the twenty-team field. John always advised Mark to forget concentrating on winning against their own teams; "What does it take to beat Germany, Austria and Italy?"

Italians, Kurt Brugger and Wilfried Huber took gold with a time of 1:36.720. Italians, Hansjorg Raffle and Norbert Huber took silver. The Hubers are brothers. Germany's Stefan Krausse and Jan Behrendt took bronze. Mark and Jonathon were fourth with 1:37.289. Chris and Gordy were fifth at 1:37.296.

We reveled as we absorbed the meaning of the pair's accomplishment by decimating a long-standing barrier. We celebrated with Mark and Jon and Jon's parents in Lillehammer. Jon's father wore a large long scarf and a furry Russian winter hat replete with Olympic pins he had bought or traded. Mark always made sure I had plenty of the most varied and coveted Olympic pins.

Meanwhile, in Muskegon, watching the luge competition on CBS, members of the luge club gathered at Diversions restaurant and bar. Diversions was one of the local luge club's corporate sponsors. Many of Mark's family and friends were there to cheer him on from home. Other local sponsors of the luge club lined up: Remax, North Muskegon, Gray's Furniture, Harbor Town Construction, Chrystal Anderson, Dog House Saloon, Americlean, Baskins, West Wind, Mr. Quick, Muskegon Community College, Bishop, Betten, Subway, Breakaway Bikes, Harold's, Fremont Public Schools, Fairway Optical, Textron Automotive, McDonald's, Jones, Northshore Sports Page, Al Perri, Meijer, Mercy, and Plumb's.

33. Aunts Peggy Schaub and Mary Kay Van Lente, Pam Schmiedeknecht, Jim Rudicil. At Diversion's on Holton Road, Muskegon, Michigan. The West Michigan luge club celebrates Mark and Jonathon Edwards's fourth place finish at the XVII Winter Olympics at Lillehammer, Norway, February 18, 1994.

In Albion, Sally Slaughter, of the *Albion Recorder*, February 18, 1994, quoted Grandma Bormann, " 'We're quite excited.' She said she never expected to see him among all the athletes. 'All of a sudden he was right there. It was a wonderful picture.' She said the camera stayed on him for quite a few seconds and she and Mr. Bormann relished every moment."[4] A photo pictured Grandma and Grandpa Bormann casually sitting side by side on their well worn couch in their living room on South Eaton Street. Grandpa's arm was around Grandma. They looked settled, but proudly engaged in their dear grandson's thrilling accomplishment.

On my visit to Lake Placid September 19, 2011, Mark said, "Mom, I remember when you and John came to a World Cup in Lake Placid in the winter of 1993 and Jon and I crashed. So, when you came to Lillehammer, we got done placing fourth and I came to the bottom of the hill and I looked at you and said, 'Mom, you didn't even watch me, did you? You came 4,000 miles and you didn't even watch me.'" I had to confess I was the troll under the bridge.

We talked about my feelings when he went off to luge in Lake Placid and the world at sixteen. Mark, in 2010, in the vantage point of head coach, spoke about how they used to wheel-train around the country and take the best, as young as ten and twelve, to Lake Placid. Currently, he told me they are drawing more locally for candidates; because the facilities are in Lake Placid it makes sense to expose local children to the sport.

A subdued Mark told the press:

> "It feels pretty good, actually." when he spoke in a phone interview from Lillehammer after he and Edwards amazed the field with a fourth place finish ... Muskegon's first ever Winter Olympian, is an unassuming, quiet, reserved, contemplative young man with an unusual knack for lying on his back and maneuvering sharp icy turns at speeds exceeding 80 mph ...
>
> Not bad for a team that wasn't expected to crack the top 10. Written off by most luge observers, Grimmette and Edwards put together a pair of solid runs and finished 0.3 of a second away from a bronze medal.
>
> "The press and public wasn't expecting us to do well," said Grimmette ..." But Jon and I knew all along, even when we were really doing badly, that we could go that fast. It just happened at the right time." [5]

A lot of practice goes into making a good doubles team in luge. Determined, Mark told me, "We want to be the best in the world, not just the United States." In doubles, however, the smallest mistake can result in a crash. The top driver points the sled. But he remains high off the ice, so he doesn't have as much feel for the sled as the bottom driver, who is four inches off the ice and in more contact with the sled.

·:·

Victories sell papers. The last question of an interview was usually, "Are you going to continue in luge?" Mark, twenty-three, could smell the medal at Lillehammer. Tom Kendra, consummate assistant sports editor, quoted Mark as saying he "wasn't into big splash and hoopla at all. It feels good just to get back to the real world and relax." [6]

Apparently, he was having car trouble with the silver Quantum and he wasn't at all sure it would even start, let alone make it to Muskegon. Kendra quipped, "Same old car. Same old guy." [7] Mark confided to Tom Kendra, "Right now, we're hovering right outside the medals, and I'd like to go for it again in 1998." [8]

What Mark claimed was of course true. His self-proclaimed reticence when talking to a camera in his face was in evidence in 1994. No one accused Mark of being boastful. Actually, his public remarks were reliably down-to-earth. Still, later, he certainly took advantage of opportunities as they presented themselves such as wearing his medals when he met with presidents and first ladies for photo shoots.

Mark's appearances were all over the media: TV, video, print, in person. The Olympians were invited to Washington, D.C. where they were treated like royalty throughout the tour. They attended a funny play at Ford's Theatre. The next day they stuffed themselves at a barbeque just before meeting President Bill Clinton and First Lady Hillary Clinton at the White House for individual photo shoots. The Clintons shook hands and personally greeted each Olympian. After having eaten barbeque, they considered how they must have smelled while meeting the Clintons. Mark had already previously met the first lady in Lillehammer at the Olympic Village during the games.

Mark joyously returned to Muskegon for a hero's welcome May 26, 1994, beginning his rounds at his alma mater Reeths-Puffer High School. He was the guest of honor at the annual Pride Day celebration. The thousands of students sported his name on tee shirts.

Later that evening, a recognition ceremony was held at the L.C. Walker Arena Annex. Family, friends, local and state dignitaries celebrated Mark's achievement. The plaque North Muskegon Mayor Sabina Freeman presented to Mark in 1994 recognized his accomplishment in Lillehammer by saying:

To Mark Grimmette:

The First Winter Olympian From Our Area who has become renowned far beyond the borders of North Muskegon and brought great honor to his community and his country; who has competed in champion fashion in the luge, one of the most precise sports in the world...

achieving the best U.S. finish in 86 years of Winter Olympic competition... the city of North Muskegon and all its residents hereby acknowledge this talented Olympic athlete and honor his extraordinary achievement!

Mark traveled to area schools to meet with aspiring young athletes. He was on hand at his native home track at Muskegon State Park.

Sunday, the bulletin at First Evangelical Lutheran Church on Whitehall Road praised Mark:

> CONGRATULATIONS, MARK GRIMMETTE! Today has been designated "Mark Grimmette" Sunday. We are all so proud and thankful to have had Mark as part of the U.S. Olympic Team in Lillehammer. Many years of long, hard work and commitment paid off for Mark. He certainly is a heroic model for our young people, proving that goals can be reached! May God continue to bless Mark as he goes forward in his career. You may wish to take time to greet Mark during the coffee hour honoring him in Fellowship Hall following the 10:30 worship service.

Mark responded: "A big thank you to you all at First Lutheran for your special cards and well wishes to me. We were grateful for all the Muskegon support! Sincerely, Mark Grimmette."

The end of June, Mark came back to Muskegon to be the grand marshal of Muskegon's Summer Celebration parade. He dressed in a beige Stetson and his frequently seen lustrous red, white, and blue USA Olympic jacket. The Stetsons were worn by the entire team at the opening ceremonies to fit in with the theme at Lillehammer. Sidelines were thronged with people on a sultry, summer day. My eyes stung at a vision that etched itself into my memory. And I ran down the street out of breath to keep pace with his float. Surprising to me was the energy and fervor Muskegon put into celebrating Mark's luge achievement. After all, he hadn't won a medal. But he and Jonathon had indeed broken a national barrier. The accomplishment was not lost on our cozy community nestled around Muskegon Lake, whose channel led to Lake Michigan's lapping, lazy shoreline.

Sought

You can't imagine how hard it is
to put two good runs together.

Mark R. Grimmette
1988

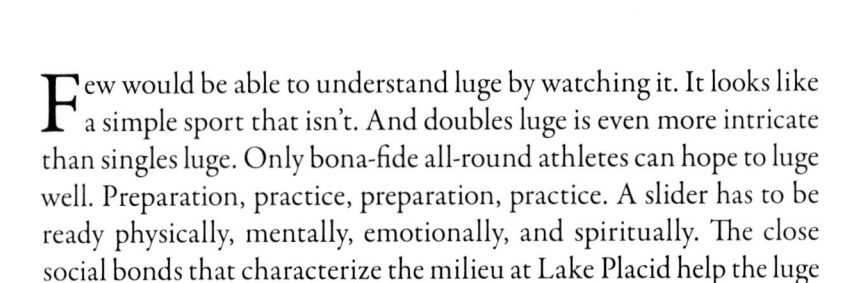

Few would be able to understand luge by watching it. It looks like a simple sport that isn't. And doubles luge is even more intricate than singles luge. Only bona-fide all-round athletes can hope to luge well. Preparation, practice, preparation, practice. A slider has to be ready physically, mentally, emotionally, and spiritually. The close social bonds that characterize the milieu at Lake Placid help the luge "wannabes" by encouragement to develop their skills for the ready.

Many a young Prometheus luger may be emboldened to steal fire from their heaven of sheer youth, but will soon be bound again by observing the experience of the older lugers around them to keep them in their places. Though beginners may feel, at times, the eagles are eating their livers of confidence, during the process of living and working together true young sliders will find their lives of luge restored and enhanced as they all help one another.

February 13, 1994, Jill Sidock wrote in the *Chronicle* about the techniques of luge:

> Relaxation and visualization are critical in the luge. A rigid, tense body tends to "telegraph" sled action down to the blades, causing them to dig in and reduce speed. You'll know the winners by their smooth, aerodynamic form. Legs are evenly extended, arms tucked in, head held back and the body held ramrod straight, even in the turns. This precise alignment cuts wind resistance and can make the difference between the fastest sliders and the rest of the field.
>
> In contrast, the luge start is an aggressive, explosive series of movements. So, the luger must be mentally and physically flexible enough to explode with the start and then settle in immediately and relax, staying focused without getting distracted.

Steering is subtle, with slight leg pressure on [flexible levers] the kufens [or shoulder pressure by the bottom driver in doubles]. Lugers want subtle changes. The slider that seems to be working hard probably waited too long to begin the turn and is trying to make up for it.[1]

Preparing the sled blades consumes an inordinate amount of time for lugers. Racers spend four or more hours honing the "steels" for track conditions. They use a whole range of sandpapers and finishing pastes. United States sliders have used wax compounds employed by the National Aeronautics and Space Administration on their sleds' steel runners. Sleds and blades are carefully examined not only before, but after each run by race officials.

Lugers can't look up, because optimum speed is attained while lying flat on the sled... Lugers wear tight suits with no exposed buttons, zippers, or decorations, which would slow them down. Rider weight is critical. Lugers are allowed to wear weighted lead vests that serve to even the odds among people of different body weights. Each racing class has a specific amount of weight that is permitted.

Grateful acknowledgment is given to the *Official Media and Information Guide of the United States Luge Association* for 1999-2000 as edited by Gordy Sheer for the nuggets about the sport of luge and for permission to reprint various parts of it:

> A new era in training began for the sport of luge October 16, 1992, when the United States Luge Association formally opened the $1.1 million York International Luge Training Complex in Lake Placid, New York... The York facility is the only indoor start track in North America and just the fourth worldwide (others are located in Austria, Germany, and Latvia)...
>
> Based in York, Pennsylvania, York International has developed and refined the innovative refrigeration technology through both luge and other prestigious projects. York engineers designed and built the refrigeration systems for the Olympic tracks at Lake Placid, Calgary, Lillehammer, and Salt Lake City. York has also designed air conditioning systems for the White House and the

Kremlin, as well as the cooling system for the tunnel beneath the English Channel...[2]

The start track area is controlled for temperature and humidity to ensure that conditions remain frost free. Through modern computer software, a slider's start time is recorded at three intervals on video footage... The athlete completing a training run, can return to the start position, and immediately watch a replay of that run. Bright television lighting creates a modern setting that illumines the intricacies of the luge start.

Luge and short track speed skating are the only Olympic sports timed to the thousandth of a second. Still, with stringent means of timing, even to the "millisecond" it happens that races are won or lost by .001 or even tied after some cumulative minutes of racing.

Another article in the same booklet shared technical information concerning the "start":

> It is very easy to see why the luge start is the most critical part of the overall run. It is the only part of the run where the athlete has control over the acceleration of the sled. Once into the racing position, the athlete must drive the fastest line down the track, but it is gravity that provides the speed. There are six basic parts to the start: Block, Compression, Pull, Extension, Push, and Paddles... Generally, 3-4 paddles are performed depending on the start ramp. [Gloves with spiked fingertips are worn to grip the ice for an explosive start.]

> In general, remember that the sled should be accelerating every moment the athlete is in contact with the start handles during the forward motion. The maximum speed should be achieved at the moment of release from the handles.

> The start is a very dynamic and explosive movement. Though it looks simple, it requires a great deal of technique work as well as physical training to help develop explosive power.[3]

DOUBLE ARM CABLE PULL

START POSITION

FINISH POSITION

34. Mark in start position.
35. Mark in finish position of start maneuver.
36. Below: Mark and Brian with an explosive start.

9.8 Meters Per Second Per Second signifies the acceleration of gravity. Gravity pulls the sliders down the track. Every one thousandth of a second is important in luge competition. And those in the sport try endlessly to reduce air resistance. Tight, sleek clothing, proper equipment, and the perfect posture are all essential and closely scrutinized.

Mark warns that their descriptions of how doubles lugers work together on the ice, though recondite, are extremely simplified in the telling. One version holds that the top driver pushes lightly against the tip of the left kufen (German word for runner) with his left calf toward the inside of the curve. Simultaneously, the bottom driver exerts slight pressure with his right shoulder toward the outside of the curve. Hopefully, the synchronicity brings them as straight as possible down the track. On-lookers on the sidelines never see these subtle actions.

In doubles with Jon Edwards in the 1994-1995 international luge season, they were seventh in the world. They thought they were becoming more consistent than they had been. Mark and Jon loved the Lillehammer track because the ice stays consistent down the length of the track. They finished regularly in their races in the top half of the pack. Their best showing for that season was a sixth place January 26, 1995, on the natural track at St. Moritz, Switzerland.

The U.S. team in 1994 had one head coach, Wolfgang "Wolfi" Schädler from Liechtenstein, one assistant coach, one strength and conditioning coach, and two managers. Dmitri Feld and Lin Hancock first introduced Mark to strength and conditioning in Lake Placid. Steve Maiorca took Mark to another level after 1993. In 1995 Mark learned from Jeff Scheuer. Dan Smith began when Mark doubled with Brian Martin. It was the transition to Scheuer and Smith when Mark began a lot of his own conditioning with their assistance. Others were Jon Osbeck and Kevin Ebel.

Athletes in luge are required to follow a rigorous training schedule. The USLA's *Official Media and Information Guide*, 1999-2000, explains rudiments of preparing for luge:

> Luge is a complex and demanding sport. A national team athlete is required to participate in a prepared training program 11 months out of the year. National team athletes begin structured training in March or early April.
>
> The start motion requires power, explosiveness and speed. The muscles of the legs, back and arms must be trained to exert a maximum amount of force in a minimal amount of time.
>
> Athletes typically perform a group of core exercises to promote general strength in these areas such as deadlifts, rows, and arm extensions. Then they attempt to use this strength in more start specific movements, such as Olympic-style lifts, explosive extensions and pulls, and actual start exercises ... The start motion itself is a highly technical event, requiring years of practice until it is effective and competitive.[4]

By training, aerobic and anaerobic fitness is maintained. The workouts include a daily flexibility program. Many other amateur and professional sports require much less.

The only time when the need to relax wanes is when the sled must be steered, thus, learning to relax and hold the body in an aerodynamic position is crucial. Neck, abdominal, and leg muscles have to be ready to hold a contraction 50 seconds. This is how long the average run takes to finish.

Sit-ups and neck exercises promote stability and control enough to hold a perfect sliding position. Agility and balance repetitions increase the luger's spatial awareness. Gymnastic exercises help prepare a luger to sense where his/her body is when in a curve or unable to see.

Lugers learn that training recovery is also important, such as getting plenty of rest and eating frequent, small meals to regain their energy.

Mark's only break from conditioning all year was from the end of the season in March to April. Otherwise, Mark worked out every day. He also used the York International Start track in Lake Placid daily. Mark and Brian reached the summit of fast starts from all their practice and hard work.

September 27, 2012, I joined Keela, Mark's wife, to watch the national start competition at the York Start facility in Lake Placid. I hadn't seen it in awhile and I could not help but be thrillingly borne away all over again by the crowd of all ages, the bells sounding, the blaring loud speakers, the loud music, the artificially wrought cold, and the glistening ice shooting from three simulation track starts. The steels running along the bottom of the tipped-up sleds shone as brightly as mirrors. Gordy Sheer taped the action and Mark, out of sight, manned the controls. In dignity, the first three places of each category received their medals around their necks.

Young "crazy" lugers imbued the space with a spirit that carried me back twenty years. The rest of my nostalgia fastened on "forever" faces: Ron Rossi, Gordy Sheer, Dmitri Feld, Fred Zimny, Bill Tavares, Ashley Hayden-Walden, Bangt Walden, and John Fee. A "family" portrayed itself here. I completely understood Mark's feelings of belonging, so intrinsic with the sport.

Mark attended Muskegon Community College for an equivalent of a freshman year of credits. Spring of 1994, he enrolled at the University of Denver, Colorado to study engineering and he made the honor roll. He and Brian Martin lived together in Colorado.

It was in 1988 that Brian and his mom, Nancy, tried the sled on wheels in Palo Alto, California, on Sand Hill Road in a parking lot. The event was sponsored by former luger, Bonnie Warner, to try and find potential, talented athletes. Brian showed promise. He was named to the USLA Junior Development Team in 1989. Fall of 1989, Mark was made a member of the USLA Junior National Team.

After sincere talks with coaches and teammates, Mark made a commitment in 1995 to stick with luge for the next three years and hope to compete in the 1998 XVIII Winter Olympics in Iizuna, Kogen in Nagano, Japan. His decision delighted Coach "Wolfi" who told us, "I wish every athlete would work as hard as he does."

Mark made a decision. "'Jon and I had been together seven years and we just weren't progressing like we should have been,' said Grimmette."[5] I remember Mark sitting with us in Cape Coral, Florida in our condominium solemnly, yet with bold certainty, telling us of his decision to try different partners the next season. He loved doubles: the intricacy, the aerodynamics, the camaraderie. He definitely wanted to continue in doubles.

World Cup racers Mark Grimmette and Larry Dolan teamed up in spring 1995, to capture the race at the Nynex National Luge Championships in Lake Placid. Mark and Larry were the 1996 Bell Atlantic National Champions in doubles. But, their time together was short.

Mark acted. He gave a call to Brian Martin spring 1996. Mark, 26, and Brian, 23, of Palo Alto, first luged together fall of 1996. They were unfunded and expected to pay their own expenses to Europe for the beginning of the 1996-1997 World Cup season. Mark and Brian worked in odd jobs to fund themselves for the new season. Mark roofed, Brian drove a beverage cart at a golf course, and they painted. As it turned out, they were on their own only a month in Europe in October.

I had to admire Mark's decisiveness in taking the actions he did in order to progress in the sport he loved. Nothing was guaranteed. Brian's receptiveness and willingness to go toe-to-toe with Mark was equally admirable. It's not easy to make a team where considerable sacrifice is assured.

·:⁙:·

Mother's Day, I received a wrapped gift in the mail. Unwrapped, a Sleepytime tea box appeared with a note from Mark sending his love. I thought, "Well, he thought about me," and I put the box in the cupboard. I'm more of a coffee drinker than a tea drinker, so the box just sat there. Six months later, Jane came to visit us in our condo in Florida. Jane is a tea drinker exclusively, so I offered her a cup. When she opened the box to pull out a bag, she exclaimed, "What's this?" I saw her grab a beautiful sterling luge pendant from Lake Placid's most treasured jewelry shop. That was Mark's gift to me in a tea box, almost lost forever.

I included them in my prayers, but in reality, at that time, I wasn't at all sure where God was leading me. Or was it that I was too stubborn in my own will to be open to being led? It was a confusing, harrowing, vacant time in my life. "Empty nest" was well under way. Mark was sixteen when he had "flown." By 1992 the girls were graduated. I felt ripped wide open. Life changes followed.

Circumstances had rendered my house torn apart inside while we were in Fort Myers, Florida. The house was aged twenty years in eleven months. Upon my return to Muskegon, I spent five solid years restoring our home on Fenner. Mark freely gave what his time allowed to help me with house repairs and to reinforce that he cared about my well-being.

I decided to read the *Holy Bible* cover to cover, an exercise I look back on and see was the most valuable thing I could have done with my life.

My prayers for my grown children were not like my prayers when they were growing up. Now my prayers were with the knowledge I had no control anymore … over anything. Complete trust – or more complete – was to come a few years later with a lot more peace as well.

At this juncture without a job and without a phone, I didn't really know much about Mark's life. He had to be greatly influenced by his friends and colleagues. And he had to be influencing his friends. They were always together. They were constantly driving together a hundred miles an hour around Europe. Self-confidence was an important part of development in his sport. All of them were young, strapping, and perpetually conditioning. They were encouraged to be self-reliant, to be the best, the best in the whole world. I believed Mark would be blessed. All went well for Mark for a long, long time.

Grandma Bormann frequently expressed to me that she wondered when "the other shoe would drop" for Mark. By that I supposed she meant when his "luck" might turn. My thinking was not really like hers. I never came from the same place she did. I was never afraid to wish him well or expect that he would do well. At the same time, I was cognizant of the fact that neither amateur nor professional athletes are amateur or professional forever. It was all in God's hands. Besides, Grandma Bormann died before "the other shoe dropped" for Mark. She had no reason to burden herself by dampening and compromising her great joy with her fears.

Tom Kendra drew a picture with his article, February 13, 1998, showing how Mark and Brian bred themselves together as a competitive-worthy team:

> During those mornings last summer, it was just the two of them. It was like a scene out of the original "Rocky" movie, two guys motivated to reach the top and determined to outwork everybody else to get there. The duo worked religiously on the drab disciplines of the sport. They spent full eight hour days breaking down the mechanics of the luge start... During their free time, they lifted weights and rode mountain bikes... "Brian and I really clicked," said Grimmette. "We're both pretty good at breaking things into steps and taking our weaknesses and turning them into strengths." [6]

They were rapidly able to make a team. They learned to use their nervous energy in a positive way. Mark was 6'1" and 196 pounds as top driver. Brian was 5'8" and 160 pounds as bottom driver. Mark said Brian was "solid and coordinated." Manager at the time, Russian Lenny Kasten stopped Ron Rossi, Executive Director, and said, "Try those guys; they'll surprise you."

Some of what is little known about luge is noted here. The pod has two seats for doubles sliders. Also, Brian, along with Mark's primary efforts, has straps that he pulls to help gain momentum in the doubles luge starts. Two steel bridges connect the two kufens on each sled, front and back and hold the shell or pod. The hollowed out section of the runners into which the gummie and bridge legs fit is the "box." The "bow" is the shape built into the steel runner. The slight arc allows the sled to steer. When pressure is put on the front or the back of the sled, the site where the steel touches the ice rolls forward or backward. The pod is attached to the bottom of the racing sled and provides the seat for the slider. Sliders lie in a pod sized to their body types.

October 9, 2012, Mark explained to me how sleds were made during his luge career. At the time he and Brian Martin slid together, their coach, Wolfi Schädler, built all the sleds for the lugers on the senior U.S. team. While Wolfi was home summers in Liechtenstein, he built the kufens, bridges, and pods. Septembers, the parts Wolfi constructed he sent to the U.S.L.A. senior sliders in Lake Placid. Mark remembers it was like Christmas when they received their sleds. Once in a great while, Wolfi sent a completely new sled to them, but more often, every new year a new element would arrive for the old sled. Wolfi returned to the United States Septembers, in time for each new season.

When they arrived, the sleds were not assembled yet; they came in parts. Mark and Brian, more hands-on than most U.S. athletes, liked working with their hands. The two began assembling the parts, personalizing the assembly so that the sled would fit them well. Their sled had to be comfortable and work thoroughly with their sliding style.

The steels were ordered from a company. Brian and Mark fit the steels to each sled after assembly. Wolfi tweaked the steels the way Mark and Brian liked them.

A tremendous amount of individualization went into putting the sled together. Mark's strengths went into a lot of assembling and rough fitting of the sled. Brian was good at preparing the steels for race day. They "changed out" parts often on seasonal trips and made alterations where necessary. Mark explained he was giving me a simplified overview of how their sleds were made, although the actual process was infinitely more complex. I understood why the slider cannot be separated from his/her sled.

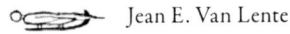

December 8, 1996, the *Chronicle* put out the congratulatory news that doubles lugers for the United States secured 1-2-3 for the World Cup at Hunderfossen's Olympic chute in Lillehammer, Norway. Mark and Brian were third.

In their first major competition appearance together, Mark and Brian finished third in the Lillehammer, Norway World Cup. Their finish contributed to a U.S. sweep for the medals, a historic first for any nation. Christian Niccum and Matt McClain won the event. Chris Thorpe and Gordy Sheer won second and went on to win the overall World Cup standings for 1996-1997. Mark and Brian's third place finish proved they could compete on the international scene and solidified their funded status on the United States luge team.

Mark and Brian nerve-rackingly worked out conditioning and improving the all-important start. August 23, 1997, the *Chronicle* began reporting for the 1997-1998 luge season by playing up their unexpected victory. They "pulled a surprise by edging World Cup champions Gordy Sheer and Chris Thorpe in the International Start Championships at Lake Placid."[7]

By the 1997-1998 World Cup season, the U.S. doubles finally had "depth" with Mark and Brian, Chris and Gordy, and Christian Niccum and Matt McClain. "Depth" was so important to the success of the program. All the European teams had "depth."

December 14, 1997, the *Chronicle* whetted appetites of luge enthusiasts: "The U.S. doubles luge team of Mark Grimmette and Brian Martin put down the two fastest runs of the event Saturday to win the All-Japan Championships, a tune-up race on the Nagano Olympic track... They defeated two-time world champions Tobias and Markus Schiegl [cousins] of Austria by almost 0.7 seconds."[8]

The 1997-1998 World Cup season Mark and Brian won four World Cups and one silver out of six World Cup races. They were the winners of the World Cup standings, even though they had come out of practically nowhere. Their swift ascent caused a lot of "buzz" among the foreign teams. They had won in Königsee and Sigulda and Calgary. Mark was especially happy about their outcome at Calgary:

> At Calgary they beat German powerhouse Stefan Krausse and Jan Behrendt and Italians, Gerhard Plankensteiner and Oswald Haselrieder with 1:29.316 to 1:29.388 to

1:29.667. Mark was happy they won in Calgary "because our other wins came on driver's tracks and this is definitely not. This run is like Nagano at the top where you have to relax in the upper turns, glide and steadily gain speed." [9]

They wrapped up an Olympic berth by winning the fourth World Cup at Calgary on December 21, 1997. The first time Mark and Brian set a track record at Calgary their time was 44.444 seconds. During the 2002-2003 World Cup season, they finished second after two runs at Calgary. But the most significant statistic of that race was that they achieved a time of 43.564 seconds on the second run. That track record at Calgary has never been broken; they still hold the Calgary track record as of October 12, 2012, after nine years.

February 8, 1998, Tom Kendra tantalized his reading public in the *Ann Arbor News*: "By that time, Grimmette and Martin were the talk of the luge world ... 'The Europeans are scared,' said Suckow, a medal candidate in men's singles. 'Even at the men's start they are talking about Mark and Brian. You can feel this generate through all the teams...'" [10]

Grimmette and Martin finished the World Cup season in style, finishing second in Altenberg, Germany on January 18 and winning the final event in Winterberg, Germany on January 24. "One thing we're doing better than most of the teams in the world is just letting the sled run," said Grimmette. "If you try to control everything, that means you're slowing the sled down by trying to drive the perfect line and always correcting..." [11]

The Associated Press picked Mark and Brian to win the gold, with defending Olympic gold medalists Kurt Brugger and Wilfried Huber of Italy picked for the silver and Thorpe and Sheer the bronze. There are a couple of factors that may work against them: "The first is pressure. The duo put together their dream World Cup season under very little pressure. They were nobodies ... Heading to Nagano, that is all changed ... Pressure is a huge factor in luge because the sport is so precise." [12]

The second factor involved is history: "The U.S. has never won an Olympic medal in luge and Grimmette and Martin have only been sliding together for two years." [13]

Mark and Brian and Chris and Gordy lived together in Lake Placid. They pushed each other, but also had maniacal fun together. For instance, on nice days they took friends out on Mirror Lake in their glass-bottom boat. Before these trips they would dump dressed mannequins into the lake to add spice to the trips.

Their enjoyment of Lake Placid included many fishing excursions on Mirror Lake, especially for Gordy and Mark. Eventually, Gordy, Brian, and Mark bought a cheap old motor boat with an old motor that they named "Ship O' Fools." The boat provided wet raucous fun for the bantering gang. Behind the derelict boat, they rode a surfboard back and forth across Lake Placid. Routinely, the decrepit motor fizzled, bringing the surfer down into the lake. They would roar up the motor again to full blast, pulling the surfer up, up out of the water for a few more momentary thrills.

Fishing reached new heights when the guys made their way to Alaska. They flew into Ketchikan and then flew to the small town of Craig, where they presented themselves at the Kingfisher Lodge Charter Boat business. Chuck was their captain. They caught halibut, king and silver salmon, red snapper and lingcod. Mark reminisced that king salmon put up the biggest fight; once, he pulled in a huge ninety-eight pound halibut. Fishermen in years past pulled in seven hundred pound halibut, but now landing a hundred pound halibut is rare. One year, a member of the group hauled in a halibut that was one hundred sixty pounds. Mark most enjoys eating halibut.

Gordy went once, Brian went once, and his mother, Nancy Martin joined them on the first trip. Mark has gone to Alaska fishing three times. Dmitri Feld has made the trip dozens of times to fish the "big ones."

❖

Mark kept in close contact with us, especially when he had a good finish. For being together only a year, he and Brian were beating all odds to be doing what they were doing. Nancy Martin was generally everywhere her son was competing, especially the Olympics. She is a traveler. She is also attentive, effervescent, and a wicked wit.

About this time, because I did not have a phone for quite a while, Mark would call Grandma Bormann whenever he had good news or just to chat with her. I was still faxing messages to the hotels in

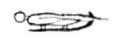

Europe where he stayed. Recently, Mark exclaimed to me, "When you didn't have a phone, that was frustrating."

A big change about this time was the "personal computer." I began getting information from my sister, Deb, off the Internet. I thought the black-rolled-on-stark-white sheets lacked character. I always preferred the *Muskegon Chronicle* for zest, originality and straight-forward news.

Mark has seen some history come and go. Shocked, he bemoaned the destruction of his favorite luge track at Sarajevo, Yugoslavia. He witnessed the security change in competition venues once the threat of terrorism became prevalent.

·:::·

December 19, 1997, Tom Kendra predicted with good reason, since Mark and Brian had captured the 1997-1998 World Cup standings:

> Mark and Brian are expected to be named to the U.S. Olympic Luge Team on Saturday night. "I'm a little more confident right now than back in 1994. I know how to train a little better. I try not to make predictions on what place we'll get. The best thing for us is to focus on ourselves." That strategy has made the Grimmette-Martin pairing the hottest luge team in the world...
>
> Grimmette's strong work ethic and strict attention to detail makes him a natural at luge...
>
> Grimmette has applied his love of physics to the sport and has spent a lot of time studying the aerodynamics of the luge start, and he is now one of the world's fastest starters.
>
> "Mark is a very motivated guy," said Martin, who will be competing in his first Olympics. "Luge is an extremely mental sport and no one prepares better that way than Mark. We're aiming for the top." [14]

"9.8 Meters Per Second Per Second is what the luge sport relies on," signaled Mark. "Luge wouldn't be possible without gravity pulling on us, that is, without speed."

The U.S. luge team went to the "spiral" for an inspection walk along the 25 million dollar track. The Nagano track was considered a difficult and demanding one with fourteen curves. There are two unique uphill parts. Curve 7 leads into the first uphill portion of the track. Teams that come out of 7 slowly, will lose momentum further by the uphill slope. Curve 8 is uphill in and downhill out, so mistakes there especially multiply the rest of the way. Sliders face a sharp right hand turn at Curve 10, followed by a long right-hander heading into the second uphill. The vertical drop is one hundred fourteen meters [374 feet]. The second uphill has a fourteen degree rise. Two physicians were posted at Curve 11 because of the risks there.

Doubles teams were not allowed on the track on the days before competition. Mark and Brian prepared by being focused beforehand. They worked on "mind-runs" down the slope. They visualized together their motions on each curve so it would be very familiar to them for the race. Mark did not even speak to his girlfriend before the race.

Mark and Brian drew the last possible position they could have drawn, which was number twelve for the first heat. On the second heat, places are decided so that slowest go first and fastest go last. Mark told us the ice gets knicked up slightly with each run. Weather also makes a difference on the track. Snow is slow, rain makes it slippery, warm weather cuts in making it soft and slushy, and cold makes it hard and fast. Hard and fast is most desired by lugers.

Three Winter Olympic sports had a record where no American athlete had ever won a medal. Before the Nagano Olympics in 1998, those sports were Luge, Biathlon, and Nordic combined.

February 10, 1998, Tom Kendra interviewed family and friends. Fawn was quoted from Florida, " 'This is the first time we realized just how big of a deal this is... We're more excited than he is. He's real humble. He'd rather hear how we're doing than talk about luge.' Karrie, also in Cape Coral, heralded that her brother is the most focused person she's ever seen. 'I know he'll be ready. Mark ponders things all day long. He likes to think things through from every direction, so he's ready for anything.'"[15]

Even the *Albion Recorder* of Mark's grandparents' hometown of Albion featured an anonymously written article: "Luger with Albion Connection Could Win Gold in Nagano," February 12, 1998. The article described Grandma and Grandpa Bormann as being excited and that was an understatement. Grandma and Grandpa loved to bask in Mark's exploits in luge.

Chris and Gordy had had a rough year. They had been struggling on their sled. When Chris fractured his right wrist, the pair switched partners for some sliding with Mark and Brian to rule out sled problems as the cause of their struggles. Mark doubled with Gordy to take down their sled. Brian took Chris down on Mark and Brian's sled. This helped Gordy and Chris to improve their sliding together. Mark enlightened me by using this as an example of the teamwork that occurred between these two redoubtable doubles teams.

27

Shoot the Chute

"Book XIV: The Conquests of Aeneas"

Then she instructed him to wash Aeneas
Clean of mortality, its taint, its sorrows
Down quiet streams to secret ocean wells.
The hornèd god of the river took his orders;
And all the mortal features of Aeneas
Were washed away in silver-flowing waters.

Ovid
The Metamorphoses
8 A.D.,1958,1986

The race was scheduled for Friday, February 13, 1998, at 2 p.m. Japanese time, which was midnight, February 13, Muskegon time. Race day was warm and sunny. Some of the thousands of spectators were in shirtsleeves. The day before had seen a lot of rain. Each team would run twice down the track and the team with the fastest combined time would win the gold medal:

> On the first run, Grimmette and Martin started well but had a poor turn about halfway down and lost speed the rest of the way... on the second run, the team had a great start and was on record pace before bumping into the wall coming out of Curve 11, which leads into the steepest uphill section of the course. Despite that, the team got back on track and finished... a Nagano track record.
>
> "After we hit the wall, we knew we just had to relax and suck it up," said Grimmette... [1]

Stefan Krausse and Jan Behrendt of Germany won the gold with 1:41.105. Krausse and Behrendt had been a doubles team sixteen years. This was a second Olympic gold for them. The first was six years ago in Albertville, France. They won silver at Calgary in 1988 and bronze in 1994 in Lillehammer. In Nagano, they flawlessly raced to gold.

Silver went to Chris Thorpe and Gordy Sheer of the United States with 1:41.127. Bronze went to Mark Grimmette and Brian Martin of the United States with 1:41.217. Mark and Brian had been a team only two years. Silver and bronze were the first ever medals for the U.S. in luge in a Winter Olympics. "The two teams from the U.S. won America's first two Olympic luge medals in the 10th Winter Olympics of trying. Sheer and Thorpe lost the closest luge race in Olympic history, missing the gold by 22-thousandths of a second." [2]

The foursome were exultant and giddy. Mark, with his unzipped fluorescent green sleeve, pumped his fist high in the air. They held U.S. flags, unfurled, in front and behind on the dais. Freelance photographer, Nancie Battaglia, gave the four the large American flag to drape behind them for her photo shoots. The famous victory photo of the four lugers after the race, all smiles, were credited to several photographers: Nancie Battaglia, free-lance photographer; Tao-Chuan Yeh with the Agence France-Presse; Laszlo Balogh of Reuters; David J. Phillip, Associated Press. The photos shone from the front pages of many United States newspapers. They were classic.

The front page of the *Muskegon Chronicle*, February 13, 1998, declared in bold: "I'm just thrilled,"[3] with a photo of Mark as he appeared February 8, 1998, in Kevin Kyser's splendid drawing of Mark on the "Olympic Pullout Section": "It was the first time an athlete from the Muskegon area has ever won an Olympic medal. And it was the first time the United States had medaled in luge... 'I'm real happy for both our teams,' said Grimmette... 'We competed hard with each other, but we also helped each other out so much.'"[4]

He especially thanked "all his family and friends in Muskegon, where he started in the sport in 1984."[5]

⁂

The Canadian Broadcasting Company carried the race live. But Michigan results were not available until after 3 a.m. on the Internet. Information was available by phone for overall luge results and local reports of Grimmette's performance and for Grimmette's comments. Jim Rudicil, Muskegon Sports Complex Executive Director and childhood friend of Mark's, made use of the Internet to get the results from Mark's race. He was downloading pictures within two minutes after they received their medals. Jim, perhaps in exaggeration, mentioned to me he was "extremely geeked."

Grimmette's home club in Muskegon had a rousing party in the lodge near Muskegon's track... Local ABC and CBS news affiliates reported the good-time, well-attended event. After the medal-winning performance, Mark was connected to the lodge via cellular phone for the crowd to hear his reactions. Jim Rudicil, savvy in communications, expertly organized the big bash.

During closing ceremonies, Mark and Brian helped carry the

banner in front of the cameras with the message: "Thank you, Nagano; See you in Salt Lake City!"

Mark basked in all the adulation from winning the bronze medal in Nagano. He cordially, in high spirits, made himself available to one and all after his race. And Gordy Sheer "played drums for local school children."[6]

> IBM touted its FanM@il program and reported more than 300,000 e-mail messages received at the Winter Games. Messages were accessed in the "Surf Shack" set up by "Big Blue" in the Olympic Village. Five hockey federations, two Nordic ski teams, one bobsled team and a figure skating squad ranked ahead of the USA luge in the final tally.[7]

"Mark led [the lugers] by receiving 279 messages at Nagano."[8] Children at Central Elementary School sent four hundred "good luck" messages to Mark in a box before the race. He seriously responded to cheering fans from everywhere.

Mark shared with me the USOC gave the fabulous four a message with a number on it, telling them that Vice President Al Gore called, asking to talk with them at the Olympic Village. Mark said he jammed the message into his pocket because they figured it was a joke. Hours later, Mark pulled out the message from his pocket and thought: "Maybe we should call the number." Mark called and heard over the line: "White House Operator. Who are you?" He answered, after which the operator responded: "One moment, please." He was immediately patched through to Al Gore. Mark recalled he spoke with each one of the medal-winning lugers. "Vice President Al Gore called both doubles luge teams to say on behalf of the country, he wanted to thank them for doing such a good job."[9]

With further adulation, "The two teams were on CBS *This Morning*, NBC's *Today Show*, CBS *Primetime*, and the Turner Broadcasting live afternoon show from above the city near Zenkoji temple. The last segment was taped at Olympic Village with Dave Letterman's mom for the *Letterman Show* on CBS."[10]

The lugers did not strike it rich, but, "Mark raced to $7,500.00 from the U.S. Olympic Committee's Operation Gold program. He received a matching $7,500.00 from the U.S. Luge Association for a total of $15,000.00"[11]

Mark said the happy "Arctic Evel Knievels" sang the theme song they had concocted with Mojo Nixon on the way over to Japan. Mojo, the "alternative" rocker, was their official team captain. He had done satirical, "Debbie Gibson is Pregnant with My Two-Headed Love Child." With further explanation:

> Sheer, who plays drums in a band called "Jim," decided to send a letter to singer-songwriter Mojo Nixon, awarding him the title of U.S. Luge Captain. Sheer liked his lyrics. Sheer's favorite was "Elvis is Everywhere."
>
> "We said, 'You're the captain,'" Sheer said. "'Congratulations.' We heard from his manager saying he'd talked to Mojo and that Mojo was out of his mind he was so happy. Now Mojo won't answer unless we call him 'Captain.'"[12]

The *Muskegon Chronicle* added to the story about Mojo Nixon, too. While in San Diego waiting to leave for Japan:

> The American lugers got together with cult musician, Mojo Nixon, and recorded the song, "Arctic Evel Knievels," which became their theme song. Sheer played the drums and Thorpe, Grimmette, and Martin sang backup vocals. "It was basically just screaming 'USA!' in the background, because none of us knows how to sing," said Grimmette.[13]

Mark clued us in that Gordy Sheer is good friends with Mojo Nixon. At the "South by Southwest" band meets in Austin, Texas, Gordy, as drummer, sees Mojo and knows him quite well. When the lugers go to San Diego to use the wind tunnel, they stay in Mojo's backroom to save money.

The lugers enjoyed a week of rest and relaxation in Hawaii. Just following the two doubles teams' double medal wins in Nagano, the four lugers undertook an interview with an Hawaiian news station. The next day they were surprised to receive a call from a public relations person from the U.S. Navy. He invited them to come to Hawaii to tour a naval destroyer and a Los Angeles Class Attack submarine: the U.S.S. Honolulu.

First, they visited the U.S.S. Arizona Memorial and they viewed the U.S.S. Missouri, on which Japan surrendered to General McArthur in August 1945. Mark always demonstrated a deep interest in events of World War II. He gladly received his Grandma Bormann's love letters Grandpa Bormann sent to her from Oran, Africa and Rome and Naples, Italy during WWII. The pair shared a secret code together wherein Grandma would know exactly where Grandpa was located each time he wrote. Mark always took keen interest in these stories.

Mark described the tour aboard the naval destroyer as "pretty cool." After they walked aboard the attack submarine, they learned the sub was scheduled to fire twice. When offered, Mark and Gordy jumped up to enter the torpedo room. There they each had an opportunity to push the button that launched the tubes.

Before leaving, the four met some of the crew and they dined with the captain of the submarine. Mark remembers a five-course meal with many spoons and forks and knives. The crew members serving them wore Hawaiian shirts. Mark shared what he thought surreal decor as they visited the sub, because from their first step onto the sub until their last step off, Hawaiian music played. Here was an attack submarine that was used to hunt down other ships during WWII surrounding them with swaying, Hawaiian serenades. Deeply impressed, Mark claimed what an honor the private tour proved to be.

The Olympians visited Washington, D.C. They were celebrated at a Bell Atlantic party in Arlington, Virginia. On a visit to the White House, the athletes were presented to President Bill Clinton and First Lady Hillary Clinton. Mark, among all the Winter Olympians, shook their hands and individual photos were taken with them. Vice President Al Gore and Mrs. Tipper Gore, also present, permitted individual photos with themselves and each athlete.

A large crowd turned out at the Muskegon County Airport the middle of March to welcome Mark home. "Mark received a symbolic key to the city of Muskegon from Mayor Fred Nielsen, then a gold medal from the Muskegon luge club representative, Larry Page."[14]

A week of festivities was planned with Jim Rudicil and Peggy White Knight in the forefront. Mark had already received honorary plaques from state, county, city, and the park rangers at Muskegon State Park four years earlier for his performance at Lillehammer. What more could be said?

Ronda Howell of *The White Lake Beacon* picturesquely described:

> Mark received a thunderous ovation when he was honored at his alma mater Reeths-Puffer Schools before 3,500 students, faculty members and guests. He received a plaque naming him, "Alumni of the Year."
>
> The office of Peter Hoekstra also made a presentation to Mark, which was the flag flying in Washington, D.C. the day of his race. When Mr. Dan Beckeman, High School Principal, asked the crowd if they wanted to see Mark in the 2002 Winter Games, the students exploded one last time.[15]

The splash at Reeths-Puffer cannot be overstated. Mr. Beckeman handled the event masterfully. The only time I can think of that exceeded the effect of 7,000 feet stomping was the reception at his alma mater four years later after he had won silver. The whole celebration was just more than I could take in honestly. For some reason, I don't remember it entirely clearly; it's a bit of a blur. But I recall the over the top sound.

One evening Mark spent as guest of honor at the Furies hockey game. He signed autograph after autograph for hundreds of children who displayed untold affection for him. Mark attracted the children and he was drawn to them. Later on, professionally done postcards of Mark and Brian were produced which he could sign, but in 1998, he signed shirts, hats, balls, shoes, paper scraps – anything presented to him. The tone was reverential. Obviously, Mark enjoyed this exercise. I enjoyed watching from the sidelines.

The open house at the Muskegon Sports Complex brought many many fans to see and touch Mark's bronze medal. He bent down for short ones to see and touch.

The occasion was made extra special with the unveiling of the oil commissioned by Peggy White Knight and masterfully and beautifully done by Lee Ann Frame. Lee Ann Frame, who lived in Fruitport, Michigan at the time, used a photo to render the painting. Her works have been shown in numerous competitions across

Michigan, including first places and theme awards. Her paintings appear in private and corporate collections across the United States and Italy. Lee Ann attended the Kendall College of Art and Design 1979-1983. She received an Associate of Arts degree from Muskegon Community College in 1984.

She lives with her husband and two sons and she wrote:

> Mark Grimmette,
>
> I am very honored to be able to use my gift of painting to help record your history-making event. I will try to show your focus as a young boy, your determination to reach your goal, your vision that came true.
>
> It is so encouraging to me to see someone of your dedication to yourself and to your country, also for my boys to look up to. Jacob did go down this winter; it was fun to see him and think of you.[16]

The oil painting occupies a prominent spot in the lodge, hung high in the rafters, at the Muskegon Sports Complex. The public event was hugely enjoyable. Celebrating Mark's medal and Lee Ann Frame's lovely oil painting together made for high recognition for talents displayed.

Peggy White Knight, hostess, always had a way of drawing people in to enjoy themselves and that's exactly what she did at that party. I'll never forget her verve and charm and her endearing winning ways. Everything she undertook came off with command and style. A letter of March 16, 1998, to the Muskegon County Board of Commissioners shows the efforts and planning that Jim Rudicil put into the lavish welcome home for Mark. My sister, Deb and her husband, Ed were present. Ed Halcomb, consummate, ever ready photographer made the event history by snapping one brilliant shot after another.

"Mark flew five times down the Muskegon 583-foot track and once lost his helmet. 'It's good to be back,' Grimmette said."[17]

First Evangelical Lutheran Church ravenously heaped laurels on one of their own. I am grateful and happy that Reverend Bill Uetricht kept in contact with Mark. Mark has been happy for his interest and contacts, too. His personal messages have meant so much to Mark.

37. Reverend Bill and Bev Uetricht, First Evangelical Lutheran Church, serving as clergyman at the induction ceremony of the Muskegon Area Sports Hall of Fame, Harbor Holiday Inn, June 5, 2010.

The "thank you" letters of March 18, 1998, shine the positive light on the decision made by the Muskegon County Board of Commissioners to send young boys on probation to Lake Placid. They luged, supervised by luge coaches, and Mark took special time out to meet with them while they were there. Deborah Jensen, IITP Coordinator, sent the letter of thanks on behalf of the young men who had the opportunity to go.

Because of his dedication to the sport, Mark underwent RK eye surgery in Waukegan, Illinois the summer of 1998 to eliminate the need for glasses. The surgery made it easier for Mark to see distances, which is so important in the sport of luge.

After Nagano, Mark and Brian committed themselves through the 2002 XIX Olympic Winter Games in Salt Lake City. The U.S. Luge Association prepared for 2002 by buying Kitchell Lodge. "The house was 5,000 square feet at Jeremy Ranch. It was less than a ten minute drive from the lodge to the new track at Bear Hollow Utah Winter Sports Park in Park City, Utah." [18]

Bounding Boundaries

9.8 Meters Per Second Per Second:
That's what we rely on.

Mark R. Grimmette
October 9, 2012

The 1998 Nagano U.S. doubles medals raised the bar considerably against which other doubles teams would strive to best. The younger doubles team of Christian Niccum and Matt McClain contested successfully against Brian and Mark and Chris and Gordy the beginning of the 1998 fall practice season.

In October 1998, the United States luge team opened the eight-day pre-season training camp on the new track in the Wasatch Mountain resort of Park City, Utah. They had six runs per sled. The lugers all did singles first. As they became comfortable, the doubles teams resumed on the doubles sleds. Single men soared 85 mph in the speed-trap between the final two turns of the course. The only run Monday, Mark and Brian were .07 seconds behind Niccum and McClain. Thorpe and Sheer were another hundredth back.[1]

Mark exclaimed, "Ice conditions were perfect for race-offs." Niccum and McClain set a doubles record over the Olympic silver and bronze medalists. Mark and Brian were second; Thorpe and Sheer were third. By midweek, the U.S. coaches finished their roster for the U.S. World Cup team. The three doubles teams would be competing 1998-1999.

In the first competition for USLA luge since the 1998 Olympic Winter Games, Mark and Brian won the Doubles Start competition. Mark reassured me, "I felt pretty strong despite my lower back problem. My flexibility is coming back. I've just started doing starts again. We're getting closer to being where we should. Our timing and coordination as we pull off the handles and paddle still needs a little work."

The 1998-1999 new World Cup season was off and running at Mark's favorite track:

> In fall of 1998, a training week was held at Königssee, Germany, where most lugers feel is the most technically demanding on the World Cup circuit. All three doubles

teams were trying to come up with a strategy for dealing with the start curve. "In the past, doubles teams would paddle twice, settle in the sled, and drive the rapidly approaching start curve," stated Sheer... "With the World Championships to be held on this track, however, many competitors are trying to get an edge. In training, we were trying to paddle around the corner instead... We all tried different methods, but reached no conclusions as to what worked best."[2]

From Königssee, the team headed north to train at Altenberg, Germany. Then, they returned south to Igls, Austria in Austrian Tyrol, and stayed through the first World Cup race. In Igls, November 14, 1998, the American doubles teams would have to fend off two-time world champions Tobias and Markus Schiegl, racing on their home track. Surprisingly, the American doubles team of Niccum and McClain won the race at Igls. Mark and Brian were second.

⁂

At this time, The *USLA News Stories* announced Walter Plaikner would be hired as part of its coaching staff:

> Walter is one of the top racers and coaches in the sport's history. Italian, he was 1972 Olympic gold medalist in doubles. He joined as Assistant Coach upon the expiration of his contract with the Japan Luge team. He was Italy's head coach from 1976 to 1992 leading the Italians to four Olympic medals. Plaikner teamed with Paul Hildgartner for the doubles gold medal at the Olympic Winter Games in Sapporo, Japan. That was in the era when luge timing still went to the hundredths of a second. Their sled actually tied for first place with East Germany. Both teams were declared Olympic champions. Timing changed to thousandths in 1976.[3]

With a full complement of high-ranking staff, "He will be part of a U.S. coaching staff that includes Head Coach, Wolfgang Schädler, Assistant Coach, Hans Sparber, Head Trainer/Strength and Conditioning Coach, Dan Smith, and Team Manager, Fred Zimny."[4]

⁂

The 1997-1998 World Cup season had been the first season Mark and Brian won the World Cup title with: first at Latvia, first at Königssee, seventh at Igls, first at Calgary, second at Altenberg, and first at the final World Cup.

They reigned again the 1998-1999 World Cup season. The last World Cup was at Nagano, where they won bronze and clinched the 1998-1999 World Cup title, their second. "They finished with 513 points compared to 511 points for cousins Tobias and Markus Schiegl of Austria."[5]

Mark and Brian placed third for bronze at the Luge World Championships in Königssee. They were the top American doubles luge team. " 'Brian and I are doing really well together,' said Grimmette... 'We have gelled really well and communicate really well with one another. That has made us good.'"[6] Patrick Leitner and Alexander Resch of Germany won the gold; Austrian cousins Tobias and Markus Schiegl won silver in Königssee.

Mark and Brian won the 1998-1999 Bell Atlantic National Championship by shattering the Park City track record by .8 of a second. Their speed was 80 mph. This was their second consecutive national doubles title.

⁃:⁃

October 22, 1998, after fourteen years in luge, Mark wrote me that he was having back problems:

> I am struggling with a bad back – pulled a muscle a couple of weeks ago. It's getting better though and I'm back to doing "starts" at 80%. We are also testing some new runners. Instead of fiberglass and wood, they have a carbon fiber outer layer. If they are not fast, they are at least the coolest looking runners on the hill. The track conditions are the best we have ever seen this early in the season. That should give us an edge when we leave for Europe.
>
> We've been too busy for me to go anywhere here, but when we come back, I'll see if I can get leads on places to stay.
>
> Take care! Love, Mark.

1999, the local reports hit the press that "*Chronicle* Gets Award":

> Members of the Virginia Press Association judged more than 3,000 entries submitted by 137 newspapers in Michigan in the 1998 contest.
>
> Awards won all around. It was delightful to note the praise the "Sports Feature" category won for a special section on Olympic luger and former Muskegon resident, Mark Grimmette.
>
> "This story is well-researched, strong writing that attracts a broad spectrum of readers. It's a well-told story," judges said.[7]

⁂

Mark and Brian were named February "Team of the Month" by the United States Olympic Committee. With the USLA, they were elected "Team of the Month" in all but a couple of months since 1996.

Mark and Brian and Chris and Gordy were among the "Top Sports Personalities of 1998" according to the latest edition of the *Wall Street Journal Almanac*. They were in the illustrious company of Michael Jordan, John Elway, Sammy Sosa, and Mark McGuire.

"Grimmette addressed a group of U.S. Congressmen who toured Lake Placid's Olympic facilities last weekend."[8] They planned to resume their training schedule June of 1999.

Mark and Brian were pictured smiling, red-jacketed with Bell Atlantic black caps and Federation of International Luge bronze medals around their necks on the front cover of the *Official Media and Information Guide of the United States Luge Association*, 1999-2000. Mark is listed as "Athletic Representative on the USA Luge Executive Board."[9] He served in that capacity at least fifteen years. Mark clearly shared his feelings October 12, 2012, that he enjoyed serving on the board: "During that period the people on the board were great examples of positive leadership and I felt a lot of respect for them."

By 2000, sharp copies of U.S. Luge Association schedules and newsletters were rolling off luge websites. Gordy Sheer retired after eighteen years luging and he became Marketing Programs Manager. In Fall 2001, he became Acting Marketing Director until 2002, when

"Gordy became Marketing Director".[10] The entire scope of the USLA was looking more and more sophisticated than in times past.

Also, in 1999, Lake Placid tore down the 1980 Olympic track to resurrect a new state-of-the-art course. The cost of the updating was estimated at $20,000,000. It was incumbent upon Lake Placid to keep up with Park City's track. The new reconstructed track at Lake Placid opened for the inaugural 2000 Winter Goodwill Games. Mark and Brian won the 2000 Winter Goodwill Games, standing tall on the dais below the new track.

Mark and Brian were given an opportunity to see the Manned Space Flight Center in Houston, Texas. Astronaut Scott Parazynsky, who had manned five space shuttle flights, gave Mark and Brian a tour of simulated shuttles and the center premises.

•:¦:•

It was in March 1999, that Grandpa Bormann died at 87. After having survived colon cancer at 85, he suffered from adhesions two years later and did not survive the healing post-surgery. Pneumonia set in and took him as I sang "Jesus Loves Me" to him while he became increasingly slack-jawed. My dearest father died. Mark came to his funeral and grieved his loss. Many many good times with Grandpa Bormann over the years were not wasted on him. And Grandpa had been so proud of him.

•:¦:•

By 1997, the luge team's budget was $2.3 million. It was fourth among the United States Winter Olympic federations. A brilliant roster of sponsors contributed mightily to the ascendance of the luge organization. "Bell Atlantic became the team sponsor bringing the luge team into the modern era in 1985."[11]

"For the top fifteen senior athletes, the World Cup season cost about $300,000 including travel and living costs. That did not include training, equipment, coaching salaries or staff."[12] Mark informed me luging sleds cost $2,500 each. Suits cost $300.00 each. Their luge suits were purchased from a company. Mark said he sent them his measurements from twenty different areas of his body. But he added that his suits often came to him needing some alterations, so he used mint dental floss to sew them up. Mark said he thought besides significant Bell

Atlantic support, the U.S. Olympic Committee gave an annual grant of around $450,000 and the Luge Foundation gave $50,000 a year.

As Mark became more and more immersed into the luge program, Bell Atlantic was generous:

> Bell Atlantic enabled the Association to provide world class coaching and training. USA Luge provided a strong national recruitment program through the Bell Atlantic Junior Luge Series... The USA Luge was able to maintain a year round operation and training program for its athletes.
>
> In addition, the Bell Atlantic Win-At-School program helped students and teachers in inner cities by telling them that the discipline and commitment needed to be successful in luge is the same as what is necessary to win-at-school.
>
> [1983: Erica Terwillegar captured the first international medal in team history by taking silver in the junior division of a major event in Igls, Austria. 1984: Doug Bateman and Ron Rossi, current Executive Director of the USLA,... finished ninth in the Olympic doubles race in Sarajevo, becoming the first American sled to break the top ten at the Winter Games. p.3]
>
> Bell Atlantic first celebrated when the doubles team of Miro Zayonc and Tim Nardiello secured the initial World Cup medal for USA Luge in 1985. Then came the team's first ever World Cup triumph achieved by Duncan Kennedy in 1991, followed by Wendel Suckow's 1993 World Championship.[13]

In expensive wheel-luging programs almost eight hundred kids, 10-14, took part in 1996 all around the country. Maybe seventy or eighty came to the Lake Placid camp for two weeks to try the track. Only about twenty advanced to the Junior Development team.

I enjoyed meeting Chuck and Sandy Yanke, the owners of Vulcan GMS, Inc. from Milwaukee, Wisconsin, when Mark introduced me in 2010. Since 1990, they have supplied the official lead weights for the luge team. In a personal way, they have been friends and confidants to Mark over the many years.

Autoeurope supplied the rental cars from venue to venue in Europe. All Nippon Airways was the official international airlines. DMT produced the official diamond edged tuning equipment. Ericsson has the official portable radio. LaCross Footwear made the official winter boot. Manco sponsored the official office and tape products. Norton supplied the official abrasive products. Reusch supplied the official glove. Team Air Express was the official cargo carrier. Uvex supplied the official eyewear and helmet. Wigwam supplied the official knitwear products.[14]

To help support the USLA: the United States Luge Federation Foundation, a separate non-profit organization, was formed in 1985. Their purpose is to oversee and manage assets of the USLA. "They make financial grants to help the USLA run its programs. The latest form of assistance after the Nagano Olympics was to purchase a house named Kitchell Lodge near the 2002 Olympic track in Park City, Utah to be a base for preparation for the Salt Lake City Olympic Winter Games."[15]

Race equipment and sled maintenance are subject to many international rules [See appendix C]:

> The only piece of safety equipment that every luge racer is required to wear is a helmet. In FIL sanctioned competitions, all athletes are required to wear the same brand and model luge helmet, which is made out of a combination of fiberglass and kevlar and is extremely lightweight. The weight of the helmet is critical as there is no headrest on the back of the sled to compensate for the high "G" forces felt in the tighter curves.
>
> Attached to the front of the helmet is a form-fitting face shield. It is constructed of a polycarbonate material. It is virtually shatterproof.[16]

Mark wore neither neck strap, which keeps the neck from being dragged back, nor mouth guard. He held his neck in position by his own strength. His face shield did crack once in 2010 in a race at Cesana Pariol, Italy. He scratched his nose, but fortunately, not seriously.

"Luge is not a thankless sport, as the Olympics proved. But [Gordy] Sheer estimates that a luger who wins every World Cup race and the Olympics would probably make $60,000 or so a year." [17]

Furthermore, the International Luge Federation announced:

> [There would be] a 207% increase in prize money for the 1998-1999 season in both Olympic style and natural track luge. World Cup race winners Olympic style each receive $900 per singles victory and $600 per athlete for a doubles win. The top three sleds in each discipline were to be paid.
>
> The overall World Cup champion got an additional $3,600 in singles and $2,100 per racer in doubles. The top overall singles lugers got paid, while the top three doubles sleds overall achieved bonus money.
>
> Helmet manufacturer, UVEX, also announced a schedule of monetary awards. A world championship was worth $1800, second gained $1,200, and third place received $600. The winning world championship doubles sled split $2,400. The silver medalists got $1,800, while the bronze medal winners shared $1,200. UVEX paid the top three in the overall World Cup similar amounts.[18]

Can an athlete live on luge alone? If the athlete has a high level of commitment and performance, they certainly can. Gordy assessed that one of the 1998 Olympic luge medal winners and defending World Cup overall doubles champs would have won $12,300 from the FIL and UVEX. Their four wins, a second place and a seventh would have brought them an additional $14,500 from the American federation. Add their combined Olympic bonuses of $15,000 each racer from U.S. Luge and the U.S.O.C., USA Luge marketing monies and a salary/stipend... the total earnings would easily exceed $60,000. The increased revenue was a major step toward permitting elite athletes to luge long-term. Then it was possible for them to train intensely without worrying about how they would live.

An example is Mark Grimmette who "lives in Lake Placid and supports himself on grants from USLA and the U.S. Olympic Committee and the stipends from those organizations for top finishes."[19] In addition, "those organizations also cover his training expenses and some of his living expenses. The United States luge athletes also received sponsorship money [as of 2001], primarily from Verizon and York Refrigeration along with eleven other smaller companies."[20]

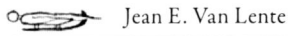

⁂

Mark and Brian led in winning the doubles division of the York International Luge Start Championships for 1999. Theirs was a track record start time of 1.270 seconds in Lake Placid.

Unfortunately, Mark broke his right elbow in December 1999, during his first run at a World Cup race in Königssee. His untreated injury compromised the team's starts because Mark had less ability to drive and paddle at his best. But he changed his start technique and came back for his second run that same day as the team took third place.

Mark and Brian were third in the 1999-2000 World Cup luge season. Mark summarized for me that he had been stuck in "third gear" with numerous bronze wins this season. They were third in Sigulda, eighth in Oberhof, third in LaPlagne, fifth in Igls, first in Nagano, fourth in Park City, and eighth in Lake Placid.

In February 2000, Mark and Brian won the York International Seeding Race in Park City. They were 2000-2001 Challenge Cup overall silver medalists. Challenge Cups were still being held that year.

Mark elaborated, the International Luge Federation (FIL) continually tries to find new styles of races to make the sport more attractive and to enable more events. The Challenge Cups represent one of those attempts to create a new style of race, which ended at some point and are no longer held by 2012 (except on the junior levels).

The premier events in luge include the World Cup races November through February numbering six to ten races each season. For example, in 2012-2013, nine World Cup races are planned. One World Championship is held every season, except in Olympic years. Of course, every four years an Olympics occurs. To enhance the excitement of the luge competition in total, the FIL, April 6, 2011, announced a team relay will be a new medal event in the Olympics in 2014.

February 2014, the Winter Olympics will be held in Sochi, Russia. Mark, just returned from Sochi, October 4, 2012, reported the temperature was 80° every day, palm trees waved and he swam in the beautiful Black Sea. Whatever the weather, we look forward to a new landscape and another new Olympics.

·:·

The USLA monthly newsletter sadly read: "In September 2001, the U.S.A. Luge athletes wish to convey their deepest sympathy for those lives touched by the tragic events of September 11, 2001." [21]

The USLA designed a sticker that was placed on the bottom of their sleds "in remembrance of the victims, their families, and the tireless efforts of the rescue workers." Mark read the sticker to me after he had attached it to his sled. "The USLA staff joins the athletes in extending our thoughts and prayers to all those affected by the attacks on the World Trade Center, the Pentagon, and the American spirit." [22]

·:·

"Mark and Brian won silver in Meransen, Italy in the Annual Start competition on September 1, 2001." [23] First at Calgary for the 2001-2002 World Cup season, Mark and Brian took bronze. Fall/Winter 2001, their results were 3rd, 8th, 3rd, 5th, 11th, 1st, 4th, and 8th before the 2002 Winter Olympics. In the World Cup standings, they were fourth overall.

I was fortunate to have been in majestic Park City just after the New Year 2002. I witnessed the Olympic lugers practice on the Park City track. Sliding, at 85 mph, the sleek sleds came into the finish. This was very fast. Mark always thrilled at the increased speeds; I cowered. Mark introduced me to all the Olympic team members chosen to compete in February at the XIX Winter Olympic Games in Salt Lake City, Utah. When each luger finished, into the covered benched track transport they went in anticipation of climbing to the top and making another run. Luge life is not always glamorous. The warm-up houses at the end of the luge tracks are sparse. Lugers don't seem to spend much time in those warm-up houses, unless it is really cold. Sliders who are dressed in their sheer, lycra-type, stretch textile-based outfits acclimate to most temperatures in winter regions.

About this period Mark began his many trips to the San Diego Low Speed Wind Tunnel near the San Diego airport. The tunnel's identifying advertisement was, "test where champions test." Sixty mile per hour winds blow in the tunnel. Mark on his sled, with his suit on was given the capability to observe how the wind rolled over the top of his body on the sled. He felt the wind and he saw himself on video. The tunnel looks like a giant fan at one end with him on his sled in the middle.

To prepare himself for visits to the tunnel, he spent four to five hours sewing various lengths of black yarn onto his suit. In hanging off his suit at different lengths, the blowing strings helped him observe what the strong winds were doing while blowing over him. Mark compared the effects of the wind year to year and took advantage of the aerodynamic lessons.

Maybe fifty years ago, in the mid 1900s, wind tunnels were built around the country to test airplanes and cars; aerospace engineers used them to design Tomahawk cruise missiles. Now the old tunnels, such as San Diego's, are somewhat obsolete. San Diego is more for use by sports athletes, such as cycling athletes, lugers, bobsledders, and skeleton.

·:·:·

Planning for the XIX Winter Olympics at Salt Lake City, Utah was under way. Statistics were available relative to the costs of the Olympics: "The Salt Lake City Olympics will be the most expensive Winter Games ever, costing nearly two billion dollars – or $791,667 per athlete – to stage 17 days of skiing and skating. Nearly $1 of every $5 will be picked up by U.S. taxpayers..."[24]

> The XVIII Winter Olympics in Nagano, Japan seemed costly at 1.14 billion dollars to Olympic officials. Salt Lake City figures eclipsed Nagano. The federal contribution of 380 million dollars equaled five times what taxpayers paid for the 1984 Summer Games in Los Angeles and twice as much as the federal government spent on the 1996 Summer Games in Atlanta. The 1.91 billion dollar Salt Lake City budget approached the cost of staging the Summer Olympics just six years ago [in 1996 in

Atlanta], which was 2.4 billion dollars when adjusted for inflation...[25]

However, the Atlanta Olympics brought 10,332 athletes to compete at 29 venues, while Salt Lake City served only 2,400 athletes at 10 venues.

The security budget, "just over 300 million dollars, is nearly triple what was spent in Atlanta... and 13 times in inflation-adjusted dollars what was spent at Lake Placid [in 1980]"[26]:

> "The athletes' housing was the only thing where you went through a security check," recalled James Rogers, Chief of Protocol, for the 1980 games. "At the venues there was nothing. The only military presence was a national guard MASH unit to treat any injuries."
>
> Rogers said Lake Placid tried to focus its spending on athletes, while leaving others to pay their own way. "We probably had the last true Olympics for the athletes," he said.[27]

Still and all, the Salt Lake City Winter Olympics of 2002 reportedly turned a profit by the end of the games.

·:·:·

Major news came in November 2001 about Mark and Brian. Mark informed, "We secured a spot on the Salt Lake team with a third place finish behind Germany's Patric Leitner and Alexander Resch and Andre Florschutz and Torsten Wüstlich. The luge team is being chosen from the first five World Cups through December 16."

Mark also informed me after ten U.S. lugers are selected for the Olympics, their names are sent to the U.S. Olympic Committee for approval. He confidently promised his fans: "We will be ready for the Olympics. We're just trying to perfect the little things right now."[28]

With regard to Mark's penchant for work, the staff seemed to think well of him: "Mark is a true professional," said U.S. Luge Association spokesman [for media relations], Jon Lundin. "He approaches everything like a business. He is always prepared and you never see him surprised by anything, on or off the track."[29]

In Europe, Mark was said to be something of a "globe-trotting celebrity." He competed for gold medals against the best from Germany and Austria, where luge is a national obsession. According to Mark:

> "Coming home to race is nice in a lot of ways," said Grimmette. "The best part is that it gets the Europeans away from Europe, so they have to deal with travel like I've had to the past ten years... I love the sport itself but I also love the struggle involved in it, " said Grimmette. "I'm always trying to better myself and even after five years together, Brian and I are still finding ways to go faster."

The danger of the sport can truly be understood only when standing next to the sheer ice track and watching competitors whiz past. It's an experience that makes you believe one of the USLA's promotional slogans: "One second from gold ... One inch from disaster." [30]

In December 2000, "Grimmette burned a hole through his racing suit and severely scraped his left arm when they crashed in Sigulda, Latvia." [31]

Review of Park City in 2001, showed "while Grimmette and Martin had good speed, they were slowed by slight 'looping' on several curves. 'Looping' occurs when a luge sled goes up and down through a curve, instead of cutting a straight line through it." [32]

Mark told Tom Kendra, *Chronicle*, they would be taking " '... a lot more runs on this track and testing a lot of different sleds.' Their starts were reported to be ninth and fourth and represented slips in the [critical] start speeds." [33] I wondered if Mark's back was giving him more trouble. He was thirty after all. He didn't complain. I really didn't know how his body was holding up, but I knew a lower back problem had not magically gone away.

They drew twelfth spot for the first run. "They prefer early when the ice is hardest. Then, there was the tenth of a second slower start followed by a little hiccup on the tricky 13th and 14th curves." [34] Mark, fourth, was shown in the "Sports" section of the *Chronicle* hugging his Reeths-Puffer counselor, Bruce Galland, who attended the World Cup race at Park City that day.

"The foreign teams seemed to delight in beating the Americans on their home turf. 'I guess I'm a little sad for them,' said Tobias Schiegl of Austria with a smirk."[35] The Germans, Italians, and Austrians start young and fight for their positions every day. In luge, the competition is fierce; anyone who views international luge in action does not have to be told. 9.8 meters per second per second: any advantage to give a team an edge.

But now, the winning German team would have to deal with what became known as the "pre-Olympic omen." "No doubles team has ever won a World Cup event on the track that will host the Winter Games the next year and then returned to win an Olympic gold medal, largely because of the additional pressure of being the favorites. The team's [Leitner and Resch] top speed Sunday was 85 mph, 5 mph faster than the best sled from another country – which happened to be Grimmette and Martin."[36]

The track at Park City was completed twenty-one years after the first completion of the track at Lake Placid. Now we had two sophisticated tracks compared to the many in Europe.

·:·

By the time Mike and Peggy White Knight took the van load of boys out to Lake Placid in 1987, the USLA was only eight years old. They were headed east, rather than west, to a virtual frontier. The organization had had its first World Cup medal just two years prior in 1985 and it was in doubles. This chapter has elaborated on some of the factors crucial to the growth and expansion of the USLA. Mark, Brian Martin, Gordy Sheer, and Chris Thorpe all entered the scene roughly around the same time. How many times and places can one be on this planet and be considered part of the "ground floor" up? Mark, truly blessed, found his niche at just the right time. And he knew it. No wonder he always thanked everyone who had helped and supported him in his quest.

Poured On a Pod Down 30 Stories

The climax was crossing the finish line
and knowing we had a medal.

Mark R. Grimmette
October 7, 2012

Little did we know how far Mark would carry the sport of luge. He was like a kid with a top that just never wound down. He was 13 and then all of a sudden he was 31. Tom Kendra summarized Mark's early dream: "Grimmette, 31, decided back in 1988 as a senior at Reeths-Puffer that he was going to go for the gold – and he has remained remarkably focused for the past 14 years. 'The first time I went out to Lake Placid and saw that my times were right up there with other kids, I knew that at some point I would have a chance to go to the Olympics. That was a rush.'"[1]

Dedication and determination were a large part in Mark's pursuit of his dream. Compliments in recognition of more stellar traits abounded for Mark in his quest: " 'Mark is absolutely the nicest guy you'll ever come across,' said Muskegon Winter Sports Complex Executive Director, Jim Rudicil, who grew up with Grimmette. 'I remember he always wanted to be an astronaut or an engineer. That was hard for him when it came down to giving those things up to focus on luge.'"[2]

Gordy Sheer, always a deep personal friend and colleague, remembered: " 'Grimmette... is so serious his... teammates love to [rib] him.' Gordy laughs as he recalls Grimmette's encounter with Matt Lauer of *The Today Show* after the 1998 Olympics. 'We all had earplugs in and Mark's fell out just as Matt Lauer was asking him a question... So Mark had no idea what he said. He just took a stab at it and ended up saying something totally out of context. It was classic.'"[3]

The late Coach Roger Chiaverini weighed in:

> Grimmette made an impression on ex-Reeths-Puffer football Assistant Coach Roger Chiaverini during his two years on the varsity in 1987, 1988, and 1989. "Oh yeah, I remember him very well," said Chiaverini, who coached

Puffer's defense. "He played defensive back on jayvee, but I made a defensive end out of him. I needed someone who could play the option against Grand Haven."

"Grimmette ended up doing an admirable job for the Rockets as a 2-year starter at defensive end, helping R-P to a 9-0 regular season in 1988. But that was the end of Grimmette's football career. He didn't even stick around for the playoffs..."

"He came up to me after we went 9-0 and he was very apologetic, telling me he couldn't play in the play-offs because he had to go to Germany to luge.... I told him to go after his dream."[4]

Mark took a road trip May 22, 2001, with his father out west for a week to get away for a while. The *Detroit Free Press* made a story of it, "Traveling with Dad, Grimmette Hopes He's on the Road to Gold," by Jo Ann Barnas: " 'I'm positive I'll be able to prepare myself as much as possible before the Games,' Grimmette said. 'The goal is to give myself the best possible chance to win. That's what [I'm] trying to do.'"[5]

Jo Ann Barnas reported, "Their coach, Wolfgang Schädler, was revising the fiberglass shell of their racing sled in an attempt to make them faster... But in the meantime, Grimmette has made some personal changes. Away from the track, he said he had developed his other passion – woodworking – into a full-fledged hobby."[6]

Mark loved woodworking long after he luged, and still does. His projects have produced Adirondack porches, headboards, dressers, lamps, tables, cedar quilt chests, frames, games, and a multitude of other pieces. He constructed a screened-in porch for Ron Rossi. Eventually he garnered all the tools and machinery a woodworker would ever want or need.

October 13, 2012, Mark invited me to his basement heavily furnished with woodworking tools. I watched him plane bare boards with one of his large assortment of planes. He showed me one plane, which is so sharp the wood slices off finer than toilet paper. Using the plan in his head, he took hold of his Forsner bits, clip rings, saw, router, and drill bits to construct a combination shelf and dowel piece for his wife, Keela to exhibit her vases on and to hang curtains from. Mark has Bill Tavares's old drill press, but Mark said, "He lets me use it."

After construction, Mark used his enormous vacuum to clean up the mess. I let him know I thought the environment in his basement was very neat, peaceful, and inviting. He replied, "I made it that way."

In the woodshop, he works alone and the solitude brings him relaxation and peace. It had been my hope for him since he was a toddler. What reassurance and joy to know God keeps our fondest dreams close to His heart to simmer and resurrect when the time is right, if the dreams are true. Speaking in 2012, if you ask me what my son is probably doing at any given moment, I'll consider the season, look at the date and time and within a couple choices, I'll tell you what he's doing. He is that predictable and content.

·:¦:·

It was February 2002; planners found themselves on short notice to finalize details for the XIX Winter Olympic show:

> After 24 hours of confusion, criticism, and compromise, the International Olympic Committee relented Wednesday and agreed to let the tattered flag from ground zero be paraded around Rice-Eccles Stadium by an American honor guard...
>
> "We had a great deal of discussion as to how to honor the flag as a symbol of the heroes of September 11," said Mitt Romney, president of the Salt Lake Organizing Committee...
>
> At the airport, on a Wednesday night, the World Trade Center flag arrived in Salt Lake City to cheers from hundreds of people. Port Authority police Sgt. Tony Scannella, accompanied by Officer Frank Accardi, carried it in a wooden triangular container that was wrapped in blue nylon cord...
>
> The 12-foot-by-8-foot flag was buried in rubble for three days and was torn in two places. Rescuers turned it over

to a National Guard Colonel for a ceremonial destruction. The colonel gave the flag to the Port Authority Police Department. The Port Authority of New York and New Jersey owned the trade center.

The flag flew over a World Series game at Yankee Stadium last fall and was included in ceremonies at last Sunday's Super Bowl.

Now, the Olympics gets its chance... [7]

The eight athletes who would carry the flag at the ceremony were being picked by the U.S. team to be announced later... When the flag is displayed Friday night, it would be something special, carried by athletes from the U.S. team and accompanied by police and firefighters from New York.

President Jacques Rogge of the International Olympic Committee empathized: "Your nation is overcoming a horrible tragedy – a tragedy that has affected the whole world. We stand united with you in the promotion of our common ideals, and hope for world peace." [8] Experts determined that, "The 12' x 8' flag could not take the stress of flying on the pole." [9]

The honor guard of eight athletes chosen to carry the tattered flag included:

> ...a soldier, taking time off to ski and shoot for gold. Another was Ohio Firefighter of the Year in 1999, now ready to slide headfirst down an ice chute at 80 mph. A third was in New York when the World Trade Center was attacked.
>
> Biathlete Kristina Sabasteanski, skeleton racer Lea Ann Parsley, and figure skater Todd Eldredge all have links to the events of September 11 and the patriotic outpouring that followed...
>
> "It's pretty special for me to do this," said Mark Grimmette, three-time Olympian in luge who also was picked for the honor guard. "It's very emotional. To be representing all the athletes by carrying that flag will be a very special moment."
>
> Other athletes chosen by their teammates were ice hockey

gold medalist Angela Ruggiero, curler Stacy Liapis, speed skater Derek Parra, and snowboarder Chris Klug.[10]

On a clear night before the start of the celebration: "New York City police officer Daniel Rodriguez sang a stirring rendition of 'God Bless America.' The crowd, some waving American flags, joined in during the final verse."[11]

Spectacular in its simple dignity:

> The ceremony officially got under way with a clang of chimes as skaters glided onto an ice rink, looping around the field. Fireworks exploded overhead, ushering in the entrance of Bush and the World Trade Center flag.
>
> In a powerful display that launched the nation's first Winter Games in 22 years, an honor guard of U.S. athletes... entered Rice-Eccles Olympic Stadium clutching the tattered flag... in front of 55,000 people and a worldwide televised audience of 3 billion.[12]

Tom Kendra, not to miss a beat, related: "Mark was captured by NBC cameras clutching a portion of the flag with a solemn look on his face. Mark was training in Lake Placid on September 11 and remembers the empty feeling in his stomach when he first heard about the attacks. 'The flag doesn't only represent the United States. It represents all the victims that were at the World Trade Center who died that day.'"[13]

Mark will never forget the eerie silence as he helped carry the tattered flag "... into the opening ceremonies. 'I expected the crowd to be loud, but when we walked in, the only thing we could hear were our footsteps. It was a pretty powerful moment and it's something I definitely will never forget in my life.'"[14]

The ceremony "culminated with the arrival of the Olympic flame, following a 13,500 mile journey through 46 states and the lighting of the cauldron by ... the 1980 gold-medal winning U.S. ice hockey team.... Athletes from 77 countries strode in behind their national flags. Greece, as always, led the way, with the home team bringing up the rear."[15]

The prominent five rings of red, green, black, yellow, and blue derive from the colors that appeared on the international flags in the late 1800s. 1896 held the first official Olympics in the modern era according to Mark. Baron Pierre de Coubertin of France is credited as the founder of the first Olympic Committee. His field of endeavor was education and history. The five circles symbolize five continents or five main regions in the world: Africa, the Americas, Asia, Europe, and Oceania. Today, at least one color of the circles is in every world flag.

⁘

February 15, 2002, the roar of the 15,000 spectators and the din of the home crowd at the Park City track was deafening. Mark and Brian's second run materialized as a rare perfect. It was enough to slide them through to silver:

> "I knew it was pretty good," said Grimmette about his and partner Brian Martin's second and final run Friday in the Olympic luge doubles competition.
>
> Pretty good is an understatement.
>
> It was the race of a lifetime, an inspired performance under extreme pressure, which gave Grimmette and Martin a stunning silver medal in front of a rowdy crowd ... at the Utah Olympic Park ... [16]

The favored German team of Patric Leitner and Alexander Resch won the two-run event with a ... time of 1:26.082 seconds. Grimmette and Martin were a scant 0.134 behind at 1:26.216. U.S. Chris Thorpe and Clay Ives were bronze with 1:26.220. Germany's Steffen Skel and Steffen Woeller were 4th with 1:26.375.

Mark pumped his fist in the air and let out a howl after the race as the patriotic crowd, stacked in eight-deep at the finish, chanted, "USA! USA!" " 'The feeling, the energy at that moment was incredible,' said Grimmette, 31 ... 'It was such a relief to know we were guaranteed a medal. We just didn't know what color it would be.'" [17]

Mark and Brian had the second fastest run among 17 sleds – two crashed and were disqualified. Thorpe and Ives, at the end of their second run, dropped a spot ... "The favored Germans, whose country has won 10 of the 12 Olympic gold medals in luge doubles history, nearly lost their hold on first place when they brushed the wall coming out of the harrowing 14th curve on the 15-curve, 1,140 meter track.[18]

Mark described his immediate reaction, " 'We were thinking for a second there that we might have the gold,' said Grimmette during a telephone interview on Friday afternoon. 'The Germans had a little bobble there, but they overcame it.' "[19] Mark called Tom Kendra just "two hours after his silver medal performance."[20]

Tom Kendra, in full realization of their accomplishment, reported, "But one of the first things he did during our Friday phone conversation was thank all of the people at the Winter Sports Complex, his alma mater of Reeths-Puffer and all those in town who supported him."[21] Mark was appreciative of everyone who had helped him. He never lost sight of who he was representing. It was an honor that he took seriously.

Mark and Brian received their silver medals in front of thousands in downtown Salt Lake City. Then they relaxed and enjoyed the band "Smashmouth" with fans. A group of 20 people from the Muskegon Luge Club… held banners with "Muskegon, Michigan" proudly displayed.

Fourth in Lillehammer, third in Nagano, and second in Park City begged the question about 2006 in Turin, Italy:

> "I can honestly say we haven't decided on that one yet," said Grimmette who will be 35 in 2006. "Brian and I need to sit down and talk after the games are done."
>
> Grimmette… was extremely nervous before the team's first run. They turned in a solid first run of 43.111 seconds, which put them in third place.
>
> Grimmette said before his second run he thought of a passage in a business book he's currently reading that stated: "Don't let the fear of failure exceed the excitement of winning."[22]

Mark confessed to me, "I was driving defensively on the first run. We attacked the course on the second run and that's what got us the silver." The duo turned in a sparkling time of 43.105 on its final run, the fastest of any of the 19 sleds in the final round.

The team discovered "during its pre-Olympic practice runs they were getting faster times using a luge with a little more suspension... The new sled bounced a little more on rough spots on the track, cutting less ice and keeping speed. They used that new luge in Friday's race.[23]

Mark rounded out his information about the team's new sled. He said it was not a sled that was different from all other sleds, but the sled was different from sleds Mark and Brian had been using. They were not able to continue their new sled after the Olympics due to new regulations governing sled suspension. Nevertheless, Mark and Brian continued to use a legal variation of the new Olympic sled.

Mark called Grandma Bormann right away, of course, to tell her the good news. Grandma was overjoyed, yet she always wondered when the "other shoe would drop" for Mark in his career. " 'I've got to get back to Lake Placid and finish the table I'm making for my grandma,' said Grimmette, an accomplished woodworker. 'Then I'm going to put it in the trunk and drive to [Albion] and give it to her.' "[24]

Comparing times, Tom Kendra explored the habits of the hummingbird:

> It's difficult to fathom what can happen in 0.134 seconds, the time separating the gold medalists from the silver medalists in the luge. For some help, we turned to the hummingbird. In 0.134 seconds: wing flaps: eight times while in normal flight and up to 26.8 times while performing courtship dives.
>
> ...Heartbeat: 33.4 times while at rest, 163.5 times while in flight.[25]

Back home in Muskegon, "Peggy Schaub, Grimmette's aunt, summed up the mood of the evening when she said, 'This is great.' "[26] That pretty much summed up the celebrative spirit of Mark and Brian's luge runs. Even Tom Kendra resorted to superlatives:

> Mark Grimmette proved Friday that he is one of the world's greatest luge athletes, winning an Olympic silver medal to go with his bronze from four years ago. But he's an even better person. That's what makes his story special.

And that's what makes his silver medal with luge doubles partner Brian Martin at the Winter Olympics here in the U.S. one of the most memorable moments in Muskegon area sports history.[27]

The XIX Winter Olympics was a roller-coaster ride. Mark embraced the gamut of emotions from carrying the flag to a perfect second run. The moniker "Light the Fire Within" fit Mark's experience. He and Brian were ignited to perform the way they did in the doubles luge. Mark found it somewhat difficult to describe to me, when I asked him how he felt about winning the silver medal. In summation of Mark and Brian's stunning second run at Park City, Utah, he laughed heartily that "the climax was crossing the finish line and knowing we had a medal." For Mark, the elation of doubles luging for a medal at Bear Hollow was heightened because it was shared.

Making "merry" describes how I felt about fourth in Lillehammer in 1994. And I couldn't imagine a higher height than I felt when Mark and Brian achieved third in Nagano in 1998. But now, I was saturated with gratitude, pride, and happiness for them. I looked back and found little to compare with the sheer exhilaration that came over me as I saw them charging like a bullet down the Park City track, rumbling like thunder, front and center for a silver medal.

I learned that the sound of the luges on ice varies depending on the ice itself. October 7, 2012, Mark had me watch a luger sliding down the Lillehammer ice track as displayed on his laptop. The run sounded like sparks crackling up from a campfire or water thrown into a frying pan full of hot oil. The luger wore a camera on his forehead. Of such marked the first time I ever saw or felt what it must be like for a luger plunging down the wondrous slope, curve upon curve of shimmering ice, while lying feet first on a bouncy little sled. The "trip" vicariously filled me with excitement, but also with images of moving artistry and beauty.

With luge, it takes imagination, and quick imagination at that. I could line up photos of seventeen doubles lugers luging side by side and you just wouldn't know who was who. You can't see their faces and you can't see the entire run live. With skaters and skiers and snowboarders and curlers you see them all. Emotions are bared by facial expression and body language. Not luge. Heads are covered. Faces are shielded. Movements are subtle and, for the most part, invisible. You know they're going 85 mph, but they don't look like it.

So I use my imagination big time. I am horrified to see them off the start handles on the big screen, then I pray and then I enjoy seeing them grab the kufens at the finish. No matter what place they're in. Imagination... Indeed, watching sliders slide can be unendurably breathtaking. Inasmuch as they bounded their boundaries, it was all the more thrilling with a big dose of trust and imagination.

Jill Hinde wrote for the *Albion Recorder*:

> By her own admission, Albion resident Leona Bormann is on cloud nine these days. Her grandson, Mark Grimmette, won a silver medal in men's pairs luge last weekend at the Winter Olympics in Salt Lake City. And she was able to share the moment vicariously via cell phone. "My daughter [and Grimmette's aunt], Debra Halcomb, was also in Salt Lake when he won the medal and she called me on her cell phone so I could hear the crowd cheering. It was almost like being there."
>
> "It's amazing to me that he's brave enough to do it," she laughed. "But I've heard him say how much he likes the speed of the sport."
>
> After winning his silver medal, Grimmette called his grandmother to share in his Olympic glory. "He called me Saturday afternoon after the race and was a pretty happy guy," Bormann said. "But he also called me after the opening ceremony and said, 'Grandma, did you see me on TV?' after he helped carry in the flag from the World Trade Center."
>
> Though the silver medal is quite an accomplishment for Grimmette, Bormann treasures also his bronze medal, because it is the one that her husband Henry Bormann got to see before he passed away two years ago. "My husband really enjoyed seeing him win the bronze medal,"

Bormann noted, "He would have loved to see him win the silver medal this year."[28]

Grandma Bormann showed her insight for Mark and his sport by calling out the speed of luge as his delight. 9.8 meters per second per second pulls the luge down the hill. Mark loved the speed of the sport, "the fastest on ice."

Mark's event was unique locally. "Grimmette is the first local athlete to ever win an Olympic medal. Muskegon Heights boxer, Phil Baldwin won two bouts as a 147-pound southpaw at the 1960 Olympics in Rome and Fremont archer, Glenn Myers took 12th at the 1984 Olympics in Los Angeles."[29]

When probed, Mark stopped short of saying that he and Brian were committed through the 2006 Olympics in Turin, Italy... " 'We have our sights set on 2006 and Turin, but we'll stay focused on one season at a time,' said Grimmette. 'I'm not one to talk about goals publicly, but there's more to accomplish before we leave the sport.' "[30]

Commenting on Mark and Brian's stature among their teammates, John Lundin asserted: "Mark and Brian will be the leaders of the team, no question about it... No one can match them when it comes to being prepared mentally and physically. They are quiet leaders but they set a great example."[31]

Mark was in the position by now of being the "elder statesman" of the USLA lugers. Young colleagues called him "Papa Mark" and sang, "Time is on My Side" to him and he would oblige with "Rock-a-bye Baby." "The reason to return can't be because I want gold – that's just setting yourself up. It has to be because I still love the challenge, the journey and the work it takes to get there."[32] Mark, locked in on process, would make a decision by June, but he said the only partners he would continue with are Brian Martin or Nagano Olympic silver medalist, Gordy Sheer.

Mark is featured luging on page 92 of *Welcome 2002 Souvenir Guide*, published by Prestige Event Publications, Salt Lake City, Utah. The magazine includes many photos of the four hundred seventy-seven Olympic medals:

> Olympic Victory Medals were designed by Axiom Designed Communications and produced by the O.C. Tanner Company in Salt Lake City. The article, "Answers

Written in Stone: What Makes the Medals Precious?" on page 2, explained that "Olympic gold and silver medals have a core that is at least 92.5 pure silver. Gold medals are plated with six grams of 24-karat gold. Twenty hours of handwork went into each medal [477] after the process of creating the medals, which took thousands of hours.[33]

※

My heartfelt gratitude goes out to the individuals who religiously gave me clippings and articles published and printed about Mark's career: Jane Kane, Jim and Bette Westgate, Lyle and Martha Graham, Bob Laban, Lorna Wilson, Gregg Zulauf, Elaine Brevick, Gwen Glatz, Eunice Beck, Deb and Ed Halcomb, Kathy Montgomery, and Alice and Jim Schneider. If I have forgotten anyone, forgive me and know how grateful I am for your thoughtfulness and generosity.

Sore Soaring

"Nothing Gold Can Stay"

Nature's first green is gold,
Her hardest hue to hold.
Her early leaf's a flower;
But only so an hour.
Then leaf subsides to leaf.
So Eden sank to grief,
So dawn goes down to day.
Nothing gold can stay.

Robert Frost
Frost, Collected Poems, Prose and Plays
1970

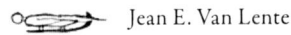

Mark was very busy after he and Brian won silver. Mark made appearances on behalf of U.S. luge and its chief sponsor at the time, Verizon, in New Hampshire, New York, Boston, Washington, D.C. and Providence, Rhode Island.

The Winter Olympians were guests of President George W. Bush and First Lady Laura Bush at the White House in 2002. The Bush visit did not strike Mark as as personal as the visits to President and Mrs. Clinton. They all were assembled outdoors on the back steps of the White House. President Bush made a speech standing behind the Olympians. After his speech, a big photo shoot was taken of the whole group together. President Bush did shake hands randomly at different points. They all were given tours of the White House.

He flew to California to appear with Martin in his partner's hometown of Palo Alto and in several other cities as part of a Verizon Luge Challenge recruiting tour. Mark and Brian both received $15,000 from the U.S. Olympic Committee for their silver performance and an additional stipend from U.S. luge.

"It's impossible to stay competitive at this level and hold down a 'real job.' My year-round job is training." Mark eats his meals at the Olympic Training Center and he said he "gets a little bit of money from a lot of different directions."[1]

Mark flew to Muskegon March 27, 2002. A public welcome home ceremony was held at the Muskegon County Airport. Muskegon by now knew Mark as a "favorite son."

"The next event was a giant pep rally with Reeths-Puffer's 4,500 students. 'Mark personifies the idea of chasing your dreams. We want all the kids to see him and see that reaching your dreams is possible,' said Reeths-Puffer High School Principal Dan Beckeman."[2]

Susan K. Treutler described the reunion March 30, 2002 in the *Chronicle*:

> Thousands of students... screamed, clapped and pounded their feet on the bleachers as they paid tribute to Mark Grimmette, their very own Olympian.
>
> In the dim high school gymnasium, packed literally to the rafters with students, film of Grimmette on his second-place run in Salt Lake City ran on an enormous screen. The Olympic theme blared from loudspeakers. A converted floor lamp served as a substitute Olympic flame. Students led a procession carrying the U.S., Michigan, and Olympic flags. Grimmette, wearing a leather Olympic jacket and his silver medal, followed to a stage where his sled and luge uniform rested...
>
> [High School Principal] Beckeman, saying he wanted the children to be able to see the silver medal more clearly, relieved Grimmette of his jacket and then put it on himself as the students roared. He then offered to relieve Grimmette of the heavy silver medal.
>
> "I think I can bear the weight," Grimmette said.
>
> The medal was key to Grimmette's thanks to the community that supported him so well through the years.[3]

The welcoming for Mark was spectacular. Youngsters grabbed for his jacket, his helmet, his hands. He was open and made himself available. Treutler insightfully concluded: "The message was clear... It [the medal] was something he wanted to share. He wanted people to feel its heaviness, run their fingers along the figures in relief, and know what it means to have earned it. "Light the Fire Within" is inscribed on the back of the medal."[4] The cheers and the stomping feet were deafening. And there was no mistaking what decision about the future the students wanted him to make.

Mark presided at the March 29 Muskegon Fury hockey game against Port Huron. He signed autographs for hours beginning at the intermission in the L.C. Walker Arena corridor. Now there were splashy photograph cards to sign and pins to give out. Thanks to Gordy Sheer.

March 30, Mark appeared at the Muskegon Winter Sports

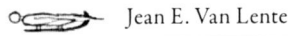

Complex luge run at Muskegon State Park where he had begun his career seventeen years ago.

※

Politically, the International Olympic Committee government is an evolving entity. In November 2002, a significant change in control processed through the ranks. Previously, the IOC president appointed the chairs of all the various commissions of the IOC. The change meant that athletes would be choosing the head of their own commission in the IOC.

※

Mark, with full beard and mustache, began the 2002-2003 World Cup season. He and Brian won first place in Park City, Utah. "They earned silver in the second World Cup in Calgary. December 9, they had fourth in Oberhof to take the lead in the standings with 245 points. Germans Patric Leitner and Alexander Resch had 219 points."[5]

December 14, the *Muskegon Chronicle* reported a temporary lurch backward: "Mark and Brian finished 13th in Altenberg, losing their lead in the overall standings. They had 275 points to 304 points for Alexander Resch and Patric Leitner."[6]

January 7, 2003, a photo appeared in the *Chronicle* of the medal stand with Mark and Brian in second place at Igls, Austria. Austria's Tobias and Marcus Schiegl placed first. Italy's Oswald Haselrieder and Gerhard Plankensteiner were third.[7] Grimmette and Martin, once again, led the overall season standings with one race to go.

They won gold at Winterberg, Germany and became three-time winners in the overall World Cup standings with 545 points. Patric Leitner and Alexander Resch had 536 points overall. "Martin said, 'This was such a fun season; it was a fight between the two of us all year long.'"[8] They weren't finished yet.

As Mark told the story from Winterberg, Germany:

> "We were in the leader's box after our second run [in Winterberg], and Leitner and Resch were coming down the track. It was going back and forth between us, the way it can happen – a couple of thousandths ahead, to two hundredths behind."

What happened next was almost unheard of...

... The numbers that flashed on the scoreboard for the combined time of the German team in relation to the Americans were 0.000.

That's right. A tie.

"Everyone went crazy." Grimmette said... "This has been one of the most enjoyable seasons I've ever had," Grimmette, 32, said from Germany... [9]

Remarkably, they had won their third overall World Cup season. Mark and Brian were ebullient. " 'It always feels good to beat the Germans because they are formidable competitors. You know you're doing something right when you beat them,' said Grimmette." [10]

·:·

Tom Kendra reported October 22, 2003, that Mark "ruptured a disc in his lower back during a medicine ball workout earlier this month. 'I can't do much of anything right now – no lifting or training – and that just means that I'm falling further behind,' said Grimmette who was recovering at home in Lake Placid." [11]

It was true. Mark was hurting from the injury. During the ball toss, he felt a sharp and dramatic pain in his lower back. He knew something was wrong. It caused him to miss the first two World Cups for 2003-2004 at Sigulda and Altenberg.

He tried to meet up with his team at Calgary for the third World Cup. The races left were Calgary, Oberhof, Königssee, Igls, Winterberg, and Turin. They won gold in a Park City race and a silver in Winterberg. Mark confided they were tenth overall with his back injury having prevented their participation in the first three races.

It was a difficult time for the doubles team. " 'We knew going in that our start was not going to be our strong point like it usually is,' said Grimmette... 'That forced us to really focus on being more aerodynamic and [to] drive great lines.'" [12]

·:·

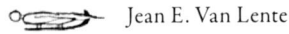

Beloved Grandma Bormann died two years later in 2004. She did not see "the other shoe drop" for Mark as she seemed always to forewarn. She did not see what 20,000 starts were doing to Mark's back or how he gradually slowed as he aged. I would sit and perform motions similar to "start" movements and immediately my back felt tense and tight and vulnerable. What would 600 to 700 starts a year for twenty-six years do to the lower human back?

·:·:·

"Homologation" is the term that refers to the process the FIL decision-makers undergo to certify a new track is ready for luge athletes to come and compete. They want to make sure there is nothing inherently dangerous about making a run on the track, that it is safe to slide.

The event of luge coaches and athletes coming from different countries to participate is part of homologation. Mark remembers Chris Thorpe and Gordy Sheer helped homologate the track at Nagano, when homologation first began before the 1998 XVIII Olympic Winter Games there. Mark was the U.S. luge athlete who took part in the homologation for the track at Cesana Pariol, Italy in 2004.

Recently, Mark participated as U.S. luge coach and Chris Mazdzer participated as U.S. luge athlete in the homologation of the new luge track at Sochi, Russia in March 2012, for the upcoming XXII Olympic Winter Games in 2014. The coaches help the athletes get down the hill by helping the lugers figure out the lines of the track. When they return home, they share their knowledge with the others.

Mark informed me that homologation is more professionally done now since the XXI Winter Games in Vancouver. However, Mark averred: "Luge is a dangerous sport." The International Luge Federation fleshes out any type of potentially dangerous risks in the track the FIL is homologating, but it is impossible to foresee or predict all the ways an athlete will come down a hill. Therefore, risks and misfortunes cannot all be avoided.

·:·:·

The track in Cesana Pariol, Italy loomed larger and larger as the four years between Winter Olympics raced on. Tom Kendra kept in contact with Mark:

> Track knowledge is critical in luge, which is why Grimmette and Martin made sure they were among the first athletes to slide down the recently completed Olympic track in Italy last month.
>
> "Knowledge of the track is important," said Grimmette... "One of the biggest things I like to say about our sport is that it is a big experience sport."
>
> ...After more than 30 combined years in the sport and reaching their mid-30s, the 2006 Olympics in all likelihood will be the duo's swan song.[13]

Mark was thirty-four years old. He had been in luge twenty years. He and Brian had been sliding together nine years.

Another German team, Andre Florschutz and Torsten Wüstlich won the gold at the February 17, 2005 Luge World Championships at Park City. Italy's Christian Oberstolz and Patric Gruber won silver. Mark and Brian won bronze. Mark reported they had a chance, but he raised his head ever so slightly and looked a little bit and that slowed them down. They were fourth in the 2004-2005 World Cup standings.

·:·

In 2005, Mark made a special trip to Grand Rapids, Michigan. He was invited as one of ten Olympians to appear for the "Go for the Gold. Reach for the Stars." event to benefit the Make-A-Wish Foundation of Michigan.

> Grimmette, along with other Olympians will start with a tour of the DeVos Children's Hospital in Grand Rapids...
>
> The Olympians will then be the featured guests at a gala fundraiser at the MVP Sportsplex, where those in attendance will participate in Olympic-style games with the athletes, complete with medals.
>
> Proceeds from the event will benefit the Make-A-Wish Foundation that grants wishes to children with life-threatening medical conditions.

> He [Mark] will also make an appearance at U.S. Luge sponsor U.S. Steel's automotive center in Troy.[14]

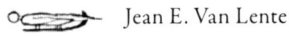

December 2, 2005, Mark and Brian won their doubles race in Calgary, Alberta. Mark and Brian secured their spot on the 2006 Olympic team by breaking out of their slump with the victory at Calgary. That race came after four lackluster races: 9th in Turin, 13th in Sigulda and 10th in Altenberg. They were also tenth in Lake Placid. Their several poor finishes were causing speculation on the luge circuit that they were losing their edge.

Of course, Mark always had a positive spin to put on his back injury, but it was really debilitating. It severely restricted what he could do. All the passion in the world wouldn't heal a herniated disc. With 20,000 starts in the average luger's career, it became clear what toll the starts had had on Mark's body eventually.

He went to Germany to cheer his teammates on at Königssee, but he didn't race. In training, he resumed his focus for the World Cup coming up in Igls, Austria January 14-15, 2005. They were sixth at Igls and only eleventh at Oberhof.

I observed over the years that the descriptions of how two sliders communicate together on a sled vary regarding how it's done. The following description by Tom Kendra seemed out-of-sync from many previous scenarios. "Grimmette, 6'1", 198 pounds, is a natural top man with his size and strength helping to pull the sled faster down the slope. Martin, 5'8", 162 pounds, tucks in and is the team's contact with the ice, doing the hard steering as Grimmette makes subtle adjustments."[15]

I'd certainly read enough describing Mark as the power steer and Brian making the subtle movements with his shoulder. So, I asked Mark. He intimated that the techniques of how doubles lugers work together are simplified for the media and the public. But, he assured me the whole process for doubles luge is complicated and it's different for every doubles team.

One month before the XX Olympic Winter Games in 2006 in Cesana Pariol, Italy, Mark missed a World Cup race in Germany due to the herniated disc in his back. "He developed back spasms over the holiday break and was being treated in Lake Placid. 'Other than missing this weekend's race, the spasms have not and will not affect my preparations for February's Games.'"[16]

Mark emphasized again the importance of experience:

> At Nagano they focused on relaxing and "letting the sled run" which German teams excel at. "It takes a number of years to see a number of different situations on the track," said Grimmette. "The more times you have those experiences, the better off you're going to be, and the more situations you're going to feel comfortable in." Mark and Brian were sequestered from the rest of the world near the luge run in LaPlagne, France – forbidden from all media and other distractions for the past week as they make final preparation for what might be their final race together.[17]

What struck me as ironic was that in 1992, Mark was in tumultuous LaPlagne as an "alternate" in the Winter Olympics, wanting so badly to be on the team. And now, in 2006, fourteen years later, he was in quiet LaPlagne to get away from all the Olympic hype to prepare himself for the fourth "fireworks" and accompanying pressures on the team in Cesana Pariol, Italy.

Tom Kendra, himself having gained much knowledge about luge, articulated: "How can you arrive at the moment you have worked for your entire life, the moment that has motivated your training for years and will in many ways set the direction of your future, and be able to block out all those 'distractions' and become 100% relaxed? Whichever luge doubles team can do the best job of that will win the gold medal on Wednesday."[18]

※

Karrie and I were on the Internet almost every single day going through the possibility of making the trip to Italy to watch Mark and Brian. We rented a flat in the nearby little town of Bardonnechia, which would accommodate ten people. In the end, only four of us could go. Karrie, Karrie's little daughter, Hannah, who was only two at the time, made the trip with Karrie's friend, Tiffanie, and I.

The trip to Turin, Italy was a charmer, but not without its trials. After flying to Paris, Karrie, Tiffanie, Hannah, and I took a train south to Bardonnechia, Italy, where we had rented a flat for ten days. When we rolled into the station, we spied a bucolic, smiling, dark-haired woman with a scarf around her head holding a sign with both hands, which read, "Van Lente." That was us!

The doors slid open as the train came to a halt. I grabbed Hannah and jumped off to the platform. Tiffanie and Karrie were left on-board to madly search for and dig out our luggage buried at the bottom of a heap. They were still struggling when Karrie saw the doors begin to close. She angrily implored the train conductor: "Don't shut that door. That's my baby out there, so don't you dare not let me off this train!" While the conductor, hollering in Italian, explained that the train must keep moving, he opened the doors again while Karrie and Tiffanie stumbled off, luggage in hand.

The Italian woman took us to our rented flat with supplied kitchenette, two spacious bedrooms and a bathroom. The cozy flat would have been perfect, except it was on the fourth floor with no elevator. Cheery curtains at the windows lent privacy. Little Hannah became fascinated with the bidet. True to form, Karrie thought she had to wash clothes. She no sooner started the miniature machine than suds began pouring out from underneath all over the floor. We scrambled to regain order.

Race day was overcast; the temperature was a damp, unforgiving cold. Tiffanie, Karrie and I took turns pushing Hannah in the Jeep stroller laboriously up a steep ungraded, rutted, rock-strewn hill in search of the track. I pushed Hannah most of the way up the steep terrain because Tiffanie was aiding Karrie, who was suffering from morning sickness. She was having a bad time of trying to keep from vomiting. She was two months pregnant at the time.

Having the Jeep stroller was a blessing in some regards, but in others, it was cumbersome. It was bulky and hard to fold up and get on a train quickly. Where we were staying there were no elevators, so carrying the large Jeep stroller was the only option.

Finally we reached the track. The mood was eerily subdued. After moving through the crowd and going through security, we noticed that the crowd really was not a huge one as people made their way up to different locations around the track. The crowd thinned out quite a bit. We huddled together three-quarters of the way down. Mark came out unsuited to assess the track. In a flash, he was gone.

On the first run, Mark and Brian came down twelfth position of twenty-one sleds rumbling closer and closer. Right in front of us at dangerous curve 14, they crashed. (In German: sturz). The term used at the Lake Placid luge course to refer to a crash is "eighty-one." They were just about to enter the "Washing Machine." The sound was like splintering wood from a swinging ax. They eventually landed, stood up, walked off and all the network cameras were turned down toward the ground. Mark and Brian were physically okay, but disqualified. Mark had warned me Curve 14 continued to give them trouble. They were riding too high and the sled turned sideways, flipped, and they rolled onto the ice.

Mark was emotionally devastated after the crash. He had only really known a rising star. He blamed himself, saying he drifted too late and he expressed sadness over having dashed Brian's hopes along with his own, which only compounded his tearful feelings of sorrow. Brian was graciously quick to reassure that he was not disappointed in his teammate of ten years.

Tom Kendra tried to characterize their profound disappointment: "Like the ill-fated slide, which ended with the longtime duo and their capsized sled careening along the icy track, Grimmette couldn't finish [at the press conference.]" [19]

The mile long track has nineteen turns. Curves 6,7 and 8 are called "Toro" and represent one of the most technical sections. Curve 14 has a sharp downhill drop and goes into curve 15 called the "Washing Machine" for its centrifugal force. Mark felt he failed to steer the sled early enough into curve 14. "This was not the ending that anyone expected for Grimmette and Martin – the top lugers in U.S. history with an amazing 61 international medals, including Olympic bronze and silver medals." [20]

Larry Page, U.S. luge official from Muskegon, gave his analysis: "Here's what happened... They were going for gold. Maybe they could have gone conservative, put down two solid runs, and walked away with third. But that was never the goal this time around. In other words, gold or bust. And they went bust." [21]

Austrian brothers Andreas Linger and Wolfgang Linger won gold. Germany's Andre Florschutz and Torsten Wüstlich were silver. Italians Gerhard Plankensteiner and Oswald Haselrieder took bronze.

At the local scene, everyone expected the best and no one feared the worst:

> Muskegon Winter Sports Complex officials hosted the party at Great Lakes Downs. [They] had taped the afternoon broadcast and replayed it on a 20-foot screen.
>
> Fans cheered mightily as Grimmette and Martin were introduced in the starting blocks. Those cheers quickly changed to groans and gasps as the team did something it hadn't done in at least two years on the World Cup circuit – wipe out.[22]

After their crash, Mark and Brian were not hurt but looked crestfallen to have their hope for Olympic gold ended in an instant. Sliders are disqualified if they do not finish on their sleds and Mark and Brian did not get a second run. " 'It's very disappointing,' said Grimmette … who is top driver and does most of the team's steering with his legs. 'But we tried hard. We did our best. It's a tough end.' "[23]

They tumbled together through the turn and slid for several seconds before finally coming to a stop. As the two men stood and brushed themselves off, they shared a few words. Asked what those were, Martin struggled. " 'I asked Mark if he was all right,' he said, his eyes welling with tears. 'That's most important …' "[24]

It was revealed that Mark and Brian had crashed during one of their final practice runs over the weekend. That experience may have left them fearful heading into the Olympic competition. Mark explained to me, "We struggled all week in training and we hoped that we would be able to put it together for two runs. But it didn't happen." Clearly, both Mark and Brian were very sparing of each other's feelings. They were a team in victory and they were a team in defeat. That's saying a lot for a twosome after ten years and a bitter disappointment. They had been top competitors on the world luge scene for a decade. And they were all heart.

I felt numb immediately after the crash. My thoughts were similar to Brian's thoughts. Were they okay and not hurt? Karrie had tears in her eyes and then spoke later about how she was happy she didn't have a job in which she worked all year for one moment, only to have it gone in one moment. I looked behind me to see my brother-in-law elbow my sister because her eyes welled with tears. We didn't want Mark to think we were disappointed in him and what had happened.

Tiffanie, Karrie, Hannah, and I refused to let the disappointment spoil our fun in Italy. We explored Turin and locations surrounding Bardonnechia. We traveled by train to Milan and Genoa by the Gulf of Genoa. Genoa held for us a view of a quaint, bustling seaside city. The hotel was across the street from the train station. We stayed the night in luxury with all the amenities. A short walk the next day took us to Genoa's grand living aquarium on the wharf overlooking crystal blue waters of the Ligurian Sea. Shops snuggled tightly together on cobbled, winding streets. We could easily have spent days there.

On our return from Genoa, Tiffanie was holding Hannah on our arrival at Milan. We all ran to catch our train. Karrie and I found our comfy, reserved corner seats facing each other over the large square table. But no Tiffanie and no Hannah. Karrie began to panic. She burst into anxious tears, just as Tiffanie, holding Hannah, came through the sliding car door.

The plenteous four-course meals did nothing for our waistlines, but we enjoyed the Italian food. Our first and final train trips to and from Paris gave us spectacular views of the Alps wherein had been the track mishap for Mark and Brian.

※

Mark and Brian wrestled with whether to continue in doubles luge, since both were having physical injuries to deal with: Brian, his arm and Mark, his back. But the *Chronicle* pealed out May 11, 2006, that they had decided to continue in the sport showing Mark with a beaming grin on his face.

In the 2006-2007 World Cup season Mark and Brian were eighth overall although in Whistler, British Columbia where the 2010 Games were to be held, they were seventh in the World Cup. Of the 2007-2008 World Cup season, Mark in 2012 responded to me he had no memory whatsoever. Mark and Brian struggled in the first four World Cups of the 2008-2009 season. Equipment problems were one of the factors.

The 2009 FIL World Championships were held at Mt. Van Hoevenberg in Lake Placid. Mark's entire family including Fawn, Eddie, their sons, Bryce and Collin, John, Jolie and Louie, and Karrie,

Shane and their daughters, Hannah and Maya, and Ricky and Merri Jo and myself traveled to Lake Placid in February for the World Championship race. John found the cheapest motel in the area where we would stay. Even in the bitter cold and snow I spied a live fly zooming between a chalky plastic covering and the window pane. The stained, buckling ceiling threatened to collapse on me in my bed the whole night. As always, to round out festivities, Jolie unloaded a car full of luscious Cajun, Spanish, and veggie dishes she had made and brought for everyone's sustenance. Bryce, 9, and Collin, 2, joined Hannah, 5, and Maya, 2, sledding on the slopes around the motel. Collin squealed with delight to be walked around on daddy's shoulders at the track. And I snatched Hannah back just in the nick of time before she got herself completely lost marching with the crush of foot traffic.

The crowd at the track was wild. Cowbells clanged. Mark and Brian responded by winning the bronze medal that day. They were buoyed and cheered by their result. It was their 6th World Championship bronze. They were happily feeling some of the old zip. We were there and we were happy for them.

December 16, 2009, the race-offs were held in Lillehammer, Norway among the U.S. teams for deciding who would compete in the Vancouver Winter Games two months later.

"After a movie and a game of 'Hearts' in their hotel room the night before, Mark and Brian emerged the next day to best Matt Mortensen and Preston Griffall. They dominated all three heats using a total of their two best runs. Mark and Brian were 1:36.989 seconds while Matt and Preston were 1:37.344." [25]

Mark and Brian explained how they felt competing on a foreign track with only their teammates for a berth on the XXI U.S. Olympic luge team upcoming in Vancouver, Canada in 2010:

> "Our runs were not perfect, but we sucked up all the issues in the track and pushed all the speed into the next turns," said Grimmette. "We have learned a lot about the sled the past 4 to 5 weeks. It's been a battle. We made some changes to it and found speed in the sled. Before, we were snowplowing too much. So, between fixing that and sliding better, both of those things made a big difference... Inter team races are tough because we're close." [26]

Martin added, "It was very quiet at breakfast. Everyone was focused and looking inward, not outward."[27] It was a very quiet day at the track. Brian turned on the lights and it was only the United States contenders. Mark told me he felt relieved when the competitions were over. It would be a fifth Olympics for him and a fourth for Brian.

Mark, 39, would be among three competitors at the Winter Games for whom it would be their fifth games. Casey Puckett and Todd Lodwick from the U.S. Olympic ski team also would be athletes competing at their fifth Olympics. Casey Puckett would be a ski cross racer at Vancouver. Todd Lodwick, 33, is a Nordic combined skier.

·:·:·

In the 2009-2010 World Cups before Whistler: Königssee is the "Olympic" track in off-Olympic years. Mark classified Königssee as his favorite track. It is the most technically difficult track in the world. Here the sliders come to prove themselves. The track is on a lake lying beneath soaring mountains. Julia Clukey said, "Right from the start you are doing something all the way down. You're kind of out of breath."[27]

Julia continued: "It requires steering through the 'S' curves as they are tight and you are high and you have to steer a lot. [The track] has a 360° turn. You are ... [steering] all the way down and pulling 4 to 5 Gs in the finish turn."[28] To "lose your head" refers to the slider who cannot keep his head up in a high G-force turn. The "kreisel," the German word for a child's toy top, describes a turn that curves back under itself, or, as at Königssee, a curve of 360° or more.

Mark and Brian were fourth in Winterberg. The snow was blowing hard. Brian thought both their runs were pretty good. They had to make small corrections all the way down: "The conditions were pretty brutal with lots of snow and wind," said Grimmette. "It was important to point the sled to where you wanted it to go, keep a good line and headed in the right direction. It was unpredictable ... Parts of the track you couldn't let the sled go, but in other sections you could."[29]

Sandy Caligiore, of the U.S. Luge Association reported:

In Oberhof, the tourist mecca, Mark and Brian were seventh, the top American finish. They pulled to the sides of the track at the start of both runs, which was a major error. Brian said he could hear the time being wasted.

But Mark preferred to look at the positive and said, "I'm happy with the direction we're headed. I learned some things with my shoulders in trying to be smoother."[30]

Again, I was confused. I had thought Brian, the bottom driver, used his shoulders. But, here was Mark saying he had learned to use his shoulders. After twenty-six years, I am left with the impression they both used everything it took and everything they had. And I still can't really conceive of how they did it at all.

"Grimmette and Martin… claimed a 10th place ranking for the [2009-2010] season with 295 points. Niccum and Joye… finished eighth in the standings with 317 points."[31]

In the face of a dismal World Cup season, Mark, 39, and Brian, 36, tried to hold steady. Just before the XXI Winter Olympics, Mark was calling me often and late, anxious to set me up for the generous $3,000 stipend that sponsor, Procter and Gamble was awarding to each Olympic mother. He wanted me to have that. I remember thinking he was losing focus and I ordered him to pay attention to what he was doing instead of worrying about me.

Vancouver would be the most populated area for a Winter Olympics. The population is over two million. Canada would be host for the third time. According to Olympic statistics, Montreal hosted in the 1976 Summer Games and Calgary hosted the 1988 Winter Games.

Whistler is a skiing resort on Whistler Mountain and Blackcomb Peak. Now Whistler would have a luge track for the games. Its location is ninety minutes north of Vancouver. The route to the track had been so underdeveloped, it had to be rebuilt and widened. Even after the improvements, it was reported there still had been rockslides before the Olympics.

Mark described the Whistler track as the fastest Olympic course. He asserted Whistler's vertical drop is 499 feet compared to 374 feet at Cesana Pariol, Italy and a 340 foot drop at Park City, Utah. By the "Wedge" curve, singles could be going 50 mph. After "Lueders Loop" and into the "Lynx" curve speeds could be 71-95 mph. The next curve is "Shiver" and the last before the elevating finish is "Gold Rush Trail" and "Thunderbird Turn," where Mark said speeds for singles might actually reach 96 mph. The finish is uphill.

Mark and Brian had qualified for an Olympic berth at Lillehammer in December. Now in February, they were in Vancouver dancing: Brian was shaken and excited and he hugged Mark as he revealed the news Wednesday night that the athletes had chosen Mark to carry the American flag into Vancouver's BC Place in front of the U.S. team during the opening ceremonies. Mark told me they were geeked for a good hour afterwards. Mark would be the third luge athlete to carry the American flag. Frank Masley carried the flag in 1984 and Cammy Myler carried it in 1994.

Mark also shared with me how honored he felt being chosen once again to carry the flag and to represent the Olympic team. He thought it was another top honor for him. I was quoted as feeling humbled upon hearing the news. Mark had had the blessings of many honors come his way over the many years. The first time Mark was chosen to help carry a flag was 2002, of course, when eight athletes were chosen to carry the tattered flag from the crumbled World Trade Center into the Salt Lake City opening ceremonies. That procession, as in a dirge, which included New York City police and fire fighters, was very somber and silent.

Brian let Mark know he was chosen during a meeting of team captains from the different sports. Then Brian humored Mark by adding that "elder statesman" was mentioned. "I hope it wasn't 'elderly'," quipped Mark. In deepest sincerity, he expressed to me he thought it was "just a great honor."

Frank Masley, former national luger, called Mark a true sportsman, a role model Olympian and very deserving. Karrie told me, "Mark left a flat voicemail for me Thursday night ... It was something like, 'I just wanted to let you guys know that I'm going to be carrying the flag in the Olympics.'" I asked him how he had been chosen again. I told him we were very proud of him.

Larry Page praised Mark. "He is what the Olympics should be about – someone who loves what he does and always puts the integrity of the sport first. He is the perfect choice as flag bearer."[32]

Tom Kendra threw in some sentimental history: "Muskegon's

Mark Jastrzembski reminisced, 'He used to come to the complex and hoist the 2-by-10-by-16 foot boards so that I could hammer them in place on the walls of the luge track.'"[33]

⁂

Even though the Whistler Resort track in Canada is the fastest and most dangerous of all tracks, no one envisioned what transpired. On Friday, the unimaginable happened. Nodar Kumeritashvili, 21, from the Republic of Georgia, flew from his sled on the luge track on a practice run coming into the finish, hit a steel post and died from the impact.

Mark was saddened at what had happened. Mark, through interviews, sent his heartfelt condolences to the family of Nodar Kumeritashvili. "[Mark] marched into BC Place Stadium wearing a pin in honor of Nodar Kumaritashvili … The tragedy has saddened athletes in Vancouver."[34]

⁂

Tom Kendra observed: "He [Mark] seemed relaxed as he appeared waving the flag before [his 216 member team] and an estimated worldwide television audience of more than three billion."[35] The stadium in Vancouver is the first one covered by a roof in Winter Olympic history. It holds 60,000. At least 2,634 athletes were present representing 82 nations.

Mark commented to me that Cypress Mountain, at 3,051 feet, had its warmest January ever. Snow had to be carted in for freestyle and snowboarding. Twice as high, Whistler Resort held the luge track. The colder temperatures prevailed there, ninety miles north of Vancouver.

Changes were made to the track. Luge officials reduced the length of the track after Friday's fatal crash. Doubles lugers were then to start in the middle of a curve between the fifth and the sixth turns. "If a doubles team steers too hard, they get too low on the track. If they don't steer hard enough, they get too high in the curve … 'We were approaching 40 runs from the proper start and we've only had 4 runs from the new start,' said Martin."[36]

The changes called for immediate adjustments by the lugers. Their start location in the track had been totally altered. The track is fast with tight curves, which makes it rough sledding. The officials quickly installed a wooden wall to cover some steel supports and padded others. Mark offered: "Officials raised the wall at curve 16. The International Luge Federation officials reshaped the ice to steer sleds toward the safer center of the track."

February 17 was clear and bright, sunny. Mark critiqued the racing after they had finished: " 'That is where the race was,' Grimmette said about the starts. 'After the starts, our runs were great. I'm definitely disappointed,' he added. 'We got the start curve down in practice and we were encouraged going into the race, but you have to do it on race day.' "[37]

They finished thirteenth with a time of 1:24.005. (They had placed second in each of Tuesday's practice runs.)

Austria's Andreas and Wolfgang Linger (brothers) won their 2nd consecutive gold medal in 1:22.705. Latvia's Andris and Juris Sics (brothers) won silver in 1:22.969 and Germany's Patric Leitner and Alexander Resch earned the bronze in 1:23.404. The top U.S. finish was 6th place by Dan Joye and Christian Niccum.

Reviewing the changes to the track and their effect on Mark and Brian's sliding, Matt Mattson wrote:

> The course was shortened upon the death of the luger from Georgia. That put an emphasis on the start, especially the first curve. Mark wistfully said they brushed the wall on the first run and pulled off to the middle on the second run, which was not the ideal path.
>
> Mark and Brian ranked 11th after their first run in 41.821 seconds. Mark seemed disappointed. On the second run, they crossed in 42.184.[38]

Mark, as always, thanked his supporters back home: " 'It's always great to represent the United States at the Olympics,' he said. 'And to represent West Michigan and Muskegon. I'm appreciative to all my fans in that area.' "[39]

"I get all teary-eyed," Dollene St. Martin said. "He's such a wonderful guy. He deserves everything he gets. He's worked so hard for this."[40] "This is great," Gary St. Martin added. "He's done an absolutely great job for not only Muskegon, but the whole area."[41]

What wonderful down-the-street upbeat neighbors we had. They were always positive and always supportive. They had seen Mark grow up alongside their son, now a pilot. Both young men followed their dreams. Surely, it seemed four fast friends in boyhood grew to fulfill their hearts' desires.

Of Mark and Brian, I felt they were somehow prepared – disappointed, but girded. I was thankful they were all right. Mark had been in luge twenty-six years. His friend, Gordy Sheer, in luge sixteen years, told Mark that being competitive in luge for twenty-six years was quite an accomplishment.

When Mark retired after twenty-six years in the sport in 2010, he called me and told me about his decision. I asked him if he was sad? Disappointed? He responded, "Mom, I've had twenty-six years in my sport; I've competed in five Olympics; I've won two Olympic medals; I've carried two flags. Now, it's time for me to retire."

For Mark, luging had always been about the process as much as the goal. He recalled playing football in high school, he was one of the few players who really enjoyed practices. He would be happy to be evolving through another life transition.

38. Mark Grimmette, Jim Rudicil, James Westgate, and Michael St. Martin at Fenner Road, March 1998.

39. Mark arrives at Muskegon County Airport, March 27, 2002.

Grab the Kufens

Everyone who competes in the games goes into strict training. They do it to get a crown that will not last; but we do it to get a crown that will last forever.

I Corinthians: 9:25 NIV

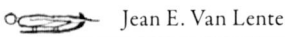

Mark talked to me after the race in Vancouver. My son sounded like an older man. He sounded acclimated to the events as they had happened. I told him I was proud of them. They did their best. Mark was still obsessing over whether or not I had received $3,000.00 from Procter and Gamble. He wanted me to have that. He sounded bent on coming home; he longed to see everyone.

Swedish 2011 Nobel Prize Winner, Tomas Tranströmer's "Homeward" spoke to Mark's deepest desires:

> A telephone call ran out in the night and glittered over the countryside and in the suburbs.
>
> Afterward I slept uneasily in the hotel bed.
>
> I was like the needle in a compass carried through the forest by an orien--teer with a thumping heart.[1]

⁘

Mark's girlfriend then, now his wife, Keela and her father, Brad Dates were at Whistler to watch the race. Jim Schneider, Alice, Laura and Ben were there. Ricky Grimmette, Mark's little brother on his dad's side, and his mother, Merri Jo were there. Nancy Martin was there. Ron Dugas was there.

Mark and Brian, after their race, were closely watching the Nordic combined race. In the Nordic combined team event, the United States won silver, the first Olympic medal for the U.S. in that event. Earlier, Johnny Spillane won a silver medal for a first ever in a U.S. Nordic combined event at ski jumping. By the end of the 4 x 5 kilometer relay, Austria was gold and the U.S. was silver for team members: Brett Camerota, Todd Lodwick, Johnny Spillane, and Bill Demong. Mark and Brian participated in the closing ceremonies.

The 2010 Winter Olympians were invited to the White House in Washington, D.C. to be guests of President Barack Obama and

First Lady Michelle Obama. They were separated by different winter sports in separate rooms in the White House. The luge team was in the library downstairs. Mark remembers President and Mrs. Obama were very friendly. They shook everyone's hands and posed for individual photos with each athlete. After the visit, they toured the exhibit of between six and seven hundred thousand stuffed birds at the Smithsonian Institute. The exhibit drew raves from Mark.

⁂

> "…These forty years the Lord your God has been with you,/ and you have not lacked anything."
>
> Deut. 2:7 NIV.

Just before the national race ending the 2010 season on March 14, Mark went to Brian's house to let him know he was retiring. Mark recalled he and Brian "were on the same page."

The day before the Nationals, March 13, 2010, Mark unemotionally and matter-of-factly shared with me that he had already talked with Brian and that he was retiring from luge. He told me the last eight years had been very rough. Of course I had known 2007 was hard on him emotionally. I had known his herniated disc caused him excruciating pain. I had been there when he and Brian crashed in Cesana Pariol, Italy in 2006. But he never talked about what these together had meant as he tried to continue to excel in the sport. Nor had he divulged that since Salt Lake, year piled on top of year, and he gradually had to admit to himself that sliding was asking more than he was able to give.

They won an undisclosed medal at the national race, their last. After the medals ceremony for the nationals, Keela told me she remembers she was standing next to Tony Benshoof, singles luger, when Ron Rossi, Executive Director, made a special announcement that led to Mark's public statement. Mark let everyone know he was retiring. Keela said Tony, in total shock, exclaimed, "What!!" Generally, the response was one of surprise. No one knew.

He wasn't looking for a sinecure. Of course, the U.S.L.A. wanted him to be sports director and head coach. So that's what he did. And he asks a lot of himself as usual. He has jumped in with both feet.

Today, Mark fills the role of sports director and manager. But he also knows perhaps too much. He may be facing another fork in the road if he doesn't produce winners. Add to that, his marriage to the lovely Keela Dates June 30, 2012. Meanwhile, he told me he thought it would be "neat to have your mother write your biography."

June 5, 2010, Mark was inducted into the Muskegon Area Sports Hall of Fame: "Mark Grimmette said that no matter what remote luge village he was in during his competitive days, 'I felt the community of Muskegon behind me in all those places.' Grimmette grew up next door to Muskegon State Park and helped build the luge run at the Winter Sports Complex."[2]

If I had read that scenario once, I had read it ten thousand times over twenty-six years, a third of a lifetime. Apparently, the compelling magic of the beginnings resonated with readers and sold newspapers. I certainly bought them!

Truly, I felt it wasn't a one-generational young lad's magical tale. Was it coincidental I had lived for awhile at sixteen as an exchange student in West Germany in none other than 1964, when luge began as a Winter Olympic sport? Did my genes soak up something in the water? Was it fortuitous that I fell in love with Lake Michigan as a waitress in the summers at the Cracker Box restaurant at Sleeping Bear Dunes in Glen Arbor, Michigan to help pay for my college education?

Was it happenstance that Mark's father found a job teaching biology at Muskegon Community College? Was it perfect timing that Jim Westgate wanted to sell a quarter of his property just when we were looking to build? And where? – A quarter mile from Lake Michigan.

For at least two generations, God's interventions had been opening up opportunities. Are all the references in the *New Testament* back to prophecies 500 to 1200 years earlier in the *Old Testament* real in showing their fulfillment in God's plan for His people? Yes, they are.

Mark told his audience: "All the way through, I tried to be humble and to represent Muskegon well." [Tom Kendra declared,] "He certainly did that."[3]

In his visit to Muskegon, "Mark cut a ribbon in the celebration of the new fiberglass track at the Winter Sports Complex. The track is the first universally accessible wheeled luge track in North America. Then he went down as the first slider."[4]

Mark also went to First Evangelical Lutheran Church in North Muskegon to speak at a special dinner in his honor. He was invited by his former pastor and ever friend, Reverend Bill Uetricht. It was time for the most decorated slider in the history of the United States Luge Association to push home.

Appendices

Appendix A:
Commemorative Plaque: June 2010

Mark Grimmette
Brian Martin

In honor of the United States' most accomplished
luge athletes of all time:

65 medals won

11 World Cup Victories

11 Time USA Luge Team-of-the-Year

8 time U.S. National Champions

6 time World Championship Medalists

3 time Overall World Cup Champions

2 Olympic Medals Won

With deep respect and a high level of appreciation for a great career, strong work ethic and wonderful memories.

Commemorated this 12th day of June, 2010
by the U.S. Luge Association's highest authority,
it's National Luge Committee

Appendix B:
Luge Tracks Around the World

Grateful acknowlegment is given to the United States Luge Association for permission to reprint the drawings of luge tracks around the world by Gordy Sheer, editor in *U.S. Luge Team: The Official Media and Information Guide of the United States Luge Association,* Lake Placid, N.Y., 1999-2000, 72-84.

The first sketch of the Muskegon luge is by Jean E. Van Lente.

Photography: Mark Kurtz, Fred Zimny, Allsport.

Muskegon, Michigan

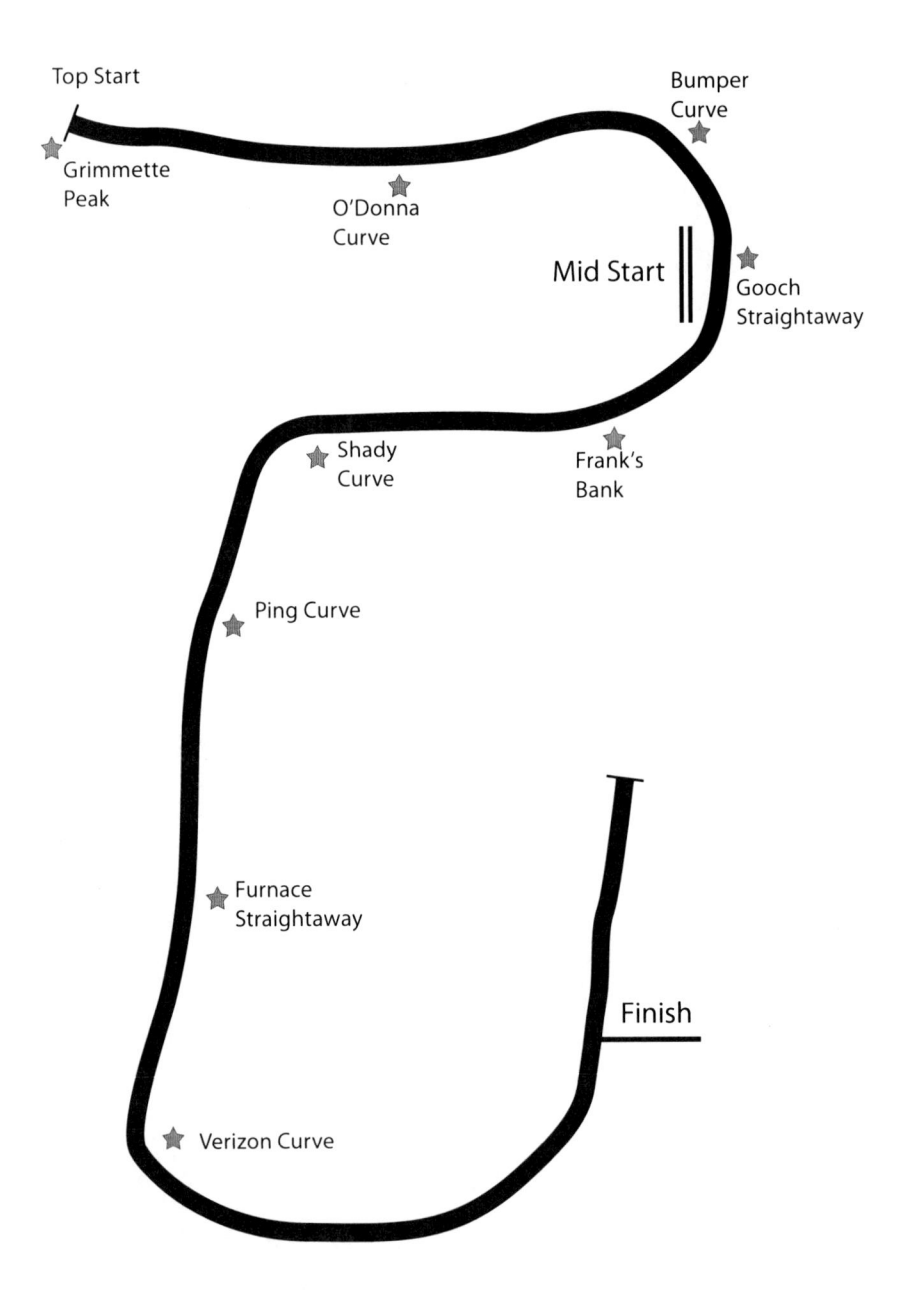

Top Start

Bumper Curve

Grimmette Peak

O'Donna Curve

Mid Start

Gooch Straightaway

Shady Curve

Frank's Bank

Ping Curve

Furnace Straightaway

Finish

Verizon Curve

1.0 Luge at Muskegon, Michigan.

9.8 Meters Per Second Per Second

St. Moritz, Switzerland

St. Moritz is located high in the peaks of the Swiss Alps and weaves through a forest of pine trees. It is one of the fastest and smoothest tracks in the world. This is ironic considering that it is a natural track made simply from ice and snow and is rebuilt completely from the ground up each year. Throw in the notorious Horseshoe curve for some challenge, and you have sliding in its purest form.

Matt McClain

4 Time Junior World Champion (Doubles)

	Length	Curves
Men		17
Women		16

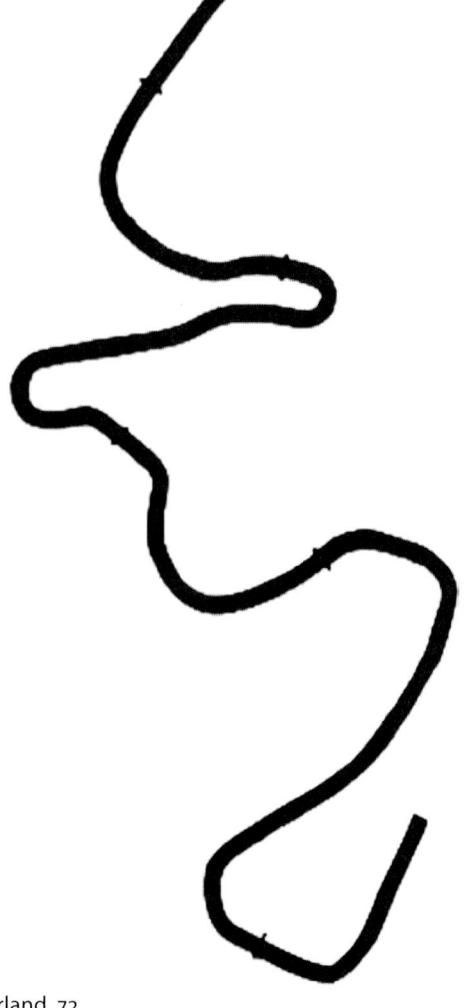

1.1 The natural track at St. Moritz, Switzerland, 72.

265

Oberhof, Germany

Oberhof is not a combination luge/bobsled track. This means that the curves can be much tighter and require a greater amount of steering. It is a fun track when you make it down clean, but believe me, it's not very much fun when you get it wrong.

Brenna Margol

Jr. National Team Member
1998-99 US National Championship Silver Medalist

	Length	Curves
Men	1130 m	14
Women		11

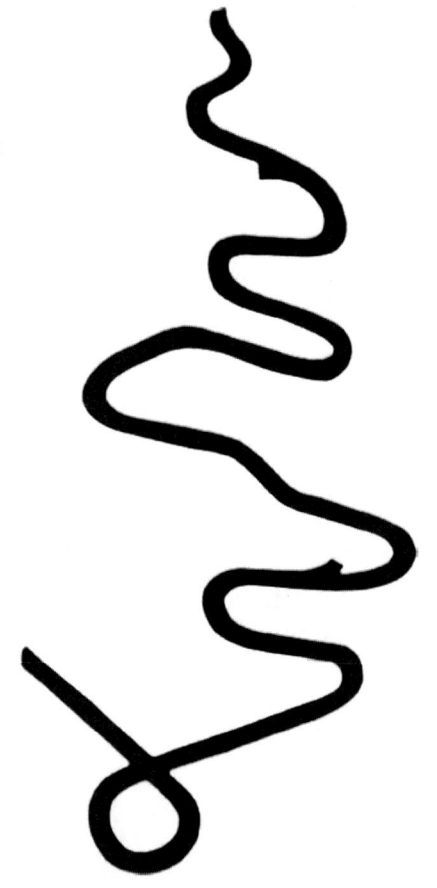

1.2 The track at Oberhof, Germany, 73.

9.8 Meters Per Second Per Second

Igls, Austria

Igls is one of the hardest tracks on which to go fast. The women's start has a tricky start curve, and curve 10 requires precision and a fine exit line. Curve 9 is also very hard, if you enter late your exit will be way off, so hold on tight for the straight-away.

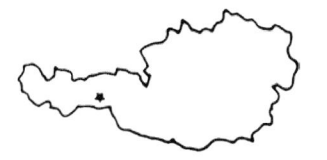

Nicole Oliveira

4 Title Gold Medalist - 1998-1999 World Cups
1998-99 Overall Jr. World Cup Champion

	Length	Curves
Men	1220 m	14
Women		11

1.3 The track at Igls, Austria, 74.

267

Calgary, Canada

Sliding at Calgary is relatively easy. A race is usually won within the first 20 meters of the start ramp because on the rest of the track, everyone's run is virtually the same. Small subtleties are important in the top steeper sections in order to gain the speed needed for the flatter lower sections. Good aerodynamics is more important here than any other track.

Clay Ives

2002 Bronze Olympic Medalist (Doubles)

	Length	Curves
Men	1251 m	14
Women	1185 m	10

1.4 The track at Calgary, Canada, 75.

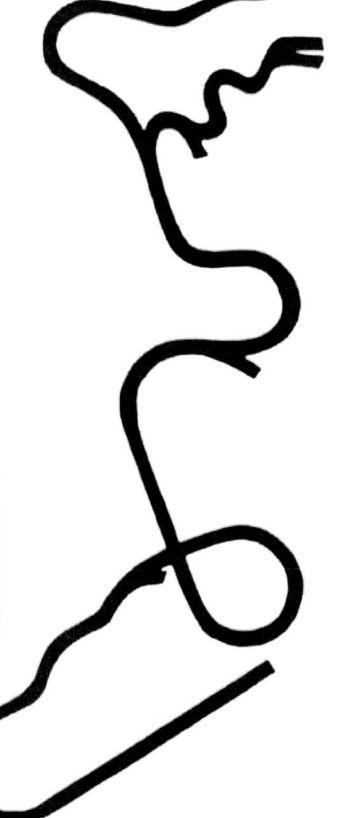

9.8 Meters Per Second Per Second

Winterberg, Germany

Winterberg, is a fun track . The men's start begins nice and slow. and the real speed starts to kick in around curve 9. From that point on you feel like you're on a rocket all the way to the finish line.

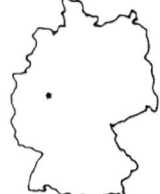

Adam Heidt

1998 US Olympic Team Member (9th Place)
3rd 1998-1999 Winterberg World Cup

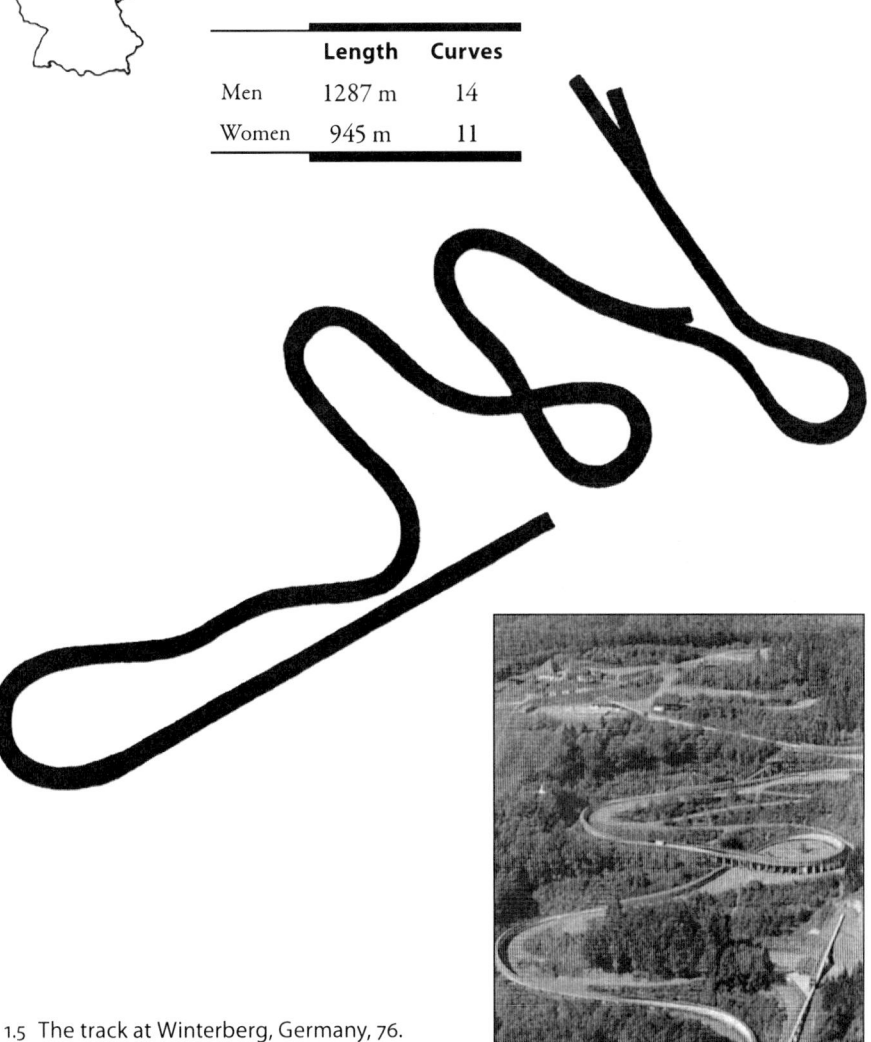

	Length	Curves
Men	1287 m	14
Women	945 m	11

1.5 The track at Winterberg, Germany, 76.

269

Lake Placid, NY, USA

The layout of the new Lake Placid track looks great. It follows the profile of the mountain, which makes for some big elevation changes and steep sections. It has both tight and open corners along with high speeds, which will make this a challenging course.

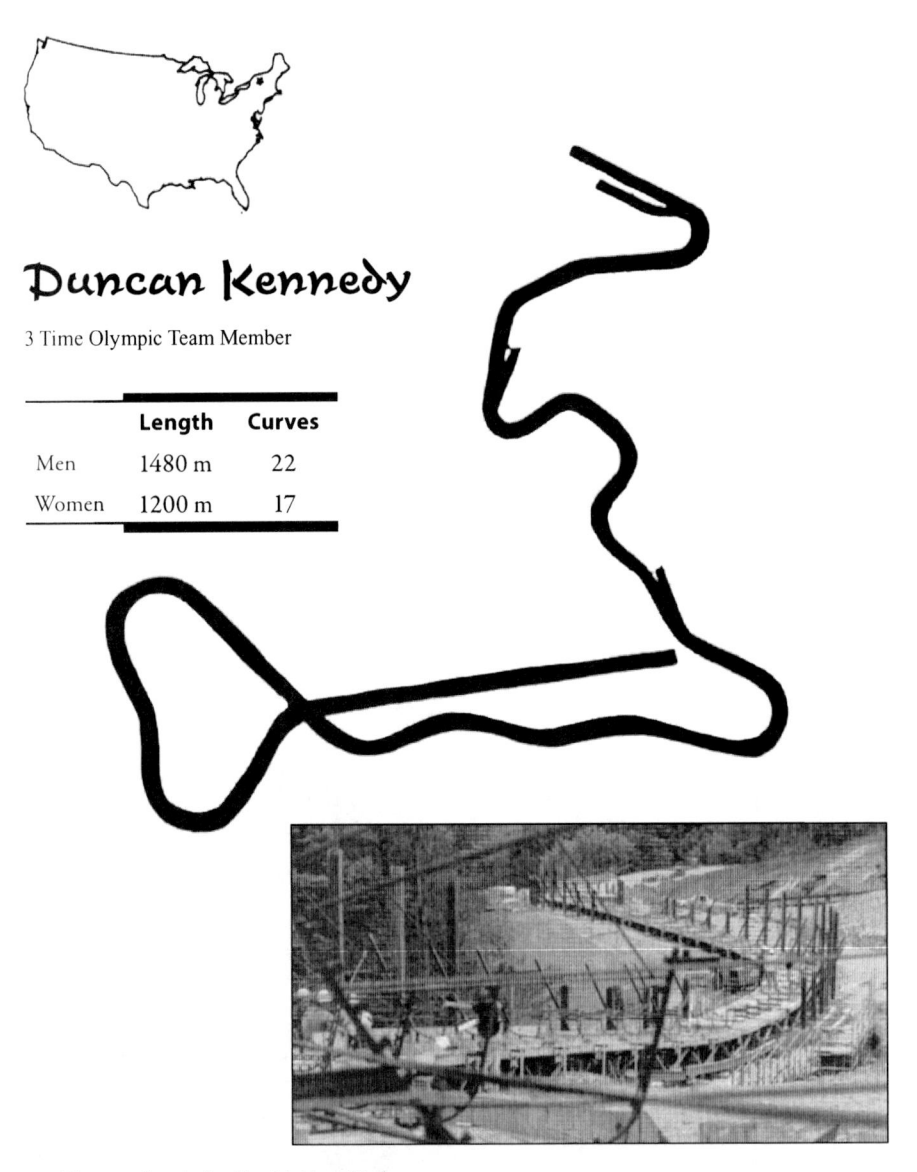

Duncan Kennedy

3 Time Olympic Team Member

	Length	Curves
Men	1480 m	22
Women	1200 m	17

1.6 The track at Lake Placid, New York, 77.

9.8 Meters Per Second Per Second

Königssee, Germany

Königssee is an amazing track. Along with the wonderful German culture that surrounds the area, every race held there always has a huge luge crowd that follows and cheers for the athletes. The track is exciting without any real straight-aways. There is always some action in the huge "S" curves. This is a track that you on your toes and brings out the true joy of sliding.

Courtney Zablocki

1998 US Junior National Champion
4 Time Jr. World Cup Medalist

	Length	Curves
Men	1264 m	16
Women	1083 m	11

1.7 The track at Königssee, Germany, 78.

271

LaPlagne, France

LaPlagne's top is slow and precise, the middle fast and the bottom long and drawn out. It will catch you by surprise if your concentration falters. Waiting for your run to start can be very intimidating; the start ramp is very steep. Your heart races... the one thing you need to do on this track is not what you would expect... instead of relaxing you must attack.

Mark Grimmette

1998 Olympic Bronze Medalist
1998 & 1999 Overall World Cup Champion (Doubles)
2002 Olympic Silver Medalist (Doubles)

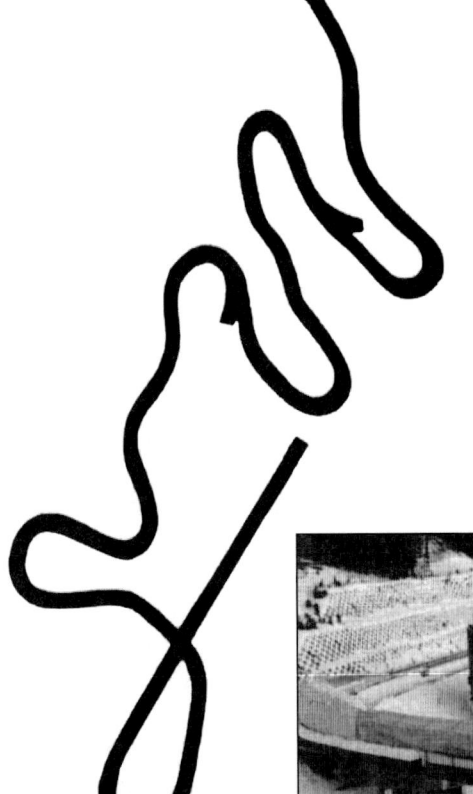

	Length	Curves
Men	1249.5 m	15
Women	11.42.6 m	14

1.8 The track at LaPlagne, France, 79.

9.8 Meters Per Second Per Second

Nagano, Japan

This challenging track lies in the heart of japan. It has unusual elevation changes and high speed. Places to watch for problems include the exits of curves 11 and 12. The team also likes going to Nagano for the great Japanese food.

Gordy Sheer

1998 Olympic Silver Medalist (Doubles)
1997 Overall World Cup Champion Length Curves

	Length	Curves
Men	1365 m	16
Women	1185 m	13

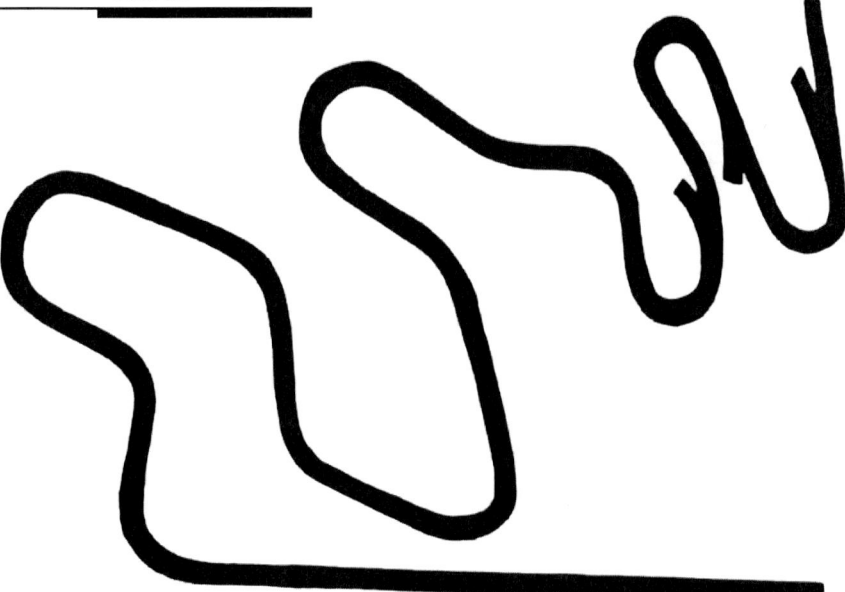

1.9 The track at Nagano, Japan, 80.

273

Park City, Utah, USA

This track drops several stories allowing the sled to gain speed with every curve. You must stay alert and react quickly, especially in the transition between curve 10 and 11. Even with the extreme speed, you must stay relaxed in order to make the finish and be fast.

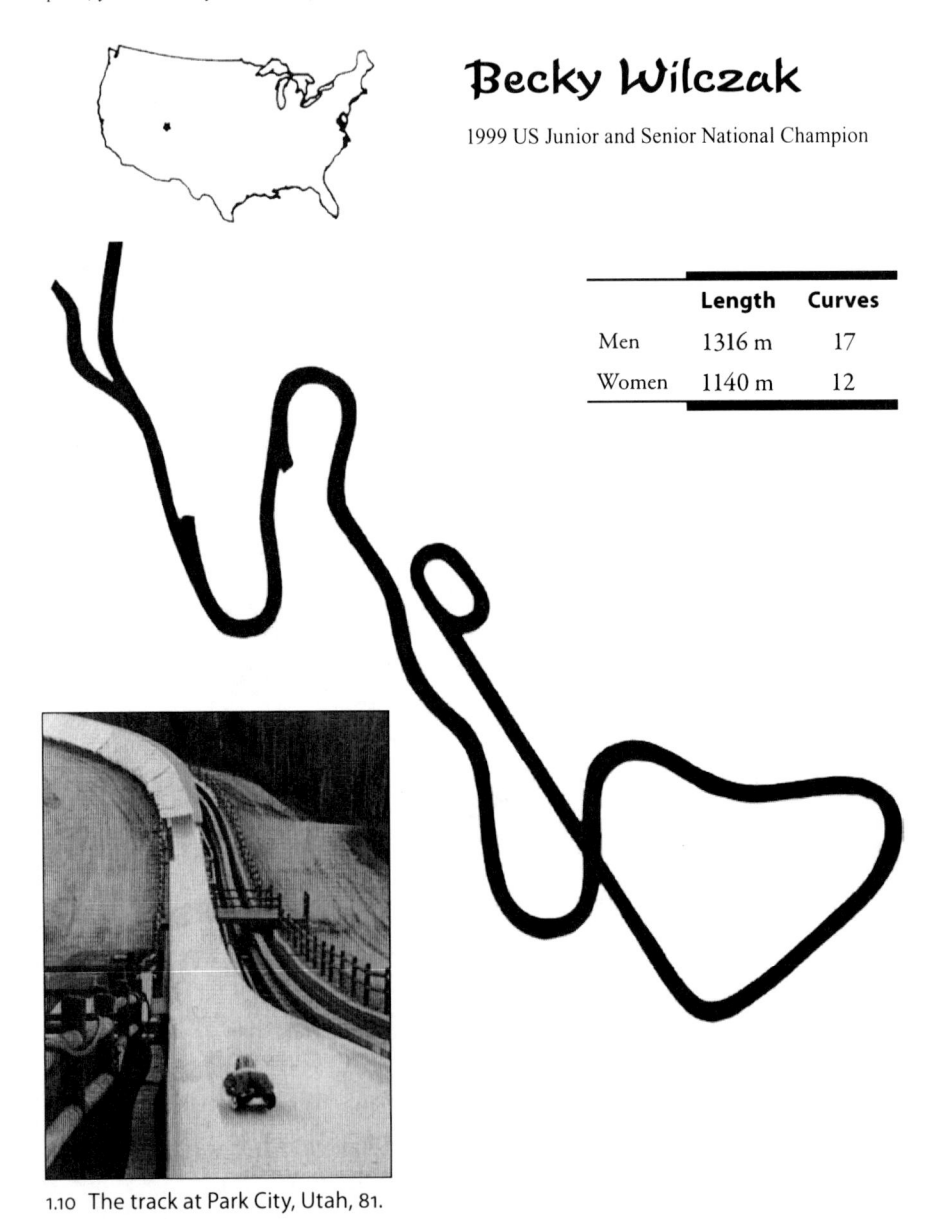

Becky Wilczak

1999 US Junior and Senior National Champion

	Length	Curves
Men	1316 m	17
Women	1140 m	12

1.10 The track at Park City, Utah, 81.

9.8 Meters Per Second Per Second

Sigulda, Latvia

Sigulda is unique in many ways. Almost every part of the track is covered, which allows the track crew to maintain consistently fast ice conditions. Tight combinations, hard drives, the 4 G-force curve 15, and two very long straight-aways keep you on the edge of your seat. It's fast and breathtaking!

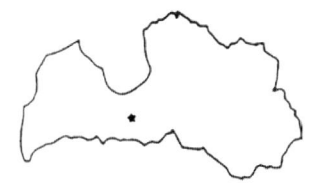

Tony Benshoof

Junior World Championship Silver Medalist (Doubles)
1999 US National Team Member

	Length	Curves
Men	1200 m	16
Women	988 m	13

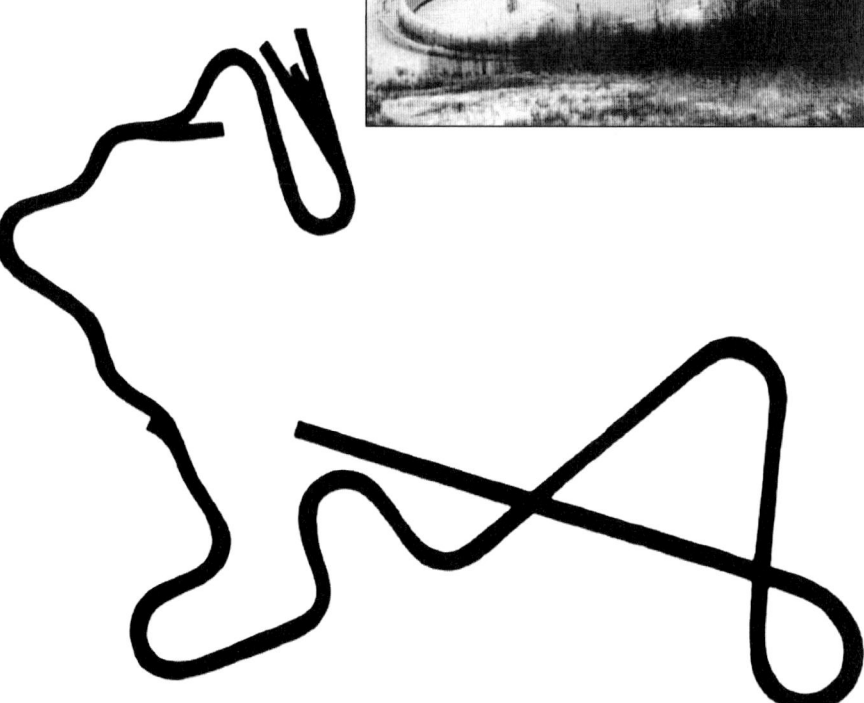

1.11 The track at Sigulda, Latvia, 82.

Lillehammer, Norway

Lillehammer is a fast and wide open track. Sliding here during the long Norwegian nights gets you used to training under the lights. The crisp air and low temperatures make the ice hard and fast. It's very important to get the curve 12-13 transition right, because a bad exit from 13 will resemble racquetball more than luge.

Brian Martin

1998 Olympic Bronze Medalist (Doubles)
1998 and 1999 Overall World Cup Champion (Doubles)
2002 Olympic Silver Medalist (Doubles)

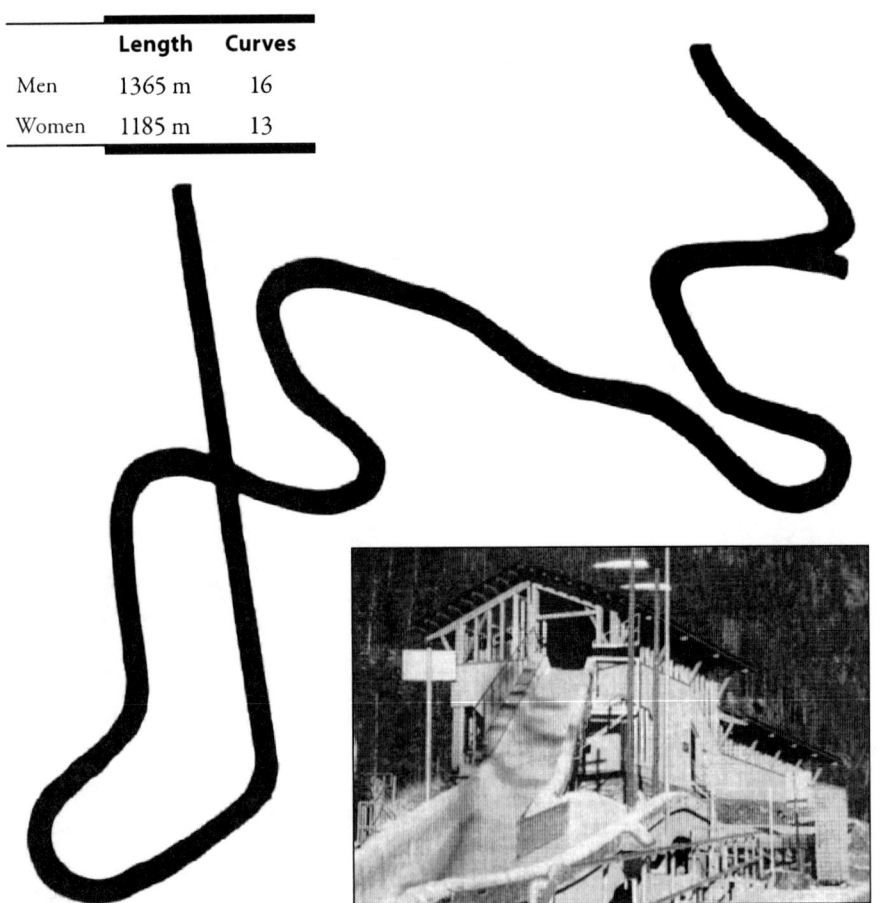

	Length	Curves
Men	1365 m	16
Women	1185 m	13

1.12 The track at Lillehammer, Norway, 83.

9.8 Meters Per Second Per Second

Altenberg, Germany

Altenberg is a track of long straight-aways. You must nail your exits so you don't have to steer in the straights. Most of the curves should be entered as early as possible. If you don't, you might find yourself on your face at the exit. Here there are always high speeds and big crowds on race day, which makes for some very exciting races.

Nick Sullivan

	Length	Curves
Men	1325 m	14
Women	945 m	11

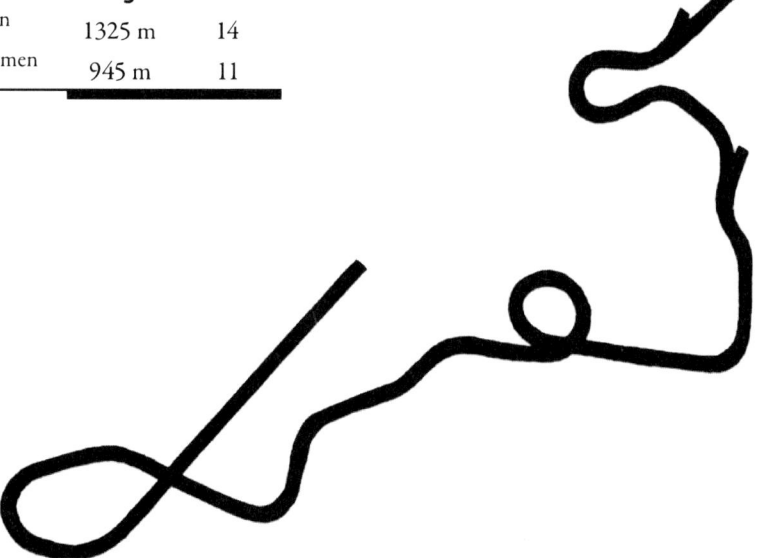

1.13 The track at Altenberg, Germany, 84.

277

Appendix C:
The Sport of Luge

Grateful acknowledgment is given to the United States Luge Association for permission to reprint information about the "International Luge Federation" 487; the "United States Luge Association," 48; the "Rules Governing the Sport," 49-51; the "USLA Member Clubs," 56; "Luge Equipment," 59-60; and "Sled Maintenance," 63-64.

The information is reprinted with permission from Gordy Sheer, editor in *U.S. Luge Team: The Official Media and Information Guide of the United States Luge Association,* Lake Placid, N.Y., 1999-2000.

Photography: Mark Kurtz, Fred Zimny, Allsport.

International Luge Federation

The International Luge Federation (FIL) is the worldwide governing body for the sport of luge. Created in 1953, the FIL not only sets the rules that all competitors and officials must abide by, but also sanctions, conducts and oversees all World Cup, World Championship and Olympic competitions.

Each nation competing in international luge competitions must be a National Federation member of the FIL. Currently there are 44 such Federations of which the US Luge Association is one.

The current list of FIL member countries include:

- Antilles-Netherlands
- Andorra
- Australia
- Austria
- Argentina
- Armenia
- Belgium
- Bermuda
- Bosnia/Herzegovina
- Brazil
- Bulgaria
- Canada
- Chinese Taipei
- Czech Republic
- Estonia
- Finland
- France
- Georgia
- Germany
- Great Britain
- Greece
- Holland-The Netherlands
- India
- Italy
- Japan
- Korea
- Latvia
- Liechtenstein
- New Zealand
- Norway
- Peoples Republic of China
- Poland
- Puerto Rico
- Romania
- Russia
- Slovakia
- Slovenia
- Spain
- Sweden
- Switzerland
- Ukraine
- United States of America
- Venezuela
- Virgin Islands

2.0 International Luge Federation.

The US Luge Association

The US Luge Association (USLA), is an Olympic-class member organization of the United States Olympic Committee and is the National Governing Body for the sport of luge in the United States. A not-for-profit organization, the USLA is based in Lake Placid, NY with a satellite office in Park City, Utah, and is the official American representative to the International Luge Federation. The USLA was chartered in 1979 as a direct result of the Congressional Amateur Sports Act of 1978. It is the responsibility of the USLA to prepare, train and equip the United States National Luge Team for international and Olympic competition, as well as to promote the growth of the sport nationwide.

Coaching, technical, marketing and administrative support are all provided through the USLA's offices in Lake Placid and Park City. Annually, a number of important competitions are held at the Lake Placid and Park City luge runs. Lake Placid has been host to significant international competitions such as the World Championships, World Cups and the first and tenth Junior World Championships. The track was also host to the luge competition during the 1980 Olympic Winter Games. During the spring and summer of 1999, this old Lake Placid track was torn down to make way for a new, combination bobsled/luge track which will be ready for the 1999-2000 season. This new track will host the inaugural Winter Goodwill Games during February 2000.

The second "newest track in the world" is in place for the 2002 Olympic Winter Games in Salt Lake City, Utah and will be the site of many recruitment and development training camps as well as National Team training, and racing prior to the Games. Utah's track has already been host to the US National Luge Championship.

2.1 The United States Luge Association

Rules Governing the Sport

As with any Olympic Sport, there exists a standardized set of rules that all competitive lugers must abide by. Below you will find a brief listing of some of the more important or interesting rules from the International Luge Racing Regulations (IRO). For a more comprehensive understanding of the rules governing luge, it is recommended that you obtain a copy of the IRO from the US Luge Association office.

Rules Governing the Olympic Games

- Each nation may enter the following number of athletes:
  - Women's singles: 3
  - Men's singles: 3
  - Doubles: 2 teams of 2 people each (any combination of men or women)
- Competition runs:
  - singles (men & women): 4 runs
  - doubles: 2 runs
- A new luge course requires an international test race at least one year prior to the Olympic Games.
- Between 50-70 officials are required for an Olympic luge competition.

Rules Governing World Championship and World Cup Competitions

- Each nation may enter the following number of athletes in a World Cup/World Championship race:
  - Men's singles: .... 5 / 4
  - Women's singles: .... 4 / 4
  - Doubles .... 3 / 3
- The defending World Champions automatically qualify for this event. Hence, some nations are able to enter five sleds in a World Championship race.
- Competition runs for men, women and doubles: 2 runs.

Regulations for Sports Equipment

- The primary components of the racing sled are: 2 composite runners, 2 steel runner blades, sling seat or pod, 2 undivided bridges.
- The luge sled must have 2 separate runners.
- Mechanical braking devices are prohibited.
- Maximum weight for a sled is 23 kg (50.6 lbs) for a singles sled and 27 kg (59.4 lbs) for a doubles sled.
- The maximum width of a singles sled is 550 mm (21.65 inches).
- The racing pod may not exceed a height of 120 mm (4.72 inches).
- In the rear of the sled the pod must not extend past the shoulders of the athlete and in the front, must not extend forward of the knees.

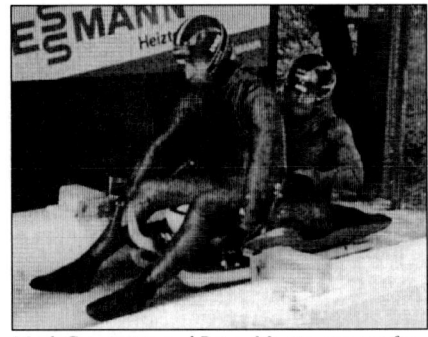

2.2 Rules Governing the Sport.

Mark Grimmette and Brian Martin prepare for a training run in Königssee, Germany. Note the straps used by the back man to help on the start.

Rules Governing the Sport

continued

Rules Governing Race Procedure

- At the start, the following equipment checks are made:
  - temperature of the runners
- At the finish, the following equipment checks may be made:
  - weight of the sled
  - weight of the athlete.
- At the start, a steel runner shall be anchored in place, sheltered from the sun, to be used as a basis for temperature measurement. The temperature of the blades on each competitor's sled may not be greater than 5° centigrade warmer than the control temperature taken from the anchored runner. However, at no time does it have to be any colder than -5° centigrade (+23° Fahrenheit). After the temperatures have been taken of a competitor's steel runners, the sled may not be removed from the designated start area nor the sled exchanged or the blades warmed.
- An athlete must leave the start handles and put the sled into a forward motion within 30 seconds (45 seconds for doubles) of the "track is clear" command, or the athlete(s) is disqualified.
- Competitions may be held in extreme weather conditions with a temperature as low as -25° centigrade (-13 degrees Fahrenheit).
- The competitor must cross the finish line in contact with his/her sled.
- If a competitor believes that he/she has been put at a disadvantage, the athlete has a right to protest. Protests must be submitted to the Chairperson of the jury within 10 minutes of the completion of the heat or event A protest fee of 100 Swiss Francs (approx. $70-$75) must be paid at the time of the protest, which will be returned if the protest is upheld
- A three-member jury decides all protests.

Regulations Concerning Race Clothing

- All race clothing must conform to the body contours of the competitor.
- A neck strap is permitted to help an athlete hold their head up under the high g-forces they experience, but it may not lead to an aerodynamically improved form of the race clothing.
- Other than goggles or face shield, an athlete will be disqualified for losing any item during the run.

GLOVES

- Spikes, which help with "paddling" at the start, may be worn, and can be a maximum of 4 mm long.

RACING SHOES

- The sole of the shoe may be no more than 20 mm (.78 inch) thick.
- The height of the shoe may be no more than 200 mm (7.87 inches).
- It is forbidden to tape the shoes to the racing suit.
- Any method of mechanically pointing the foot or toes is prohibited.

2.2 Rules Governing the Sport (con't.)

Rules Governing Age Requirements

Athletes who compete in youth and junior competitions must belong to the following age classes:

Youth 1	Maximum age	Year of event - 12
Youth 2	Minimum age	Year of event - 13
	Minimum age	Year of event - 14
Junior 1	Minimum age	Year of event - 15
	Minimum age	Year of event - 17
Junior 2	Minimum age	Year of event - 18
	Minimum age	Year of event - 20

During a competition taking place at the beginning of the season (1st July - 31st December), the athlete belongs to the age class valid for him/her during a competition starting on the 1st of January.

During all FIL competitions for juniors with the exception of the World Junior Championships, athletes belonging to the Youth class 2 are eligible to start in the Junior Class I (they can start with a junior sled) and athletes in the Junior Class I are eligible to start in the Junior Class 2.

Additional Weight

- Additional weight may be carried by competitors. The maximum amount of additional weight permitted is calculated based on a formula which determines how much additional weight a competitor may wear:

Category	Maximum	Formula
Men	13 kg	90 kg - body weight X 75%
Women	10 kg	75 kg - body weight X 75%
Jr. Girls	8 kg	70 kg - body weight X 50%
Jr. Boys	10 kg	75 kg - body weight X 75%
Doubles	10 kg	90 kg - body weight X 50%*

*For doubles, the formula is more complicated than shown here. Please consult the rulebook for more information.

- All athletes in all disciplines may wear race clothing in the amount of 4 kg (8.8 lbs).
- All athletes competing in a race are required to weigh in at a specific date and time prior to the beginning of the race. At this time the athlete is informed how much additional weight they will be allowed to wear during the race.
- During the race, if an athlete exceeds their maximum allowable weight, they are disqualified.

Construction of Tracks

	LENGTH	
	Maximum	Minimum
Men:	1300 m	1000 m
Women:	1050 m	800 m

2.2 Rules Governing the Sport (con't.)

USLA Member Clubs

ADIRONDACK LUGE CLUB

NEGAUNEE LUGE ASSOCIATION

WASATCH LUGE CLUB

MARQUETTE LUGE ASSOCIATION

MUSKEGON LUGE CLUB

ROCKY MOUNTAIN LUGE CLUB

2.3 USLA Member Clubs.

Luge Equipment

Helmet
The only piece of safety equipment that every luge racer is required to wear is a helmet. Helmets are required to meet certain test safety standards in order to be eligible for use. In FIL-sanctioned competitions, all competitors are required to wear the same brand and model luge helmet, which is made out of a combination of fiberglass and kevlar and is extremely lightweight. The weight of the helmet is critical as there is no headrest on the back of the sled to compensate for the high "G" forces felt in the tighter curves.

Face Shield
Attached to the front of the helmet is a form-fitting face shield. It is constructed of a polycarbonate material and is virtually shatter proof. The face shield serves 3 functions, the first two being safety.

Over the course of a normal run, the face shield helps protect the athletes from the dangerous wind chills. In the event of a crash, the athletes entire face is protected from possible contact with the sled or ice reducing the risk of injury. Finally, the face shield provides a certain degree of aerodynamic advantage in that it allows a smooth surface to be exposed to the air.

Racing Suit
Racing suits are constructed of a lycra-type, stretch textile-based material. Each suit is custom-sized to the individual athlete. Built strictly for speed and aerodynamics, the racing suit provides little in the way of comfort or warmth.

Spikes
When an athlete departs the handles after performing a start, they typically do 3-4 "paddles" on the ice to help accelerate the sled before lying down into the racing position. Spikes may be worn on the gloves to help maximize grip on the ice during these paddles. Spikes may be a maximum of 4 mm (.157 inches) long and are attached to the glove either on the fingertips or knuckles, based upon the athletes preference.

Racing Shoes
The luge racing shoe, or "bootie," is a lightweight, aerodynamic piece of equipment worn by all competitive sliders. Weighing just 3.9 ounces each, they have a smooth outer sole and no tread on the bottom (for aerodynamics). The light weight of the bootie makes it easier for the athlete to hold his/her feet up on the front of the sled as they resist the 4-5 G forces attained in some curves.

Neck Strap
Speeds sometimes exceed 90 miles an hour and G forces can reach 4-5 (meaning a 150 lb. athlete would briefly register a weight of 600-750 lbs.). As a result. even the strongest athletes require some assistance to keep their head up. To assist in this, a neck strap is worn under the speedsuit. The neck strap has two loops that go around each thigh. A single piece of strap attaches the two loops together and runs up to just under the neck where it is fed through a small hole in the suit. A clip is attached to this end of the strap, which is then connected to the neck strap of the helmet. When in the racing position and under a G force load, the head gets pulled down toward the ice which in turn pulls the neck strap tight against the thighs and prevents the head from getting pulled any further down to the ice.

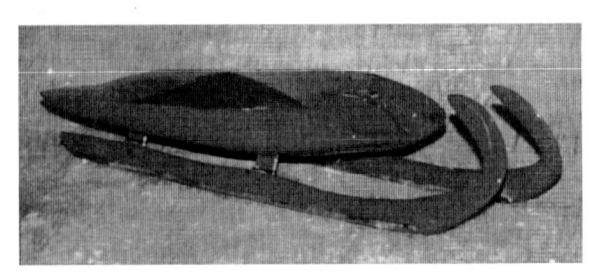

2.4 Luge Equipment

Sled Maintenance

Preparing a New Sled

A brand new racing luge sled requires a great deal of work and tuning before it is ready to take its owner down their first luge run together. Much of the work described below should be performed by an experienced luge coach to ensure safety and optimal performance from the equipment. If you are inexperienced or have any questions regarding your equipment, do not experiment on your own. Get the advice of a coach before you proceed.

Steels

It is generally accepted that the steel runners are the single most important part of a racing sled. Consequently, the steels require the most attention before getting the sled on the track. All new steels are delivered directly off the belt sander with the critical running edge (the only part of the sled that touches the ice), as sharp as a razor. This is too sharp. If you were to try to slide on steels what were this sharp, the sled would be too responsive. Any small movement by the slider would make the sled dart in that direction making it dangerous to ride. Additionally, extremely sharp steels would be somewhat slow because there would be a great deal of friction present from the steels digging so deeply into the ice.

When setting up steels, the coach's objective, taking into account the athlete's level of experience, is to create an edge that is sharp enough to give the athlete the necessary degree of steering and control, while making the steels dull enough to be fast. It is a very fine line. Also, this edge must be constantly adjusted to adapt to specific ice conditions and different tracks.

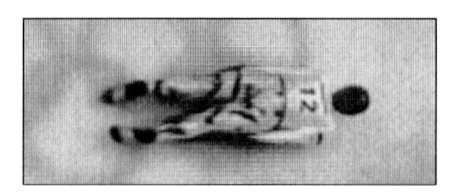

The coach uses a combination of a table belt sander and hand file to prepare the racing edge. Generally the edge will be very dull at the front of the steel, and get gradually sharper as it progresses toward the back of the sled. In the middle portion it remains quite sharp, and at the very back of the steel it may become dull once again.

Another variable when setting up steels is the "parallel" from steel to steel. Not all sleds arrive exactly parallel from the factory. Some may have a 'toe-in' condition. This is similar to a 'snow plow' position in skiing. Conversely, it may have a 'toe out' problem, wide in the front while getting gradually narrower toward the rear. Either one of these will make the sled respond erratically and slow it down. This must be corrected before the sled is ridden. The coach can adjust the toe-in or toe-out by using a belt sander. He will gradually remove steel from the inside of the running edge in an attempt to make the steels perfectly parallel in the middle section. Toward the front, he may leave a very small toe-in, perhaps only .25 mm - .5 mm to make the sled respond to steering quicker. On tracks that are high speed and do not require a great deal of hard or power steering (Calgary, Canada or Lillehammer, Norway) the toe-in will be very small. On tracks that require a great deal of hard steering (Koenigssee, Germany or Lake Placid), the coach may set the sled up with slightly more toe-in.

Once the edge has been set and the parallel checked by the coach, the athlete may begin to sand the steels with sandpaper. Sanding and polishing steels is a duty athletes will spend endless hours performing during their luge career. All performed by hand, it is laborious and time consuming but extremely important work.

To start, the athlete may use a 240-280 grit sandpaper. This is followed by 320, 400, 600, 1000, and 1200 grits, with each of these being applied to both the inside and top edge of the steel until consistent, even 'grit lines' are displayed for each corresponding grit. After the finest grits have been completed, a final application of diamond paste is applied to bring

2.5 Sled Maintenance.

the steel surface to its ultimate polished finish (Diamond paste is usually only used when preparing the sled for a race).

Shell/pod/seat

The aerodynamic shell requires some modification before being used as well. Basically, it must be sized to the athlete that will be using the sled. This may involve shortening or lengthening the back of the shell to make it fit to the athletes' shoulders, and trimming the fiberglass around the handles so the athlete can comfortably grasp the handles.

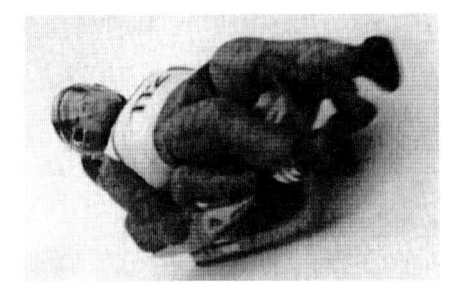

Handles

The handles are minor pieces of equipment on the sled, but can cause a great deal of problems if they are not adjusted properly for the athlete. The handles should not be so far forward that the athlete must reach for them causing the shoulders to lift up, nor should they be so far backward that the athlete cannot get a proper grip on them.

Daily Maintenance Requirements

Training during the winter season usually takes place on a daily basis with races occurring on weekends. All sleds require maintenance attention after every sliding session. After a sled has been on ice, the steels should be wiped down to remove moisture, especially if it is to go unused for more than a few minutes. This should also be done when the sled is brought from a cold environment to a warm one (outdoors to indoors). Condensation forms on the cold steel when hitting the warm air causing a build up of moisture, which leads to rusting. The steel should be wiped down every 10 minutes until the steel temperature is the same as the ambient air temperature.

The running edge of steel will usually receive at least some minor damage after just one run. It is possible that this damage may not be visible to the naked eye, but nonetheless, with races won or lost by .001 seconds, any minute imperfection in the running edge can make a difference. With this in mind, an examination of the running edge should take place after every run with a more thorough inspection occurring at the end of training. If a nick or scratch is found, it may require filing. This should be done by a coach. If it does not appear serious enough to require a file, it may at least need sanding and this should be performed before the next time the sled is used.

Generally for training, steels are maintained at around 600 grit sandpaper. For races, a much higher polish is desired.

To function properly on a daily basis, a luge sled needs to be lubricated about every 2-3 weeks. The most important area to lubricate is the inside of the "gummie" (rubber) where the bridge leg is inserted. This is located inside the "box" in the fiberglass runner. This is the area that ultimately allows the sled to be flexible. The preferred lubricant is either a silicone gel (from a tube), or, if this is unavailable, a silicone spray.

Bridge Bolts/Runner Bolts

Bolts should be checked every day before training. This is the most basic of all maintenance responsibilities. There is no excuse for having a loose bolt during a run. Additionally, these bolts should be lubricated with an oil or silicone spray every 1-2 months.

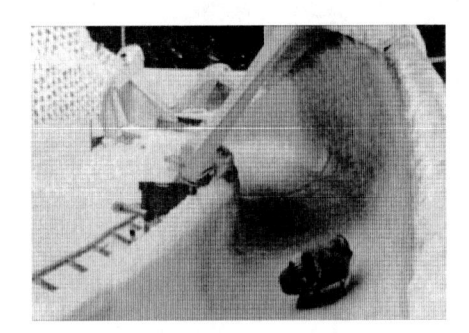

2.5 Sled Maintenance (con't).

Appendix D: Discussion Questions for *9.8 Meters Per Second Per Second*

A. Does Part I resonate with your experience on topics of senior productivity, mountain climbing, mother-son relationships and spiritual hope?

B. In Part II, how does the author use her journals to narrate childhood and maturation? Are the journal perspectives effective? Why? Why not?
   1. Is the narrative subjective or objective? Can it be both at once?
   2. What evidence do you see of Mark's sensitivities in his youth?
      a. What gave Mark joy? Fulfillment? Satisfaction? Confidence?
      b. What gave Mark fear? Anxiety? Disappointment?
   3. Is the family cohesive?
   4. Are the parents supportive? Nurturing?
   5. Are the mother and stepfather good role models? Give examples.
   6. How would you raise a child to feel secure and to be him or herself?
      a. Did Mark mature physically?
      b. Did Mark mature psychologically and intellectually?
      c. Did Mark mature emotionally?
      d. Did Mark mature spiritually?
   7. How do we know Mark's love for John is growing?
      a. How long does it take?
      b. Does the timeline correspond to the experiences of those of you who come from broken families?
   8. What virtues and skills did Mark demonstrate in his youth that helped him luge?
   9. What sacrifices did Mark make in order to luge?
   10. What part does humor play in this biography?
   11. Is the location where Mark grew up significant?

C. Is Part III sufficiently descriptive?
   1. Do you think Mark should have continued luging 26 years? When would you have retired? Why?
   2. Did Mark make good decisions? Give examples.
   3. Does Mark reflect more or less faith when his career is going well? When his career wanes?
   4. Are Mark's skills at luge inborn or developed? Give examples.
   5. What kind of a reputation did Mark have among his teammates? Foreign competition?
   6. How well did Mark deal with the arc of his career?

D. What do you like about Mark?
   1. Do you think Mark is a champion? Give examples.
   2. Do you think Mark is a good model to emulate?
   3. How did the sliders win the first ever Olympic medals in United States luge?
   4. Is luge a sport you would like to try?

Notes

Abbreviations

Grateful acknowledgement is given for permission to reprint from the following titles. After the initial endnote of each, they will be abbreviated as shown:

1. For Tom Kendra, *Muskegon Chronicle*, after the initial note, the notes will read T.K. and MC.
2. For Gordy Sheer, editor in *U.S. Luge Team: The Official Media and Information Guide of the United States Luge Association*, 1999-2000, after the initial note, the notes will read *Official Media and Information Guide,* 1999-2000.
3. For Barbara M. Newman and Philip R. Newman in *Development Through Life: A Psychosocial Approach* after the initial note, the notes will read Newman and Newman.
4. For Publius Ovidius Naso, in *The Metamorphoses*, after the initial note, the notes will read Ovid, *The Metamorphoses* (New York: Viking Penguin, 1986).

Part One: More Sparks

1: Why Not?
 1. Lawrence H. Walkinshaw, "About the Author" in *A Number of Things*, by Margaret Drake Elliott, 2nd ed. (Muskegon, MI.: Gillette Natural History Association, 1988).
 2. Anne Verne Fuller, "Foreword" in *A Number of Things*, by Margaret Drake Elliott, 2nd ed. (Muskegon, MI.:Gillette Natural History Association, 1988), 2.

3. Studs Terkel, "Street Scene" in *Touch and Go*, (New York: The New Press, 2007), 3.
4. Sylvia Nasar, "Genius" in *A Beautiful Mind*, (New York: Touchstone, 1999), 70.
5. Margaret Drake Elliott, "December: Appreciate the Friendly Sparrows" in *A Number of Things*, 2nd ed. (Muskegon, MI.: Gillette Natural History Association, 1988), 226.
6. Fuller, "Foreword" in *A Number of Things*, 3.
7. Ibid., "Foreword," 4.
8. Robert Louis Stevenson, "Title page" in *A Number of Things*.

2: Where There Is a Mountain …

1. Dylan Thomas, "Fern Hill" in *The Poems of Dylan Thomas*, copyright © 1945 by The Trustees for the Copyrights of Dylan Thomas. Reprinted by permission of New Directions Publishing Corp. (New York: New Directions Books, 1957), 178.
2. T. S. Eliot, "The Lovesong of J. Alfred Prufrock" in *T.S. Eliot, Collected Poems, 1909-1962*, rev. ed. (Orlando, FL.: Harcourt, Brace, 1968), 4-5.
3. Publius Ovidius Naso, "Book XI: Midas" in *The Metamorphoses*, translated by Horace Gregory, translation copyright © 1958 by The Viking Press, Inc., renewed © 1986 by Patrick Bolton Gregory. Used by permission of Viking Penguin, a division of Penguin Group (USA) Inc. (New York: Viking Penguin, 1986), 304.

Part Two: Ecstasies and Agonies of Childhood

3: Whee!

4: Uphill

1. Barbara M. Newman and Philip R. Newman, "Epilogue" in *Development Through Life: A Psychosocial Approach* (Homewood, IL.: Dorsey Press, 1979; Belmont, CA.: Cengage Learning, 2009), 494.

5: Mercy

1. Newman and Newman, "Middle School Age, " 236.

6: Christmas

7: Loss

    1. Newman and Newman, "Later Adulthood," 462.

8: Gone Fishin'

    1. Erma Bombeck, "Wrinkles Are Jewels Awarded Survivors" synd. in *Muskegon* (MI) *Chronicle* (Muskegon, MI.: Field Enterprises, 1978).

9: Halloween

10: "Everybody Abandon the Farted Ship!"

    Epigraph. Carl Sandburg, "Fog" in *The Complete Poems of Carl Sandburg*, © Lillian Steichen Sandburg, Trustee, edited by George Hendrick and Willene Hendrick, rev. ed. (Orlando, FL.: Harcourt Brace Jovanovich, 1970).

11: Liberation

12: "Baucis and Philemon"

    Epigraph. Ovid, "Book VIII: Baucis and Philemon" in *The Metamorphoses* (New York: Viking Penguin, 1986), 236.

13: Nice to Talk to

    1. Newman and Newman, "Middle School Age," 231.

14: Two Flat Tires

15: Just Say "No"

    Epigraph. Robert Frost, "Blueberries" excerpt in *Frost, Collected Poems, Prose and Plays*, rev. ed. (New York: Henry Holt and Company, 1970), 62.

16: A Boy's Room

    Epigraph. George Oppen, "Boy's Room" in *Collected Poems*, copyright © 1965 by George Oppen. Reprinted by permission of New Directions Publishing Corp. (New York: New Directions Books, 2008), 122.

17: 'Undertoads"

    1. Edmund H. "Tad" Harvey, "Announcing: Our Age of Electricity" in *The Quest of Michael Faraday* (Garden City, N.Y.: Garden City Books, 1961; New York: Doubleday, 1961),

28.

2. Ibid., "Most Singular Speculations," 55.

18: Losses Skirt Christmas

19: Grandmothers Hurt Too

20: All Nature Sings

21: Hugs and Kisses

22: What Generations Pass Along

Epigraph. Barbara M. Newman and Philip R. Newman, "Epilogue" in *Development Through Life: A Psychosocial Approach* (Homewood, IL.: Dorsey Press, 1979; Belmont, CA.: Cengage Learning, 2009), 460.

1. Ovid, "Book X: Cinyras and Myrrha" in *The Metamorphoses* (New York: Viking Penguin, 1986), 288-289.

23: Goings On Across the Street

Newman and Newman, "Epilogue," 496.

24: New Pursuits

1. George Oppen, "On the Water, Solid" in *Collected Poems* (New York: New Directions Books, 2008), 32.

2. Barbara J. Aardema, "Luging – A Dream Becomes A Reality" in *Muskegon Magazine*, (Muskegon, MI.: Scott Publications, December 1987/January 1988), vol. 4, no. 2, 15.

3. Ibid., 16.

4. Ibid, 17.

5. Barbara J. Aardema, "What Does It Take To Be A World Class Luger?" in *Muskegon Magazine*, (Muskegon, MI.: Scott Publications, December 1987/January 1988), vol. 4, no. 2, 16.

6. Aardema, "Luging – A Dream...," 17.

7. Tom Kendra, "It's Downhill Race for Local Olympic Luger," Sports, *Muskegon Chronicle*, February 13, 1994, 6B.

8. T.K., "Luge, Golf: Talk About 'Gripping' Sports," *Muskegon Chronicle*, February 13, 1994, 6B.

9. Gordy Sheer, ed., "The History of Luge" in *U.S. Luge Team: The Official Media and Information Guide of the United States Luge Association* (Lake Placid, NY.: USLA, 1999-2000), 46.

Part Three: On Wings

25: Upswept
1. Mike Mattson, "R-Puffer Graduate Making Impact on Jr. National Team," *Muskegon Chronicle*, January 26, 1990.
2. Ron Rop, "Luger Dreaming of Gaining Berth On U.S. Olympic Team," *Muskegon Chronicle*, 1991, 1C, 3C.
3. T.K., "Olympic Desire Still Burns for Local Luger," *MC*, December 29, 1993, 2A.
4. Sally Slaughter, "Albion Couple Has Olympic Connection," *Albion* (MI.) *Recorder*, February 18, 1994, 1.
5. T.K., "Olympian Returns to Quiet 'Real World,'" *Northshore Chronicle Shopping Guide*, Muskegon, MI., March 22, 1994, 1,2.
6. T.K. "Olympian: It's Golden to Return to 'Real World,'" *MC*, March 10, 1994, 1A.
7. Ibid.
8. Ibid.

26: Sought
1. Jill Sidock, "A Look at Luge," *Muskegon Chronicle*, February 13, 1994, 1B.
2. Gordy Sheer, ed., "York International Luge Training Complex" in *Official Media and Information Guide*, 1999-2000, 10.
3. Ibid., "The Luge Start," 57-58.
4. Ibid., "Fitness Requirements for Luge," 62.
5. T.K., "Luger Tries Hand at Singles," *MC*, October 26, 1995.
6. T.K., "Fate Deals Luger New Dream," *Ann Arbor* (MI.) *News*, February 8, 1998, D6.
7. *MC*, "Local Luger Pulls Surprise at Lake Placid," News in Brief, August 23, 1997, 2C.
8. *MC*, "Luge," News in Brief, December 14, 1997, 2B.
9. *MC*, "Grimmette Nears Spot On Olympic Team," News in Brief, December 20, 1997, 2C.
10. T.K., "Fate Deals Luger New Dream," *Ann Arbor News*,

February 8, 1998, D6.

11. Ibid.
12. Ibid.
13. Ibid.
14. T.K., "Luger Hopes for Second Chance at Olympic Gold," *MC*, December 19, 1997, 1C, 4C.
15. T.K., "Family, Friends Will Be Cheering," *MC*, February 10, 1998, 1C, 3C.

27: Shoot the Chute

Epigraph. Ovid, "Book XIV: The Conquests of Aeneas" in *The Metamorphoses* (New York: Viking Penguin, 1986), 401.

1. T.K., "Grimmette Goes Bronze; Second U.S. Team Gets Silver," *MC*, February 13, 1998, 2A.
2. Bud Shaw, "For the U.S., A Luge Deluge," © 1998, *The (Cleveland) Plain Dealer*, All rights reserved. Reprinted with permission, February 14, 1998, 11-D.
3. T.K., "I'm Just Thrilled," *MC*, February 13, 1998, 1A.
4. T.K., "Grimmette Goes Bronze...," *MC*, February 13, 1998, 1A.
5. Ibid.
6. *USA Luge Association News Stories*, "The White House Calls," news release, November 27, 1998, 31 of 48, http://www.usaluge.org/news_stories.htm/
7. *USA Luge Association News Stories*, "USA Luge Ranked High in Olympic FanM@ail," news release, November 27, 1998, 29 of 48, http://www.usaluge.org/news_stories.htm/
8. Ibid., 29 of 48.
9. *USA Luge Association News Stories*, "The White House Calls," news release, November 27, 1998, 31 of 48, http://www.usaluge.org/news_stories.htm/
10. *USA Luge Association News Stories*, "USA Luge Medals... the Aftermath," news release, November 27, 1998, 31 of 48, http://www.usaluge.org/news_stories.htm/
11. Ibid.

12. Bud Shaw, "For the U.S., A Luge Deluge," ©1998, *The Plain Dealer*, All rights reserved. Reprinted with permission, February 14, 1998, 11-D.
13. T.K., "Grimmette Goes Bronze ... ," *MC*, February 13, 1998, 2A.
14. T.K., "Olympic Hero Gets Golden Welcome," *MC*, March 16, 1998, 1A.
15. Ronda Howell, "Olympic Medalist Welcomed at R-P," *White Lake* (MI.) *Beacon*, no. 10, March 23, 1998, 1.
16. Lee Ann Frame, "Resumé," March 16, 1998.
17. T.K., "Olympic Hero ... ," *MC*, March 16, 1998, 2A.
18. Gordy Sheer, ed., "USA Luge Western Style" in *Official Media and Information Guide*, 1999-2000, 14.

28: Bounding Boundaries

1. *USA Luge Association News Stories*, "Medalists Off to Good Start," news release, November 27, 1998, 17 of 48, http://www.usaluge.org/news_stories.htm/
2. *USA Luge Association News Stories*, "Racing Season Getting Closer," news release, November 27, 1998, 6 of 48, http://www.usaluge.org/news_stories.htm/
3. *USA Luge Association News Stories*, "USA Luge Adds to Coaching Staff," news release, November 27, 1998, 7 of 48, http://www.usaluge.org/news_stories.htm/
4. Ibid.
5. T.K., "Grimmette Repeats in World Cup," *MC*, February 14, 1999, 6B.
6. *MC*, "Grimmette Third in Luge Championships," News in Brief, January 31, 1999, 2B.
7. *MC*, "Chronicle Gets Award, " Local Reports, 1999.
8. *MC*, "More Honors Roll in for Local Luger," Sports in Brief, March 10, 1999, 2C.
9. Gordy Sheer, ed., "U.S. Luge Association" in *Official Media and Information Guide*, 1999-2000, 5.
10. Ibid., 4.
11. Ibid., 6.

12. Paul Hochman, "Luge Story: Sliders and Sponsor Team Up," *Wall Street Journal*, December 19, 1997, B15.
13. Gordy Sheer, ed., "Bell Atlantic and the United States Luge Team" in *Official Media and Information Guide*, 1999-2000, 6.
14. Ibid., "U.S. Luge Suppliers," 12.
15. Ibid., "The United States Luge Federation Foundation," 13.
16. Ibid., "Luge Equipment," 59-60.
17. Bud Shaw, "For the U.S., A Luge Deluge,"© 1998, *The Plain Dealer*, All rights reserved. Reprinted with permission, February 14, 1998, 11-D.
18. *USA Luge Association News Stories*, "Pre-Season Notes from USA Luge," news release, November 27, 1998, 7 of 48, http://www.usaluge.org/news_stories.htm/
19. T.K., "Grimmette Goal: Gold," *MC*, April 17, 2002, 2A.
20. T.K., "Muskegon's Mark Grimmette Prepares for the Ride of His Life," *MC*, February 10, 2001, 2A.
21. *USLA Member Bulletin ... Keeping You On Track*, September, 2001, 1.
22. Ibid.
23. Ibid., 2.
24. Tim Dahlberg, "Olympic Budget Nears $2 Billion, Taxpayers Picking Up Part of Tab," *AP, Muskegon Chronicle*, December 11, 2001, 1C, 5C.
25. Ibid.
26. Ibid.
27. Ibid.
28. T.K., "Date With Destiny," *MC*, December 2, 2001, 1B.
29. T.K., "Muskegon's Mark Grimmette Prepares for the Ride of His Life," *MC*, February 10, 2001, 2A.
30. Ibid.
31. Ibid.
32. T.K., "A Whisker Away: Grimmette, Partner Just Miss Out On World Cup Medal," *MC*, February 12, 2001, 4C.
33. Ibid.

34. T.K., "Grimmette 4th After First Run," *MC*, February 11, 2001, 7B.
35. T.K. "A Whisker Away…," *MC*, February 12, 2001, 1C.
36. Ibid., 4C.

29: Poured On a Pod Down 30 Stories

1. T.K., "Run for Glory: Setting Their Sights on Gold," Olympic Pullout Section, *MC*, February 7, 2002, 12C.
2. Ibid.
3. Ibid.
4. Ibid.
5. Jo Ann Barnas, "Traveling With Dad, Grimmette Hopes He's On the Road to Gold, " *Detroit Free Press*, May 22, 2001, 6G.
6. Ibid.
7. Larry Siddons, "IOC Relents: American Honor Guard Will Parade Tattered Flag From Ground Zero Around Rice-Eccles Stadium," *AP*, *Ludington* (MI.) *Daily News*, February 7, 2002, B1.
8. Pauline Arrillaga, "Go, USA!" *AP*, *Muskegon Chronicle*, February 9, 2002, 1A.
9. *Ludington Daily News*, "Muskegon's Grimmette to Carry WTC Flag," *AP*, February 8, 2002, B1.
10. Ibid.
11. Pauline Arrillaga, "Go, USA!" *AP*, *Muskegon Chronicle*, February 9, 2002, 2A.
12. Ibid.
13. T.K., "Grimmette's Role Moves Many to Tears," *MC*, February 9, 2002, 2A.
14. *MC*, "Grimmette: Footsteps Louder Than Crowd During Flag Walk-in," February 11, 2002, 3C.
15. Pauline Arrillaga, "Go, USA!" *AP*, *Muskegon Chronicle*, February 9, 2002, 1A.
16. T.K., "Silver Streak: Grimmette and Martin Grab Silver Medal with Stellar Second Run," *MC*, February 16, 2002, 1A.
17. Ibid.

18. Ibid.
19. Ibid., 3A.
20. T.K., "Is a Luge Hotbed Cooking in Muskegon?" *MC*, February 17, 2002, 1A.
21. T.K., "Silver Streak...," *MC*, February 16, 2002, 1A.
22. Ibid.
23. Ibid.
24. Ibid.
25. Ibid.
26. Dick Davies, "Local Reaction: 'This is Great,'" *MC*, February 16, 2002, 3A.
27. T.K., "Is a Luge Hotbed Cooking...?" *MC*, February 17, 2002, 1A.
28. Jill Hinde, "Local Grandmother Takes Pride in Grandson's Silver Medal," *Albion Recorder*, February 21, 2002, 25.
29. T.K., "Grimmette Goal: Gold," *MC*, April 17, 2002, 2A.
30. Ibid., 1A, 2A.
31. Ibid.
32. T.K., "Grimmette to Show Off Silver Medal, " *MC*, March 14, 2002, 2A.
33. Kathi L. Whitman, ed., "Answers Written in Stone: What Makes the Medals Precious?" in *Welcome 2002 Souvenir Guide*, (Salt Lake City: Prestige Event Publications, 2001), 2.

30: Sore Soaring

Epigraph. Robert Frost, "Nothing Gold Can Stay" in *Frost, Collected Poems, Prose, and Plays*, rev. ed. (New York: Henry Holt and Company, 1970), 206.

1. T.K., "Grimmette to Show Off Silver Medal, " *MC*, March 14, 2002, 2A.
2. Ibid., 1A
3. Susan K. Treutler, "Geeked About Grimmette," *MC*, March 30, 2002, 1A.
4. Ibid.
5. *Muskegon Chronicle*, "Local Luger Slides Into First in World

Points," Sports in Brief, December 9, 2002, 2C.
6. *Muskegon Chronicle*, "Luge," Sports in Brief, December 14, 2002, 2C.
7. *Muskegon Chronicle*, "World Cup Runners up," January 27, 2003.
8. T.K., "Grimmette Slides to World Cup Crown," *MC*, February 9, 2003, 1B, 3B.
9. Jo Ann Barnas, "A Tie Goes to the Slider; In This Case It's Grimmette," *Detroit Free Press*, February 12, 2003, 9D.
10. *Muskegon Chronicle*, "Grimmette and Martin Set new Record in Win," November 24, 2002, 2B.
11. T.K., "World Class Luger Faces New Obstacle," *MC*, October 22, 2003, 1C.
12. *Muskegon Chronicle*, "Grimmette Wins World Cup Race After Injury," Sports in Brief, 2004, 2B.
13. T.K., "Still Slidin' Along," *MC*, February 1, 2005, 3C.
14. T.K., "Grimmette to Visit GR for Benefit," *MC*, 2005, 3C.
15. T.K., "Grimmette Aims to Make Games History," *MC*, February 12, 2006, 4A.
16. *Muskegon Chronicle*, "Grimmette Sidelined By Back Injury, " Sports in Brief, 2005, 2C.
17. T.K., "Grimmette Aims…," *MC*, February 12, 2006, 4A,
18. T.K., "Relax: Grimmette Has Good Shot at a Medal," *MC*, February 14, 2006, 1C.
19. T.K., "Grimmette: It's a Tough End," *MC*, February 16, 2006, 1A.
20. Ibid.
21. Ibid.
22. Ibid.
23. Ibid.
24. Ibid.
25. Sandy Caligiore, "Grimmette/Martin and Megan Sweeney Heading to Vancouver," news release, *USLA.org*, December 16, 2009, 1, http://www.usaluge.org/dyncontent.php?/articleid=944/

26. Ibid.

27. Sandy Caligiore, "USA Luge Building Steam as Hamlin Gets Bronze," news release, *USLA.org*, January 10, 2010, 1, http://www.usaluge.org/dyncontent.php?/articleid=944/

28. Ibid.

29. Ibid.

30. Ibid.

31. T.K., "Muskegon's Mark Grimmette Leads American Team Into Winter Olympics," *MC*, February 12, 2010, 2.

32. Ibid., 2.

33. Ibid., 1.

34. Ibid.

35. Ibid.

36. T.K., "Mark's Moment: Luger to Go Tonight," *MC*, February 17, 2010, B4.

37. Matt Mattson, "Not This Year," *MC*, February 18, 2010, A1.

38. Ibid.

39. Ibid.

40. Ibid.

41. Ibid.

31: Grab the Kufens

1. Tomas Tranströmer, "Homeward" trans. by Robin Fulton, from *The Great Enigma*, copyright © 2006 by Tomas Tranströmer. Translation © 2006 by Robin Fulton. Reprinted by permission of New Directions Publishing Corp. (New York: New Directions Books, 2006), 157.

2. T.K., "Area Sports Hall of Fame Honors Class of 2010," *MC*, June 6, 2010, B5.

3. Ibid.

4. Darren Breen, "Caption to Photo," *MC*, June 6, 2010, A9.

Select Bibliography

Aardema, Barbara J. In *Muskegon Magazine*. Muskegon, MI.: Scott Publications, vol. 4, no. 2. December 1987-January 1988.

Eliot, T.S. In *T.S. Eliot, Collected Poems, 1909-1962*. Orlando, FL.: Harcourt, Brace, 1968.

Elliott, Margaret Drake. In *A Number of Things*. Second Edition. Muskegon, MI.: Gillette Natural History Association, 1988.

Frost, Robert. In *Frost, Collected Poems, Prose, and Plays*. New York: Henry Holt and Company, 1970.

Harvey, Edmund H. "Tad". In *The Quest of Michael Faraday*. New York: Doubleday, 1961.

Nasar, Sylvia. In *A Beautiful Mind*. New York: Touchstone 1998.

Naso, Publius Ovidius. In *The Metamorphoses*. Translated by Horace Gregory. Translation copyright © 1958 by the Viking Press, Inc. Renewed ©1986 by Patrick Bolton Gregory. Used by permission of Viking Penguin, a division of Penguin Group (USA) Inc.

Newman, Barbara M. and Philip R. Newman. In *Development Through Life: A Psychosocial Approach*. Homewood, IL.: The Dorsey Press, 1979 and Belmont, CA.: Cengage Learning, 2009.

Oppen, George. In *Collected Poems*. Copyright © 1965 by George Oppen. Revised edition. Reprinted by permission of New Directions Publishing Corp. New York: New Directions Books, 2008.

Sandburg, Carl. In *The Complete Poems of Carl Sandburg.* © Lillian Steichen Sandburg, Trustee. Edited by George Hendrick and Willene Hendrick. Revised Edition. Orlando, FL.: Harcourt Brace Jovanovich, 1970.

Sheer, Gordy, Editor. In *U.S. Luge Team: The Official Media and Information Guide of the United States Luge Association.* Lake Placid, N.Y.: USLA, 1999-2000.

Terkel, Studs. In *Touch and Go.* New York: The New Press, 2007.

Thomas, Dylan. In *The Poems of Dylan Thomas.* Copyright © 1945 by the Trustees for the Copyrights of Dylan Thomas. Revised Edition. Reprinted by permission of New Directions Publishing Corp. New York: New Directions Books, 1957.

Tranströmer, Tomas. In *The Great Enigma.* Translated by Robin Fulton. Copyright © 2006 by Tomas Tranströmer. Translation © 2006 by Robin Fulton. Reprinted by permission of New Directions Publishing Corp. New York: New Directions Books, 2006.

Whitman, Kathi L., Editor. In *Welcome 2002 Souvenir Guide.* Salt Lake City: Prestige Event Publications, 2001.

Photo Credits

1: Photograph by Denny's. Collection of Jean E. Van Lente.
2: Photograph by Mark R. Grimmette. Collection of Jean E. Van Lente.
3: © 1998 Nancie Battaglia.
4: Photographer Unknown. Collection of Jean E. Van Lente.
5-8: Photographs by Jean E. Van Lente.
9: Photograph by Schiavone Studios. Courtesy of Ed and Deb Halcomb.
10-14: Photographs by Jean E. Van Lente.
15: Photographer Unknown. Collection of Jean E. Van Lente.
16: Photographer Unknown. Courtesy of Gwen Glatz.
17-19: Photographs by Jean E. Van Lente.
20: Photograph by Tom Van Dyke. Courtesy of San José *Mercury News*, February 14, 1998.
21: © 2002 Nancie Battaglia.
22: © 2002 Nancie Battaglia.
23-32: Photographs by Ed Halcomb. Courtesy of Ed and Deb Halcomb.
33: Photographer Unknown. Courtesy of the *Lake Michigan Examiner*, February 23, 1994.
34-36: Photographs by Fred Zimny and Jon Lundin. Courtesy of *The Slider*, February 2003, 4, 8.
37-38: Photographs by Jean E. Van Lente.
39: Photography by Ed Halcomb. Courtesy of Ed and Deb Halcomb.

About the Author

The author is the mother of Mark Richard Grimmette. She graduated from Eastern Michigan University with a degree in Secondary Education, majoring in English Language and Literature and Sociology. She graduated from Western Michigan University with a graduate degree as a Master of Social Work.

She was an honorary member of Adahi and its president at E.M.U. She published new student handbooks at E.M.U. during the period she was Assistant to the Director of Student Activities.

The author worked as a recreation coordinator, case manager, interim placement supervisor, hospital liaison, and placement coordinator for Community Mental Health in Muskegon County, Michigan. She was a social worker for Able Care In-Home Health in Fort Myers, Florida.

Her membership has been continuous in the Lutheran Church, Missouri Synod and E.L.C.A. She currently lives in West Michigan.